I0152697

Bush
Background

Adventures and experiences that
originated in Rhodesia

About the author

The author, Paul Gray, was born in Middlesex, England on the 4th of August 1942 and emigrated with his brother and parents to Bulawayo in Rhodesia (now Zimbabwe) in October 1947.

He was fortunate that they had settled close to open veld. It is this background that provided the unique privilege to get close to nature – thereby captivating and focusing his mind on the natural curiosities that it offered. This interest continued onwards through life and extended to hiking, camping, exploring and climbing. He also has a passion for archaeology and the natural environment and has served in organisations for both.

He is married to Jean and has two children Heather and Quintin, and together they have five grandchildren who are significantly treasured.

After school and despite being considered unfit for military training at Brady Barracks, he instead joined the Sea Cadets – T S Matabele in Bulawayo in 1959. He served voluntarily for a short while with the BSAP Reconnaissance group; The CF Hunter Group at Doornkop in Johannesburg from 1973 and 1974; with SAS Yselstein in Simonstown in 1975 and finally on a volunteer call up stint with the Rhodesian Defence Unit – Op Tangent in 1977.

He is a member of the Mountain Club of SA and served with the mountain rescue section for 13 years.

Amongst his other interests, he enjoys writing poetry and quotations as well as some songwriting.

During busy times including work, he and the family have been able to go on many trips to the bush and National Parks of which he never tires.

He is retired and lives in Cape Town and still planning some bush trips.

The peacefulness of it all, the chaotic grandeur of it; it creates a feeling of awe and brings home to one how very small we all are...

– a quotation by Cecil John Rhodes – of Matopos

*Overlooking Mcleme Dam – Matopos circa 1959,
Photo: Tony Gray*

I dedicate this book to my family, and especially my parents who brought me to Rhodesia; and Africa that gave me the opportunity to enrich my life and to meet and bond with so many wonderful people

Map of Rhodesia / Zimbabwe – locations guide

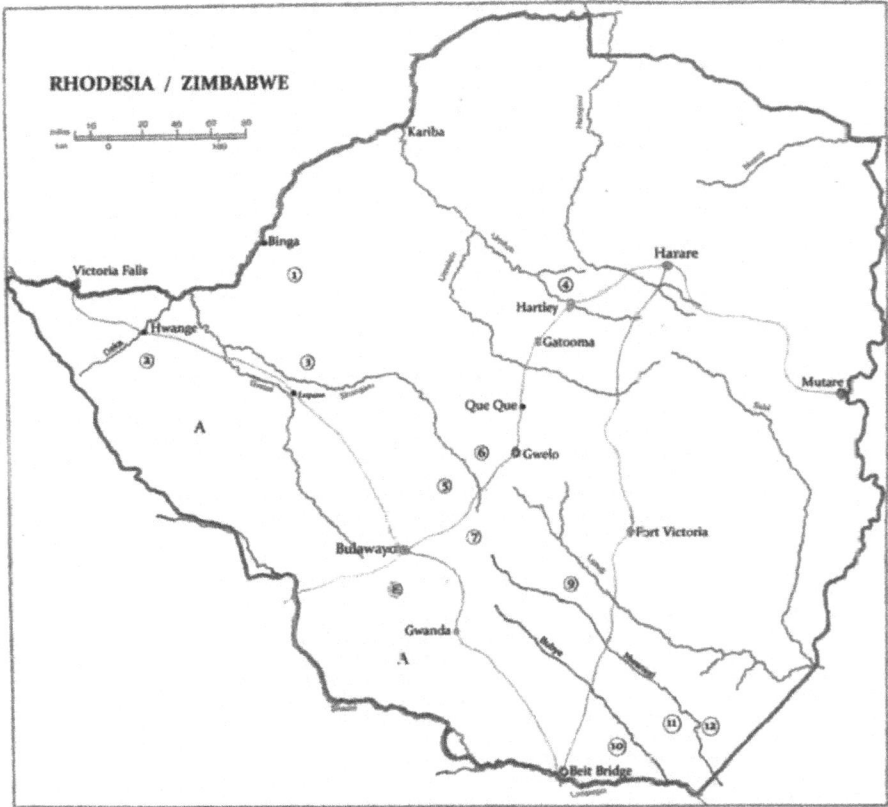

Legend

1.	Chizarira Hills	7.	Sunnyside Farm Greystones
2.	Bumbusi Ruins	8.	Matopos Hills
3.	Allan Wilson battle site	9.	Shabani Mine
4.	Makwiro	10.	Marungudz: Crater
5.	Mambo Hills	11.	Mateke Hills
6.	Somabula	12.	Buffalo Bend – Gona re Zhou
		A	Operation Tangent

NB: Most of the original place names have been retained

Bush Background

Book Cover: View across the Mateke Hills from
Lomolehoto Kopje – photo Jean Gray
Frontispiece photograph of the author overlooking
Maleme Dam – Matopos circa 1959
All photography and sketches by Paul Gray unless as noted

© Copyright by Paul Gray, 2020

All rights reserved.
No part of this publication may be reproduced,
transmitted in any form or by any means without
permission in writing from the publisher, nor be otherwise
circulated in any form of binding or cover or e-book.

Published by the author
Tel: +27 21 712 0088
Cell: +27 84 400 0088
Email: grays@yebo.co.za

First edition 2020
Second print 2021

ISBN: 978-1-77626-060-7

Book design and editing by Heather Kensley

Printed by Print on Demand
Website: www.printondemand.co.za
Telephone: +27 21 951 1464
Address: 5 Koets Street, Parow Industrial, Cape Town, 7493

CONTENTS

CHAPTER   **PAGE**

CHAPTER		PAGE

List of photographs, sketches and maps

List of photographs, sketches and maps

List of photographs, sketches and maps

Acknowledgments and thanks

Quotations and Poems: By the author and as noted in the captions

Sketches: By the author, Olivia Kensley and Sarah Mackie (assisted)

Photographs: By the author, Jean Gray and as noted in the captions

Media: *The Argus* – Rescue of Jill Graafland

The Bulawayo Chronicle/Cape Times – Paul Connolly article of leopard attack and his permission to include his account.

Maps: Battle scenes – by Oliver Ransford – *BULAWAYO Historic Battleground of Rhodesia*

To Doug Kriedemann of The Greys Scouts and his experience at the Shangani Patrol Battle site.   Ref book – *The Equus Men*.

To my wife, Jean for her support and advice.

To my daughter, Heather Kensley for her professional and tireless input and assistance in design, layout and editing.

To my grandaughter, Olivia Kensley for photo-editing the high resolution digital file of the cover image.

To Chenai Gwandure for converting the cover image from a slide-film to a high resolution digital file.

To the Gray family for valued and shared experiences.

To Paul Els for his valued guidance and assistance.

Introduction

This book is a story of my experiences and events that have left me with lasting and life-changing impressions. Generally, when they happened, they remained in my thoughts as particularly memorable. The pattern of life does not always favour happy or comfortable times, but also sorrowful and sometimes challenging, and perhaps at times just plain normal – nonetheless all a part of walking the road of life.

The wonderment and observation of nature around have always held firm. Remarkable discoveries are being made throughout the world all the time. Still, each one of us needs to discover things for ourselves, within our interests, no matter how grand or minuscule.

I have often taken for granted my interactions with people but always held dear on reflection, especially those friends that I have shared adventures and experiences with, and folk and characters that I have met.

It can be challenging to recall exact details sometimes, but oddly enough, I can picture places very accurately when events have occurred – especially in the natural environment and the bush.

Much of the treasured experiences took place in my earlier years from when we arrived in then, Rhodesia. The love of the bush is beyond question. Even world affairs and its problems cannot erase that which has been etched into my very soul. I am by nature a bit of a naturalist and have an enquiring mind, which is a blessing that while walking, hiking or exploring I can enjoy the veld, geology, archaeology, season changes and the animals and insects that form part of the earth's gift to us all.

> *'Life without adventure is like*
> *a frame without a picture'*

Books that I have read, and they are mostly factual books, which have illustrations, drawings or photographs have always stimulated the imagination – like providing a window into the scene and atmosphere of the time. I have done likewise where possible to draw the reader into and enhance the experience. Nostalgia becomes evident after the event at whatever age one is. 'I remember' seems terribly dated and terminal, so I have avoided its use where possible. Nonetheless, each one of us has memories to draw from as we journey through life. A life's experience is more often composed of many small events rather than the few noteworthy happenings, as well as and most importantly, the people and characters we meet along the way and what we learn from them. I have included some anecdotes of such special people and characters that made an impression on me, and which I believe the reader will enjoy. Perhaps some of my experiences through life thus far will stimulate and recall your own valuable experiences as you have journeyed through life. Every person has stories to tell; these are some of mine.

I have not stuck to a typical diary in chronological order, but more on subject type within phases of my growing up and journey through life. Some later references have been included to demonstrate the radical changes that have emerged since my earlier years and in addition, relate to the status of events as told. Above all, there must be adventure and some mysteries in life to explore.

1

Emigration from England – Arrival in Bulawayo

I was born in Hillingdon Hospital in Uxbridge, Middlesex on the 4th of August 1942. I was five, and my brother Tony was seven years old when we set sail from Tilbury Docks in October 1947 for Cape Town.

My recollections are plentiful with air raid sirens from the Second World War in England, tube trains, yellow buttercups growing in green grass against blue skies, the distinctive scent of canvas fabric and leather suitcases, of the sea, soap and engine smells of the S.S. Llanstephan Castle (built 1914, troop carrier and landing ship 1945, converted to passenger ship in 1947), and the scary experience of seeing the ritual of people being dunked into a pool when we crossed the equator. The sight of the vast open sea, the fascination of watching the retreating wake created by the passage of the ship and finally the first sighting of Table Mountain in the early morning in October 1947 are still with me; but left far behind after we landed in Cape Town, and headed north by train to Bulawayo in Rhodesia.

My brother Tony who prior to leaving England had just had the plaster removed from his arm which he had broken whilst playing near a wartime Canadian army depot, then, unfortunately, tripped over a watertight door frame on board ship, broke the same arm again (which did not please father!) then had it put in splints. It remained so until we got to Bulawayo where his arm was x-rayed, found incorrectly lined up, broken again (under anaesthetic) and reset...

In hindsight, my mother must have taken a lot of strain on the two and a

Gray family at Bulawayo station

half days steam-engine train journey from Cape Town to Bulawayo. October month is not kind to anyone with the excessive heat, dust and almost total absence of greenery. In fact, there is hardly a decent-sized tree between Cape Town and Bulawayo, so the adjustment must have been tough for her.

My parents decided to immigrate to Rhodesia after the war to start a new life as opportunities had been advertised for qualified artisans in the country. My father, after serving many years as an apprentice (I recollect that he had started work at the age of fourteen!), qualified as an electrician and had eventually started up his radio manufacturing business. One of the main reasons for leaving he told me was the constant labour problems, and the effect labour unions were having on everyday business. Life was hard during those years before, during and immediately after the war, and I only realised later how soon and short was the time between the traumatic years of war and their decision to move to Rhodesia. It was the same for many folk in those times.

We moved into a 'Pisé de Terre' house in Queens Park, a new suburb northeast of Bulawayo. The house was asbestos roofed and had mud-filled, cement-clad walls. The open bush was immediately across the road from our house, which provided close access to nature and my first experiences as a youngster. 'Tokkie' Thompson lived next door, and we were good friends. His father was an elephant hunter and used to stack his 'guns' against the wall in the front entrance hall – whenever I went to see him, the front door was always open. During our stay there, an elephant was seen not that far from Queens Park up the Turk, Queens and Lonely Mine road. In fact, that road beyond Inyati (the original mission station established by Robert Moffat with the permission of Mzilikazi) was called 'Hunters Road' and was the original road north. The suburb to the northeast was close to wild bush. A leopard was also reportedly seen up a tree on the outskirts of the suburb. The Thompson family seemed to have had a lot of money (no doubt from ivory hunting) because at Christmas time his father bought him a brand-new pedal car. Actually, the wheels on it were so narrow (no doubt made in England for English roads), that you could not get good traction in the dirt and soil surrounds. The effort of pushing the pedals was not worth it, so we instead pushed one another around. Later we switched to racing around with old tyres, some old motorbike tyres my father got from the police, or the more stable car tyres. These were less effort to run around with, and more fun.

Two early, memorable and giant scares I experienced were when I tried to put a small lampshade over a candle. The plastic shade was very inflammable and burst into flames, but my mother came to the rescue and put it out. The second was more serious when I had a thing about

Paul (5 years) and Tokkie playing with tyres – Queens Park West

experimenting with matches, and when I set fire to the bush opposite the house, and not realising the extent or speed in which it spread raised all concern from the neighbours available. It was eventually doused, but the heat remained on my backside from the 'pink' hairbrush my father used to quell his anger, and, my stupidity. However, and for the record, I did learn a lesson, and I did not suffer any psychological problems for the 'light' discipline I received!

The bush was always attractive to me, and undeniably set my deeper interests for the remainder of my life.

I once followed a column of 'Matabele' ants (big black and shiny ants) through the veld, and I observed that the ants were very organised and had scouts walking ahead and either side, more or less to the leaders of the column. With the rainy season upon us, 'white' ants (termites) were already building mud-sheaths around some fallen thorn tree branches. The Matabele ants boldly approached, set upon the termites and decimated them. I noted with interest that they each carried off a termite before returning to their nest. Very smart, I thought.

Bicycles were the in thing, though I was too small to ride a bike, I was in awe of those that could balance and proceed without falling off. My mother and father both had bikes as they did not own a car at that stage.

My friend and I were also very aware of the danger of snakes, so one early evening, we hid in the grass at the side of the narrow road to town. We had tied a piece of black rubber hose to the end of a piece of string and waited until a bicycle appeared, then rapidly pulled it across the track in front of the bike. It caused consternation and fear – to the cyclist and ourselves – it really wasn't that funny, I think he fell off, but we did not wait to see or hazard the consequences of being caught.

My first school was Baines Junior School, and I used to catch the bus there. I enjoyed it, and there were some very nice teachers, one of whom used to wear a very strong but pleasant perfume, so it was always OK to be standing next to her when having my books marked. One unreasonable teacher would not allow my friend to go out for a pee, and he wet his trousers and ran out of the classroom. It was true, however, that some small kids were always asking to 'be excused' for whatever reason. But he did, in fact, have a bladder problem, and it was usual for him as he told me, to have to go often to the toilet. I am sure it affected him psychologically.

It was government policy that schools had to give each child a bun and a quarter pint of milk per day. It was always welcome, and I am sure many post-war children were undernourished. At break, it was especially comforting to open the little pressed cardboard suitcase and unwrap the sandwiches. The small suitcase held a pleasant and permanent smell of bread sandwiches.

It is funny how when you are young and having fun; you are not always aware of time or necessarily any potential danger. One afternoon my friend and I set off to explore the local bush and a river (the Matsheumhlope River). It was the dry season, so we headed along the dry riverbed. It probably was not too far, but it was getting dark and unbeknown to me, my mother had already raised the alarm and called out the National Guard! I do think she had a deep fear of

Paul with his older brother Tony in the front garden – Queen's Park West

the bush, lions and other wild creatures, lurking there, ready to pounce. For example, years later when we were driving along the old strip road to the Victoria Falls, she made me stand guard against wild animals while she had to have an urgent pee in the bush – I obviously had to face the other way... Back at the river, after hearing much calling, we acknowledged our presence and received a serious telling off and yanked off back home. We were not lost, but it was too late literally for any excuse or explanation, and the sun had already set. When you are still around six or seven years old, it is a bit worrying for your parents!

The heat in summer before the onset of the rains was accompanied by the cicadas relentless high-pitched shrilling in the background, and after the rains, the appearance of Toktokkie beetles, shongololos and what we called the Christmas beetles of brown-red and light-blue colours. None of these insects posed much danger. Interestingly, if one was careful, you could pick up the shiny black Matabele ants without being bitten, and they were slower moving. You could not do that with the somewhat hairy greyish-black ants (smaller than the Matabele ants), as you would get stung very quickly and very painfully, they could move a lot faster as well. I was very wary then, and even later of the large black wasps that often came into our houses looking for a place to make a nest. They looked threatening with their black and yellow coloured banded legs dangling below them whilst hovering around. I reasonably had no reason to fear them as I had never been stung by them, but I was confident they would sting quite severely if caught. The smaller faster moving brown wasps were another story and when disturbed seemed to go directly for your face or eyes. I was stung by them much later in life, and always avoided disturbing their nests.

Tea was a regular event. The superb taste of freshly brewed tea in our translucent cloudy green glass cups was always very refreshing. It brought out a sweat, and I always felt better afterwards.

2

Illness and Ghost in Sauerstown

One day when we lived in Queens Park, I became very ill, I was around six or seven years of age, and the events around it are still blurred. I was passing blood, very thin, and eventually had to be admitted to hospital where I do remember vomiting up bright red hospital medication. I had contracted amoebic dysentery and was in a bad way. Bucket system toilets were in use in the outside PKs (piccanin kya's), so I may have been inadvertently infected.

How long it took to recover, I cannot remember. I realised afterwards that I must have experienced a delirious 'out of body' experience. I do remember the dreams of going down an extensive dark tunnel which just went on and on with no light, and the other climbing up a very long staircase up into the bright sky and clouds – I never did quite reach the clouds. Those visions have never left me.

In my weakened state, a friend of my mother Desire Metelerkamp, who also worked in the C I D fingerprint department of the BSAP in Bulawayo,

Sketch of the river crossing on the way to Sunnyside Farm, Greystones – Shangani

recommended that my brother and I go to a farm near Shangani, specifically for me to recuperate. We were met at the Shangani railway station by the Metelerkamp family after the train journey from Bulawayo and then driven to the farm by 'uncle' Gordon Eva in his model 'T' Ford pick-up. He drove us into the dark, through a long and winding bush road. The headlights pierced the dark, and the reflections on the trees, bush and tall grass seemed to close in around us in our safe truck cabin. It was very exciting, including the regular stops at streams to refill the radiator. The radiator bubbled and spluttered all the way.

The farm was called 'Sunnyside'. It was near Greystones which I suppose was named for the granite outcrops along the route.

We had a room that had sacking for a ceiling, no door, and candles for light. The sitting room at night was lit by a couple of Tilley pressure lamps that hissed and broke the silence of the night. Sleep did not come easy with the pitch-black night noises, particularly the scuffling sounds above the Hessian sack ceiling, probably rats. The creature we saw on the floor in the poor light turned out in the morning light, to be only a screwed-up ball of paper from a calendar! Uncle Gordon's mother, whom we called Granny, had a secret stash of lollipops in her drawer, which we eagerly awaited daily. Granny had a scare one day when a snake was lying across the front door to the sitting room, how it was disposed of, I am not sure, but it did provide some excitement.

The light of day brought much activity with chickens and cattle and movement. My fears of cattle were realised when I was chased by a bull which I avoided by running very fast and ducking around a haystack. You have to admit that given my size compared with such a creature, it was quite frightening. We witnessed the 'callous' removal of a chicken's head with a knife in preparation for a meal. My young mind was imprinted forever with the unpleasant sight of the headless chicken charging around for a while!

There was a small farmworkers store built on the edge of a granite outcrop which sold tobacco, soap and other odds and ends. The African dresses in striking colours hung in a line, the waxy scent of new material mingled with the distinctive smell of tobacco, probably from the small cloth bags of pipe and cigarette tobacco (I still love the smell of pipe tobacco). African wood smoke either from a kraal or a bush farm permeates one's soul. It belongs and is not pervasive – grass fires in the winter are also almost pleasant to smell.

Much time was taken up by 'uncle' Gordon tasking us with daily chores such as walking relatively long distances to fetch stores and the mailbag, regularly feeding the chickens and farm animals as well as filling the lamps every night. A comforting daily rhythm of farm life.

Gordon Eva and Paul (7 years) at Sunnyside farm, Greystones
(Tony is not pictured)

The quiet of the night seemed to close in around the hissing of the Tilley lamps – like man's comfort against the dark, and we were soon off to bed with drooping eyelids after a satisfyingly busy day. With the new experiences, fresh air and physical exercise, we slept soundly and were awake at dawn and up by sunrise.

Tony and I had a great time playing in a low-walled and roofed brick-enclosure behind the farmhouse which was filled with freshly dehusked mealie seeds from the dried mealies. Out at the back, we had a close look at the ingenious dehusking machine with its grooves that did the job. We wound the handle of another machine which then blew a strong wind into the shallow bowl. Charcoal was used to produce a high heat for working and bending metal.

Petrol was pumped by hand from a 44-gallon drum for the truck and tractor and seemed to take some time to fill.

My interest in rocks and stones started there when I found with much delight some reasonable pieces of Mica on the granite slope near the small dam.

The break did me well as it did Tony, but more than just health, it was our first experience of life on a bush farm and the outdoors. It opened a window into distant bush yet to be experienced and explored, and the myriad of things nature offered to charge the senses and the desire to explore more. Uncle Gordon left an indelible mark in my memory, and I can still recall his smiling face and hear his friendly laughter.

We moved from Queens Park to Sauerstown West which was north of Bulawayo and situated not far from the Bulawayo Spruit. The house we moved into was also a Pisé de Terre, newly built and faced the bush and was not too far from the river. Looking back, I was very fortunate and blessed to always have the open bush across the road from our house. This included later, our house in Glengarry which was four miles from town on the Salisbury (now called Harare) road.

The house in Sauerstown was part of quite a spread-out township, and it was built over the lower east slopes of Lobengula's kraal. There was evidence of old 'fired' bricks in and around the house and in the bush opposite. It could well have been some of the early European built dwellings and trading stores that used to be close to the kraal. This area which historically was called the 'Grass Town' because of all the thatched dwellings, was indicated on an early map on the opposite side of the Bulawayo Spruit and located more on the opposite South Eastern side of Lobengula's Kraal (named by him as Bulawayo).

The house even though new, was in fact haunted. When we first walked in, my mother saw an elder woman walk into one of the rooms (the lounge) off of the passage. Astonished to see this, she followed into the room, which was empty, and there was no one there! Tony sometimes heard a tap-tapping at night along the cement path skirting the front of the house. He also experienced a feeling like something pressing him down on the bed. My only experience was when one quiet afternoon in my room, I heard steady and heavy breathing coming from the corner of the room. I called my mother to listen, but she could not hear it, despite my protestations! This was obviously an unhappy spirit and could no doubt have succumbed to one of the cruel executions ordered by Lobengula.

An amusing but 'haunting' incident occurred when we lived there as one night, while my mother was alone in the lounge and while my father was on police duty, the top drawer of a chest of drawers, slowly opened. My mother related how terrified she was to see out of the corner of her eye this happen. At the time, all was quiet as she was sipping on her brandy and didn't expect such a thing to happen right before her eyes, remembering that the place was possibly haunted! In a desperate rush, she slammed the drawer shut, only to find when she sat down, that the next

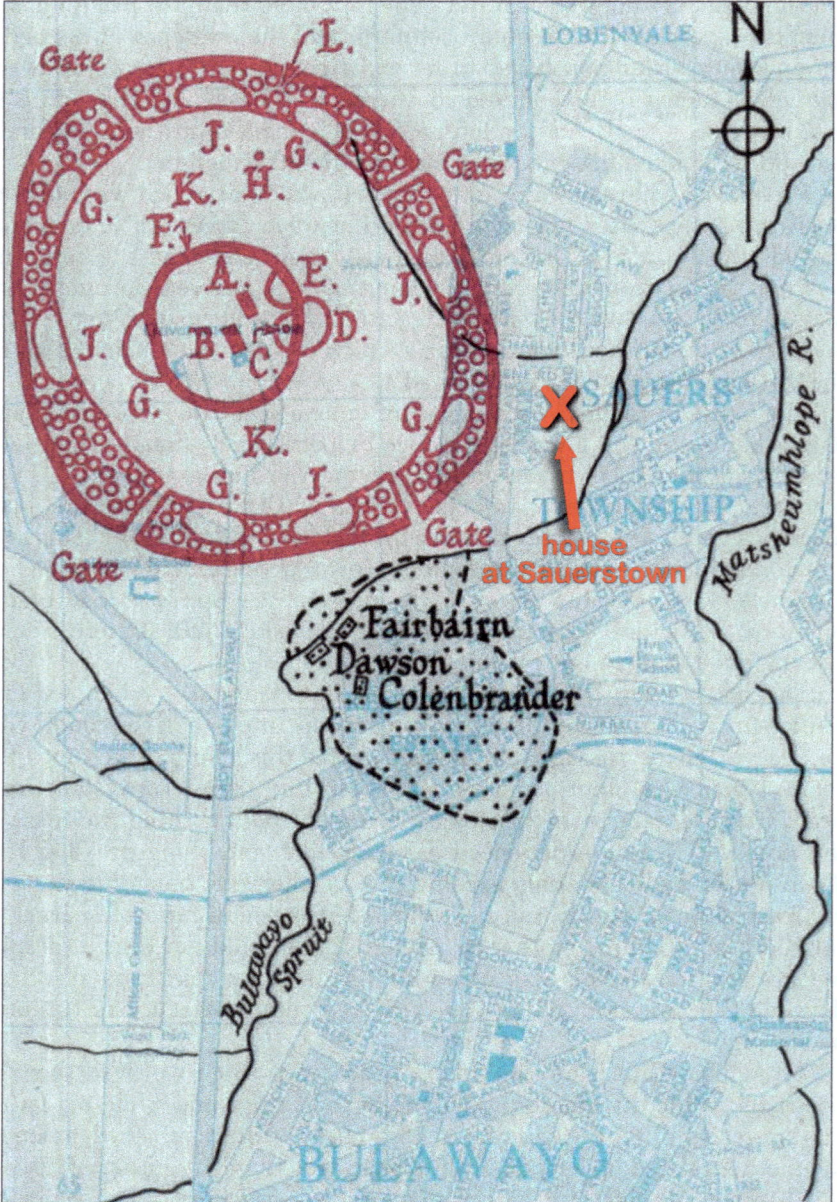

Map of Lobengula's New Bulawayo kraal – as depicted in 1893.
Our house was about 100m outside of the kraal perimeter,
above the lower RHS kraal gate.

drawer down slowly started to open. She repeated the same frightening and desperate closure of the drawer. Believe it or not, when she sat down shaking, the following drawer down began to open, and she desperately slammed that shut. She then heard a muffled cry and discovered to her now much-unnerved relief, that our cat had climbed in behind the drawers, causing the drawer to open. After a severe battering one drawer after another, it arrived at the bottom somewhat rearranged, but alive! We thought it absolutely hilarious, she did not, but the next morning she might have had a bit of a hangover from the medication!

Jean, my wife, and I visited the house 35 years later during a trip via the Victoria Falls, and we dropped in to meet the occupants. A friendly coloured family invited us in for tea. The house was still in good order, notwithstanding the mud-filled and cement-clad walls, it was surprising to see how well it had stood up to the rigours of time. However, I did not mention the haunting events, but carefully enquired if everything was OK in the house. The wife immediately responded by saying she was fine, but her husband experienced someone putting pressure on him, like holding him down when he slept!

I have heard that an expert from England had stated that ghosts live for about 400 years – how they arrived at that I do not know, but the one in Sauerstown might be there for a while still. Or perhaps it is one of the lonely lost souls that still inhabits Lobengula's old kraal, that Peter Gibbs writes of almost amusingly in his book, *A Flag for the Matabele...* it would not surprise me at all.

I at first went to Baines Junior school when we lived in Queens Park. When we moved to Sauerstown, I attended the Sauerstown Junior School up to standard 5, and later Northlea High School which was built just west of Government House (Lobengula's 'New' Bulawayo Kraal site), so walking or cycling to school was the mode of transport. The walk along the river was always enjoyable, as was the fishing which produced barbel (catfish), rainbow bream as well as in the rainy season when the river was full, hundreds of sardine type fish. The smell of decaying poplar leaves on the ground next to the river was not at all unpleasant – the rushing water when in flood also had a special odour. We caught the 'sardines' in Hessian sacks below 'First Wall', (a dam wall), and above that and further upstream, the 'Second Wall'.

There used to be a drift crossing the river, which became a hold-up when the river came down in flood, so it was decided that a new bridge should be built. So it was with great interest that I followed the progress while travelling to and from school. It was early one evening, while the contractor was feverishly working under lights and could be seen hurrying back and forth with wheelbarrows of concrete poured into the steel reinforced wood-shutterings, that I decided to have a closer look at how it was being done. They were in a desperate hurry because the rains had already started, and the river was known to come down in flood. I walked under the wood-shuttering and was amazed at the wooden props supporting the whole temporary structure. It certainly did not appear sufficient to carry the amount and volume of wet concrete. Early the next morning I passed by the bridge to check on progress and was shocked to find that the supports had collapsed in the night and that the mass of concrete and steel had settled on the river bed and... set! I think it took at least two weeks and more for the whole mess to be chiselled out, the steel removed and work to be recommenced properly. Fortunately, the rains held off, but it did provide an important lesson to me for the future in 'quality' where if something does not appear to be correct, then it probably isn't!

I had a couple of scares with snakes in the local bush, one where I had to make a call of nature and while crouched in the bush near a thorn tree heard a sort of hissing noise and to my horror saw a large snake sliding away on my left-hand side through the grass and across a path. It may have been offended by me, but I was scared witless or words to that effect! The snake must have been very puzzled and decided to move off, whilst I, in hindsight (excuse the pun) could never have imagined a person doing something so stupid, even if through ignorance. Alongside the river bank whilst walking barefoot I had to take a very long extra step when below me was a large coiled up snake in the green grass. I flew off smartly and did not wait to see if it noticed me or not.

The roar of the river in flood was always an attraction during the summer as were the veld fires in the winter. I had grown up a bit and was not responsible for starting any of the fires. It was exciting bashing out fires with bits of sack, and I felt a bit of pride in helping to prevent the spread of fire. Birds always loved the veld fires and would swoop in and out of the smoke I suppose to catch insects. There is something about the crackling of grass fires and the smell the smoke that is not unpleasant in small doses.

The summer rains brought a whole host of insects, from the different beetles, mosquitoes, flying ants, birds and of course, the cacophony of noise especially at night from the frogs at the river. I only ever saw one giant bullfrog, and it really was big, almost the size of a small chicken, but that was quite far from our house. My mother, with her green fingers, loved roses. She had numerous types of different colours and scents. I made a hobby of collecting the different coloured petals, then boiled them and stored the numerous different shades in narrow glass tubes. These I had collected from a dentist that had used them for holding the anaesthetic for dentistry. They had a small rubber plug at either end, which was perfect for containing the liquid. Against the light, they were beautiful. I must also have eaten a lot of vegetables from my mothers vegetable patch over the years directly from the garden; favourites were cocktail tomatoes, carrots and strawberries when in season and a simple rinse under the tap for the carrots and they were eaten.

Bob was the 'laat-lammetjie' of the family, and we had huge fun with him when he was big enough to sit in the pushchair. The pushchair was not really user friendly, and the frame and the hand crossbar was simply wrapped in material, no super padding. However, the body and wheels were strong, and we sometimes had races around the outside of the house, mostly on four wheels, but more often than not at the corners a controlled lifting on to two wheels. His deep 'sucking in chuckles' and laughter was totally infectious. He loved it, and so did Tony and I. He was not always very polite in his high-chair, and once hurled a spoon of mashed potato or pumpkin at our Gran (she had come out from England for a spell). It connected with her glasses and just about obliterated her vision. Everyone burst out laughing; Bob picked up on the entertainment success and could hardly stop chuckling. Gran did not think it so funny at the time, which made it worse in some perverse way.

Bob, unfortunately, was born with a hare lip, although not a cleft palate, it required surgery to be corrected. Our family was not financially well off and could not afford to have the specialist surgery conducted in Johannesburg. We were very fortunate in Rhodesia that the Lottery Sweepstake made available funds from the lottery for such causes. My parents made an application to them, and it was granted. My mother and Robert flew down to Johannesburg, and the surgeon Dr Jack Penn performed the operation, which was a success. It was Dr Jack Penn's son many years later in 2013 that was an anaesthetist during a hernia operation on me in Cape Town – a small world indeed.

Tony and I took it in turns to make the folks tea on a Sunday morning. It was all carefully laid out on a wooden tray, which fitted exactly on the arms of an occasional chair. The wooden arms were quite narrow, and one morning I was not quite so sharp and put the tray down, but not perfectly on the arms. As I turned, the tray slid down on one side and the whole lot, teapot, milk, teacups and sugar slid off the tray, on to the chair and then onto the floor. The clatter of crashing china was enough to raise the dead. And indeed, they were quickly awake, the 'lay in' moment had passed for them, and the sombre mood could be cut with a knife. The 'clean up' had to commence, and I was sorry for that lapse of concentration.

My mother made the most amazing 'bread pudding' with lots of raisins, creamy goodness and perfectly crusty on the outside. It was quite heavy and would have made excellent ballast for a boat, but it was great at school break as a substantial and filling snack. Plum jam sandwiches were the favourite but at times equally enjoyable and satisfying when jam was short, to have buttered bread liberally covered with sugar!

Christmas time was always magical, and to feign sleep was customary when the pillowcase was hung at the end of the bed. Fruit was by tradition always included in the bag. Special treats were bought, which included a case of cooldrinks, different nuts, sweets and biscuits. However, the tradition of hot meals in the heat of December was trying to say the least, but the paper hats combined with sweat resulted in various colours streaming down the brow. Paper decorations were the order of the day, and sometimes we would construct paper chains to enhance the décor. Christmas trees never lasted and would quickly shed the needles all over the place. Christmas carols were a pleasure to hear on the radio. But continually hearing the strains of *'I'm dreaming of a White Christmas'* by Bing Crosby wore very thin in the heat of Bulawayo, almost as much as hearing today the annual boring Bony 'M' Christmas renditions in shopping malls! However, discomfort only lasts so long, and we sensibly progressed to having cold meats and salads, and then followed by hot pudding with custard.

I especially recall when Bob was still very young that we asked him what he would like for Christmas. In broken vocabulary, he answered, "I want a ping pong ping from the ko-ba-haas" it was adorable and translated meant 'I want a ping pong ball from the OK Bazaars!' The OK Bazaars was perhaps the first large store in the fifties where you could with some freedom, select what you wanted and hand the goods over to the attendant for payment. Unlike some other departmental stores where you had to ask to look at or select, goods or items that were mostly under glass covers or shelved behind the attendant – these could perhaps in hindsight be called 'inconvenience stores'.

Of little importance really, but as a youngster, I often wondered why the large text under the OK Bazaars – 'Where Rhodesia shops', did not have a question mark. As if to say we were not sure where Rhodesians shopped. I did figure it out later, but they still use the same 'footer' so to speak. Had they said where Rhodesians shop it would have made more sense, at least to me.

The great event was the Coronation of the Queen. I clearly recall trying to be fully attentive to the drone on the radio that seemed to take hours. We clustered around trying to image the picture in Westminster Abbey. I think it would have even been a marathon today with modern television, even in high definition, but it would have helped. We were nonetheless very patriotic to the Queen and the royal family. After all, the Queen mother had her birthday on the same day as mine – quite a privilege! Standing to attention, proudly singing the national anthem for the Queen inside the movie-house – while she trotted by riding side-saddle on a Royal horse, all seemed quite pointless as no one was watching us, least of all the royal family. Without disrespect, the practice was dropped years later, even before UDI. We had the Coronation cups for years before the glazing eventually cracked and were subsequently lost in the number of moves we had.

I just loved Guy Fawkes. The weather was often stormy with the onset of rains, and the night could not come quick enough to light up the Catherine wheels, bangers and crackers, sparklers, rockets and Roman candles. Why they were called Roman candles is still a mystery to me, but I suppose they enjoyed them as much as us. On one such occasion, my father brought home a special rocket that would go both high and blast-off coloured lights and all. He would handle the launch because it was much bigger, and no doubt quite expensive. Despite my unqualified advice and protestations about using a bottle as a base, he pushed it into the earth; I suppose also realising that a bottle might topple over. It ignited successfully and roared into life and eventually with sufficient thrust; it parted from the stick and flew around the garden blasting impressive balls of different lights as it whirled around quite out of control. The finale of the show was over, no one got hurt and a few lessons learned but not spoken of! We never really had enough fireworks to satisfy our desires, but we also took delight in watching other impressive rockets and deep explosions from around the neighbourhood. Gunpowder has a distinct scent, especially when it is burnt – I just loved that 'after-burn' smell!

A great deal of excitement was raised in town one day by an 'adult' who had reported in *The Bulawayo Chronicle* that a Pterodactyl (a winged bird from the dinosaur era) had been sighted near the Little Umgusa River. My friend and I set out to try and find it but failed, and were disappointed. But interestingly enough, we later found out that a 'single flamingo' had been seen at a small reservoir a few miles from where we lived, the 'singular rare sighting' may very well have been the misidentified bird.

I used to shoot birds with a 'catty' (catapult) not many actually, but until one day I was coming from a small quarry where I was looking for geologically interesting stones when I saw and heard a bird flapping. Up close, I could see that it had become trapped with tree gum (birdlime) to a narrow branch. It was a lovely bird, and I carefully freed it from the gum and let it go. Seeing that fragile creature up close was an important message for me. I had shot some birds later with my pellet gun, and those were always given away to the locals, but that earlier encounter made a significant impression on me. I think it was the suffering that I saw that was cruel, like the mature elephant my wife and I saw years later in the Chizarira National park, limping along, raw around the lower leg and above the ankle. A distressing sight indeed. We reported it to the local Wardens office, and it was followed up the next day and shot. That type of cruelty goes on and on.

Pocket money was always scarce, so one of the ways I made a few shillings was to grow seedlings and sell them to the Farmers Co-op in Bulawayo where my mother worked. Seed could be bought by the ounce and seedlings sold in little wads wrapped in damp newspaper. Trying once to cut the small front lawn with scissors was not successful and was not worth the pocket money as it produced painful blisters.

Talking of money, I once walked into town from Sauerstown with a five-pound note clutched in my hand. This was a considerable amount of money, which I dared not lose. Closer to town, and where I really cannot remember whether I had to buy something or hand it over to my mother, I checked in my pocket for the money, and it was gone! I panicked, checked my other pocket, and it was not there either. I was severely traumatised until I realised still shaking, that the money was still clutched in my hand, but I had transferred the money to the other hand when I checked my other pocket. Honestly, it can happen and did to me.

When a railway line was constructed, a cutting was made just north of the North End cemetery, so a friend and I explored the cutting, and were surprised to find that some bones we felt sure were human, were sticking out of the soil near the top of the cutting. (In fact, later on, I noted on a map of Bulawayo that the railway line did cut a corner of the old cemetery). However, the much more exciting discovery was that you could find quartz crystals about a foot or two below the topsoil. They were mostly slender, beautifully clear, and a treasure.

Also, most beautiful were the agate stones that we could find in the bush behind the Garden Cash Store at the top of the hill. The stones were pockmarked, rather dull-looking pebbles, and when broken open revealed beautiful crystals pointing in towards the centre with concentric rings of agate surrounding them.

The railway line construction also provided me with my first experience of welding, which later in life, became an important facet of my profession of inspection, testing, and quality assurance. However, the lesson here was that after having observed the workers (welders) using brilliant sparklers (welding rods), we then recovered a few of the rods after they had left for the day and tried to ignite them with matches, which did not work! Obviously, but not realising it at the time, you required electric generators producing voltage and current to create the arc for welding. However, the small railcar they used for travelling up and down the constructed railway line did work. After the workers had left, we jumped onto the small railcar, pumping a handle up and down, which drove the car along the rails. It was too much hard work going uphill, so we headed downhill with much excitement. A handwheel at the back of the car was to be turned to apply the brakes. So off we went downhill with much rumbling of the wheels and excitement – ahead of us was (which I now realise) a rail-mounted welding generator. We did not realise that the brakes would only apply when the handwheel was turned down quite far! We leapt off as it banged into the rear of the generator and derailed onto the side of the track. It was too heavy to reposition, so we hastily left.

When not walking along the river short cut, my brother Tony would give me a lift on his bike. It was tough for him, who often accused me of being a dead weight on the bike. I really tried to be lighter than I was but could not logically figure out how. When dismounting, I often could not walk as the circulation in my leg had stopped because of the crossbar, and it had become numb. He developed strong legs, and I was still as skinny as a rake! When I did have my own bike, I nearly lost my manhood one day when cycling in a standing position off the saddle, and while pumping the pedals, the chain came off, and I landed heavily with legs astride on the crossbar. I swear I must have had lumps behind my ears – the pain was intense, and in a dazed state, simply careened off the path and fell into the bush, which was not nearly as painful!

One day I bunked high school with my friend Derek. My brother, who I was walking with, was astonished that I had decided to head off into the bush instead of going cn to school. Oddly enough, I had never really made a habit of bunking or pretending I was sick, but this was more an adventure. We had water, a tin of beans and viennas, built ourselves a grass shelter, and enjoyed the bush. Government House (originally the site of Lobengula's Bulawayo kraal) was about four hundred meters to the north, and they had a wonderful orchard of oranges. Oranges would have tasted so refreshing, and there were so many of them that we decided that the few we planned to take would probably only become rotten on the ground anyway, so we set off. The approach was easy as the type of sandveld supported very long 'thatching' type grass, so we were well concealed. There was no one around, so we crossed the road and climbed through the fence (not barbed, no electric fence, no CCTV or beams). We collected as many as we could carry in our shirts and when just about to return on our path, heard voices so took cover and hid in a very large cattle dung compost heap. Convict workers with a few armed guards carrying old Lee Enfield 303's, commenced working in the general area. In about half an hour, they moved on, and we scooted across back to our shelter. It was a wonderful morning, which was only clouded by a bit of boredom and conscience. The other occasions that I visited Government House and the museum were conducted formally and in the open.

School was great, apart from being bullied on occasions, I suppose because I was very short for my age. Even in Form II, I was, I think, the shortest in the school. I really enjoyed the atmosphere and location of the school set high up and surrounded by bush. I enjoyed cross country running, high jump, and long jump. Pole vaulting, I felt, was hazardous given that the landing was a hole dug in the ground and filled with sawdust, and neither did the sheet metal receptacle for the pole look inviting, and what's more, I had minimal padding. I could, though, jump my own height at one stage, no record, because I was already short. I also enjoyed boxing, and it is a great sport when you are winning, but being short, was no advantage so gave it up when I lost too frequently. My father was very keen on boxing and encouraged me because from where he came from in London, bare fist boxing in the street was popular, followed by glove boxing later on. I must say that I enjoyed the major world heavyweight title fights that were so popular worldwide in the sixties.

I learnt to type when I switched to commercial stream when our French teacher Mrs Broughton (the headmaster's wife), left. A number of the boys were asked if they would like to learn typing, so Dave Sutherland and I agreed to. We did well, and surprisingly, he and I in a class of girls achieved first and second place in the exams. I have never regretted learning to type, though learning to touch type on an old mechanical Remington typewriter without jamming keys on the platen and scratching fingers between the keys was quite a challenge. How things have changed, but we would never have known how important it would become in the future for all folk with a computer or Smartphone to be able to type – cryptically or otherwise!

I just loved chemistry and physics. This proved to be most beneficial later on in my career when I took up metallurgy and physical testing of metals. One of our classmates got quite badly burnt when he pocketed a stick of phosphorous after removing it from a jar of water! What wonderful teachers we had then, we were very blessed, and I am still thankful and privileged to have such a good education. We often played 'bok-bok' and 'kinnetjie' at a break which was good fun. I doubt if they are ever played now though. Cricket and rugby were also played, and for some reason, football was only played in junior school which I really enjoyed then, and much preferred over cricket and rugby. I lost interest in playing cricket after blocking a ball, it flew up and hit me above and between the eyes. Tony also played cricket, and I think he lost interest after sustaining a broken nose which resulted in permanent damage! I do, however enjoy watching cricket.

3

Early Bush Exploration and Prospecting –
Sputnik / Sea Cadets RSES

We moved to Glengarry when my mother fell in love with the double-storeyed and gabled thatched house. I suppose it reminded her of England. The thatching was almost intoxicating at times, and when it rained the thatch gave an even deeper and more pleasant smell. The house was on a plot of over two acres which provided lots of space for growing vegetables and to have fun. The small 'Glengarry' estate with moderately large plots was on a rise between the Intindita and Little Umguza Rivers. These two small stream beds met at the bottom of the estate and had been the site of some serious battles and skirmishes between the Matabele and occupying forces during the Rebellion of 1896. There are exciting accounts of these battles, including accounts of outstanding bravery which were well documented. However, suffice it to say, that the passage of the patrols and forces at the time actually passed through Glengarry. As described by Oliver Ransford in his book, *Bulawayo, Historic Battleground of Rhodesia*, the wide, Matabele-impis front would have advanced through our property as well. Two of the following engagement maps depict this action. There were several other military engagements and rescues in and around that area from Umvutcha's kraal close to the Umguza river to the north, Ntabazinduna, Bembesi (1893), and in the Matopos. The stories make exciting reading when understanding the risks, dangers and types of difficult terrain that had to be negotiated in those early days. The Mashonaland campaigns were no less challenging. The major engagement in the Mambo Hills and numerous battles in the Matopos.

My mother had green fingers and virtually everything she planted grew well and produced either fruit or vegetables. Red soil and well water did the trick and we enjoyed tomatoes, peas, carrots, radishes, cabbage, lettuce, strawberries and much more. My friend and I had in the past picked large mulberries from a convenient overhanging tree near Sauerstown, and I decided that we should have such a tree as well. I broke off a thin branch from the tree and pushed it into the soil in our garden at Glengarry. It took well, grew fast and eventually produced the large mulberries that were vastly superior to the small almost button-shaped ones. The leaves were excellent for feeding and growing silkworms. So, I guess the soil must have been very fertile. The well water was another story and was so 'hard' that it had to be treated to soften it. Soap would

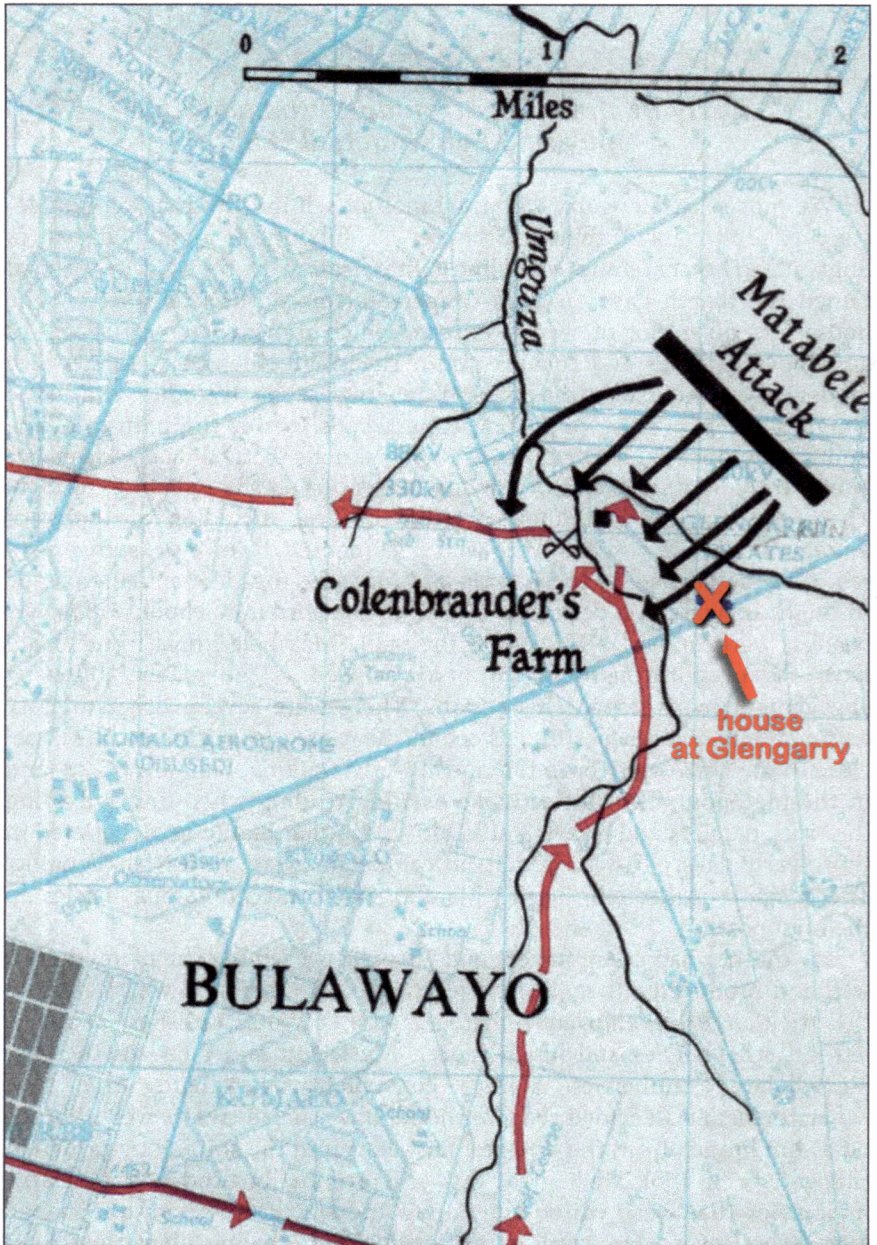

Map of first battle, action and retreat to Bulawayo by Captain Macfarlane at Glengarry – 19th April 1896

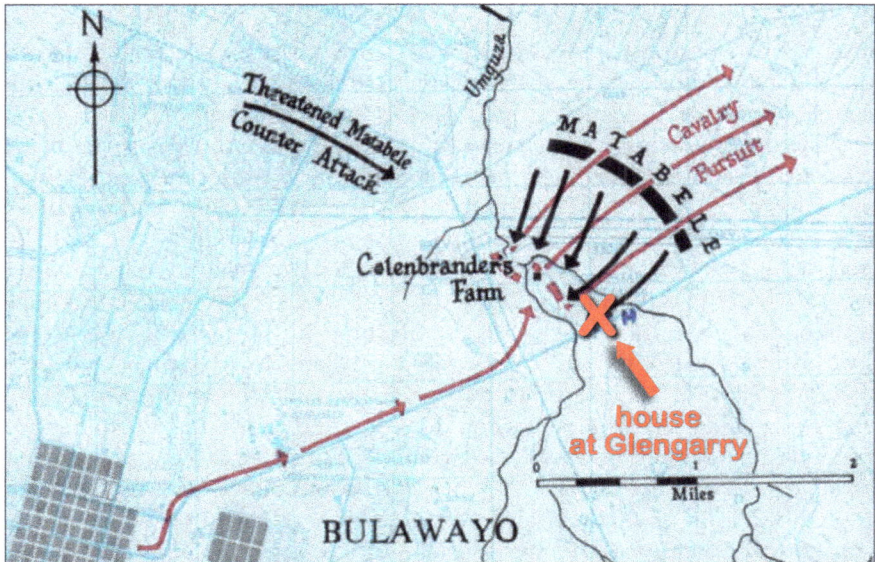

Map of second battle with the Matabele, the battle and the counter attack by Captain Macfarlane through Glengarry – 25th April 1896

never lather in it untreated, and I always blamed it for the kidney stones that I suffered years later, but perhaps that was a good excuse.

We once had a terrible drought in the area, and even the well dried up although it was said that there was a large subterranean reservoir of water in the Glengarry area, so it was a tough time carting water from town in drums and bottles for drinking. We did not have piped water at that time, but eventually, the rains came, and things came back to normal. The message from this was that I never forgot the importance of water and never wasted it by having deep baths.

The beauty of our house with its location out of town was that I could spend any free time wandering and exploring the bush. I did not have any local friends, so much of the wanderings were with my two dogs exploring old mine workings and peering down old mine shafts.

The general area was already known for gold and as a result, there were several small workings not far from our house. One was a three stamp mill on a small rise not more than half a kilometre from the house and the other across the Salisbury road where there was a five stamp mill (perhaps the 'City & Suburban Mine'). The stamp mills were not always working, but the sound never bothered me. In some way, the rhythm of stamp mill hammers was comforting, and one could tell the change in the direction of the wind by the sounds being either stronger or weaker. Most of the gold in the area occurred in pockets or 'lenses', so workings did not last too long. Both workings closed within a few years. The exception to this was the Old Nick mine some distance south towards the Harry Allen Golf course, which is still operating after seventy years of operation.

It was while living in Glengarry that I started part-time prospecting; it was almost a natural extension to exploring the bush. I did find a small flake of gold after crushing my sample with crude bits of iron and a channel iron base (a bit noisy). It was not worth pursuing due to the ratio of material to be worked. All of my samples either went to the Museum where Dr Geoffrey Bond kindly identified the different minerals (he once told me that I should have studied for Geology – I think he was right). The gold samples I dropped off at the Standard Bank in Bulawayo, and they would crush and analyse them and give me a written report, all for no charge. I paid a 'madala' African man five pounds a month to explore the general area and gather samples that looked promising. Most revealed no payable gold, but my excitement was raised when one sample he collected from a small pile of stones from a very old and narrow shaft revealed a gold content of 32 pennyweights per ton of gold, very profitable! I did take out Prospecting Licences at 5/ – (five shillings) for a few serious prospecting options. The disappointment of the great find was when I found out that the sample had been taken from a working in a proclaimed residential area (though not occupied at that time).

Sketch of an old five stamp mill – near Glengarry

Sketch of typical panning for gold scene

Apparently, the over 3,000 gold mines in then Rhodesia, were established on ancient workings. I also prospected a good quartz reef near Cement Siding and the Umguza River. Further prospecting was north of Burnside/Hillside area. Prospecting is a completely absorbing hobby. Most of the fun was quietly 'sniffing' and exploring around the bush, outcrops and river stones and finding something, rather than just the desire for wealth. One afternoon I went walking with my dog not far from the little Umguza, and upon coming across some open veld, I saw an old prospecting ditch some way off. The grass had been recently burnt, so observation was easy – however, a very strange feeling followed, a sort of presentiment of something unseen. I stopped had a look around and could not see anything obvious to be afraid of, and then proceeded towards the old working. It was relatively shallow with nothing obvious to look at but the dog that would typically follow me anywhere, would not venture forward, even after calling it. It was as if there was a long glass wall in

Lion in a cage near the Old Nick Mine, Bulawayo

front of it. It paced back and forth but would not come near. Another one of those feelings.

I returned to the spot where the dog was, which was about twenty odd metres from the working, then set off home as it was almost sundown and I was more than a bit uneased! Not far from this area perhaps a kilometre away, there was a fully grown male lion which was held captive in a small cage. It seemed to be kept there by I think, folk from the Old Nick Mine. There was always meat there which looked like donkey carcass, but the poor creature had all of its fur rubbed off from the constant walking back and forth against the square wired cage. It never seemed to mind my presence. In fact, it may have enjoyed a bit of company. I never found out what became of it, but it was unbelievably cruel to have been caged up.

It was at Glengarry near our house that I found my first stone implement (1957) probably of Middle Stone Age period. I still have it. My dear mother did not share the interest of collecting stones, and I would most often have to retrieve my samples from the garden where they had been thrown out!

The two small dogs would often go out by themselves hunting, and it was very sad when one day only one returned. Even though I went out to search, it was futile there being so many deep mine shafts dotted around,

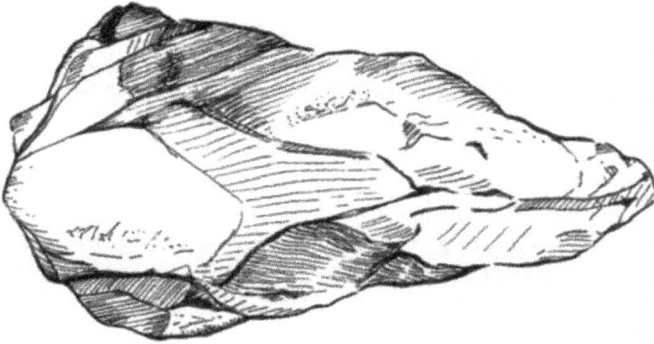

Sketch of Middle Stone Age (MSA) tool – 100mm long.
Sketch: Olivia Kensley

where I presume, she had fallen down one, or had perhaps and sadly been bitten by a snake. Talking of snakes, I was in the front of the plot with Bob, my younger brother and we were looking around at a lot of broken rock at a hedge line, when I noticed some bright yellowish coloured liquid on his right cheek. Puzzled I thought it might be from us breaking a few branches from the hedge, but, and to my horror on my immediate right I saw a movement, and a 'huge' head of a snake emerged right next to me. I leapt back and Bob followed on my heels. It was a Spitting Cobra (Ringhals). None of the venom had got into his eyes, but we carefully washed it all off the side of his face. I found later that the snake had spat on my khaki trouser leg. The sprayed area never washed out and looked like light rust stains.

Sitting on the stoep one hot afternoon, one of our small dogs came trotting along the gravel driveway but had not seen a long snake that I had spotted gliding with its head outstretched, next to a large rock. I shouted at the dog, but it took no notice and walked straight into the snake. A furious tussle took place between the surprised dog and the snake – the snake vanished, and the dog continued walking along as if nothing had happened. It did not look like a venomous snake, and the dog did not suffer any effects from the engagement. Perhaps too tired to bother!

One day near the five stamp mill mine since closed, I looked down an open working and saw a few cardboard boxes in amongst rocks bushes and debris. I was curious to find out the contents, but with caution and fear of nesting snakes, I fired my pellet gun, which was quite a powerful one, into the boxes. Imagine my surprise and horror when I scrambled down the working and opened the boxes to find that they were filled with sticks of old dynamite. I left them be, and never went back.

Our house being thatched, apart from the pleasant intoxicating smell as mentioned especially when it rained, could be a concern and worrying during hectic and violent thunder storms. Our house was struck by lightning once on the apex but being right on the top and with forthcoming rain, the roof did not catch light though a section of the thatch had burned! My room was upstairs, and I had a wonderful Pilot radio (no TV at that time) that had all the medium and short wave bands, and to improve the signal I had erected a steel pole in the garden and hung a long aerial from it through my steel-framed window to the radio. I woke one hot sultry storm brewing night to find that the whole window frame was electrically alive with sparks everywhere. The static in the air and on the aerial had caused it, so I quickly opened the window and yanked it off quite shaken, because the aerial actually passed through the overhanging thatch!

I often used to practice my Morse code by listening in to the numerous transmissions. Most of them were too fast for me to translate quickly enough, but one evening, I heard a transmission which was slow enough for me to catch most of the letters and words. I was astonished at the message; for it was from a radio ham in the Belgium Congo who was reporting that there had been serious uprising and that people were being killed. I noted what I could and would have replied had I had a Morse key and transmitter, but I did not. Early next morning I informed my father of what I had picked up, and it was only later that day that information filtered through that indeed the Congo was in turmoil and there were massacres, looting and fighting. This had followed the pulling out of Belgium from the Congo and the subsequent rocky road to independence.

Sometime after this, my father, Tony and I saw the convoy of vehicles carrying thousands of refugees from the Congo (probably from Elizabethville, as called then) pouring into Bulawayo. That must have been late 1960 and early 1961. The later reports from reliable sources such as doctors, nurses, missions revealed that the murderous acts were more graphic and barbaric than we could have ever imagined.

I was deeply interested in space events as Russia had just launched Sputnik. There was a huge flurry of night watchers to see the satellite. We were fortunate one night to see the small dot of light crossing the sky and the much radio announced beep, beep, beep of the transmitted signal to earth – so much has changed and advanced since, where now, there are literally thousands of satellites in the night sky transmitting everything you can think of. At the time however, I started to build rockets. Though they were never as successful as the bought Chinese rockets at Guy Fawkes, I did try. There was a risk of which I was sternly warned of, and that was the danger of the thatch catching light because of the rockets. Early experiments were made using gunpowder. And in those days, a chemist was a chemist where you could buy all the ingredients to make gunpowder. The purchase of Potassium Nitrate was always questioned by the Chemist to ensure that I was aware of the dangers. Those rockets never went far, in fact mostly never really took off because of launching ramp problems, gunpowder mix and rocket pressure. I did try and improve propulsion using Zinc Dust, and that worked very well. That final rocket I promised my mother I would take across the river bed away from the house. It was a grand set up, and I used Jettex fuse to ignite the fuel. She watched from the house a distance away. It roared off the ramp and blew up only about six feet above the ground. The cloud of smoke was big, and my poor mother thought that I had been burnt to a frizz, but I emerged unharmed and abandoned further experimentation. Talking of frizz though, I once bought a rocket (these were much more reliable), and carefully tied a large shiny Matabele ant with cotton to the rocket and encased in a cocoon of silver paper to avoid it being burnt. It was also some distance away from the thrust. It duly shot off in great speed to the heavens. I was impressed to see how the ant had fared... well, the thrust of the rocket tore the poor ant through the silver paper (which was lying on the ground next to me when I looked around) and hurtled it high into the air (without oxygen), while being burnt to a crisp below the flaming rocket. I felt bad about that, but I had placed it below, because at the head of the rocket it would have been crushed because those rockets always came down head first. Later astronauts were always at the top of rockets, but the rockets rarely came down head first At that time, the only creature to go up into space (not really very far) apart from my poor ant was a monkey and a dog by the Russians.

Apart from burning my big toe (deep fried) with a homemade rocket, and my finger while trying to light a failed fuse on a banger, I had a scare of permanent eye injury when during the rainy season, the white ants (termites) used to eat every bit of exposed or hidden wood or thatching. They would also sneak up inside plaster and bricks and demolish roofing timbers from the inside and while out of sight. On this occasion the ants were furiously building a termite mound with an open top out the back yard. There were thousands of them on the inside and building the perimeter ridge of the mound on the outside. So, I got a large cracker, lit the fuse and threw it down the hole. It obviously did not go off, so I looked into the hole, and bang! I thought I was blind, the rush of material and air past my face was frightening, but after extracting at least two ants from under my eye lids and suffering stinging spots on my face, feeling sorry for myself (but not the ants), and stupid for not allowing enough time for the fuse to take, I withdrew considering myself lucky that it was not worse. Fortunately, they were the smaller white ants, and not the bigger termites. There were other experiences with blowing up Harpic tins, and Mazoe cordial bottles but practices not to be mentioned or recommended here as they were quite dangerous. In those days there were no public warnings of 'Do not try this at home', so we did try them at home, or close to it! I guess my learning curve may well have been prematurely interrupted had I continued. But, I did learn a lot about chemistry, pyrotechnics and physics.

I later moved from my upstairs bedroom to the end of the house which was more convenient with a bathroom close by and on the ground floor. I could look out of my window and see the main Salisbury (now Harare) road. The traffic was never that busy then, and generally by eight o'clock at night the road fell silent, so it was never that disturbing because of noise. It was one moonlit night, very quiet and I was asleep, and in my semi-conscious state thought that I must be dying because the clock I had, a real tick tock Big Ben Westclox type began to become quieter and quieter, like fading away. And yes, indeed it was fading away, for when I awoke, I saw a young black fellow running down our front driveway, with my clock. I rarely closed my windows, or closed curtains, and in the moonlight, he was as clear as day. I could have caused a rumpus but was sort of taken aback and just watched him vanish down the service track. I was not angry because it was quite bold of him and amusing. He would have to walk through a small courtyard to my side window to have done it. Our dogs did not stir as they were at the far end of the house. We had thirteen rooms in all, so quite spread out. Early morning during weekdays, the common sight was to see probably twelve to fifteen African cyclists, with arms resting on the handle bars cycling into town. They cycled all the way from Ntabazinduna, a distance of fifteen miles from town. Their bikes were the old fashioned and very heavy roadsters with bigger tyres. I admired them greatly for their stamina and fortitude. Bulawayo can become very cold in winter with 'Guti' light rain, as well as searing heat in October, and every day they would be there going to and from town. There were literally thousands of African cyclists that filled the roads of Bulawayo daily. One could hardly cross Lobengula Street at rush hour with the constant stream of cyclists. Africans walked great distances then as there were few buses, especially out of town. On occasions one could hear one playing either a simple guitar melody or the very mellow sound of a mouth harp. The harp was played with a single wire, strung across a curved piece of light, flat wood. The one end positioned in the mouth which was tightly strung and plucked with a finger or tapped with a small stick. The resonance and sound were produced by opening or closing the mouth to produce the notes. I have never forgotten that sound. These folk were very poor but had music in their hearts! One weekend while lazing in bed I heard a bang from a passing car, and looking out my window, saw a suitcase sliding along the verge of the road and at our front entrance to the main road. The car continued, but while contemplating getting up, saw an African pick up the suitcase and carry on walking with it. I dressed and jumped in my Hillman Minx and drove up the main road to stop the removal of the suitcase knowing that someone had lost it. I came upon the fellow already well past the Glengarry cash store and recovered the suitcase and informed the chap that I would take it to the Police station. He was happy with that, knowing that it was not his. It was a rather tatty suitcase and looking inside found clothing. I handed it in at the Fife street police station, and that was that... a week or so later, I received a call from the police to come in to see them as the owner, was most thankful and had left me with ten Pounds, because they had had their jewellery at the bottom of the case! That was a huge amount of money then. I should have given a gift to the walker, who picked it up, but it did not occur to me then that he certainly deserved a good 'bonsella'.

October was an extremely hot month preceding the rains and was commonly called the suicide month because of this. Everything seemed to stand still during the oppressive heat, waiting for the welcome relief of rain. Generally, the clouds would appear on the distant horizon to the North. Distant flashes of lightning would give hope, but daily the clouds would disappear, then next day be slightly closer until the moisture laden clouds would eventually form and produce heavy thunder storms – this could take weeks to happen. During the hot build up, it was not uncommon for the tar in the roads (certainly as I had seen in Lobengula Street) to start running – car tyres would make a whishing sound as they went through the liquid tar. *The Bulawayo Chronicle* newspaper showed pictures of eggs that could be fried on corrugated iron. The swimming pools were very popular, but the harsh sun caused serious sunburn at times. A rain shower could fall on one side of the street and not the other. The drops were sometimes big and the size of half-crowns when they hit the ground and just a few could soak you through. Just before a storm one would feel tired and listless, and as soon as the rain fell, one perked up and felt alive again, often smiling! I later learnt that it was because of the positive ions in the air that made one listless, and after a storm (not the only cause) negative ions would be produced in the air that made you feel mentally alert and refreshed. I later read a scientific report that had conducted tests on folk that revealed that under conditions where air saturated in positive ions would have adverse effects on workers, and the reverse when breathing in negative ions. Too much electronic equipment in a room without adequate ventilation can also be bad for you.

Anyway, when the rain fell on our parched garden, the smell of the soil was unforgettable. Something magical happens when rain falls, the air is cool, and all life rejoices and renews. After the building and filling of Kariba dam (around 1959), I noticed for the first time, that light fluffy clouds became obvious drifting from the North during the early rainy season. I had never seen this before and concluded that they were evaporation clouds from the massive lake. The lake was then the largest in Africa and was over 300kms distant north from where we lived in Bulawayo.

Bulawayo when originally set out, had very wide streets to accommodate the turning ('U' Turns) of a wagon with sixteen span of oxen. However, they also had quite deep sloping dips at each intersection running from the West where the landscape was higher down to the lower East side of town. This was to cope with the flash floods of water from heavy rain. Apart from unsuspecting visitors that 'bottomed' out badly when speeding too fast through the dips, it was fun to splash through the rushing water... One day while in a cinema in Grey street we could hardly hear the movie due to the roar of rain on the roof, and on coming out after the show, found that the car was not on the upper side of the street, but had been swept across the road which was quite wide, to a gully on the opposite side, all due to a flash flood!

I had joined the Sea Cadets called the 'TS Matabele' which was based at Brady Barracks on the Salisbury road and just West of the Kumalo Aerodrome. I used to cycle there which was about two and a half miles from Glengarry. Going there was fine but coming back in the dark it was a bit scary. I only had a small battery powered headlight which penetrated a few metres ahead. There was mostly no traffic, no lights and thick bush either side and past the aerodrome. One night I saw a vehicle parked in the bush at the end of the aerodrome. Probably a couple having a bit of 'slap and tickle' I thought... The next day I was horrified to find that there had been a terrible murder committed there. The coloured lady was dead, and the European guy had staggered for miles at the back of the aerodrome (where there were no houses, only a rough track), to find help as he had been wounded in the assault. He I guess recovered, but I did not lose the image of the vehicle parked in the dark where the murder no doubt may have already occurred, or about to be committed. The magnitude of the murder was enhanced by *The Bulawayo Chronicle* publishing pictures of the location with bold dotted lines and 'X' marking the spot etc. The thought that there were murderers lurking in the dark there put me on edge thereafter and I used to shoot past the spot riding in the centre of the road in the blackness and only felt at ease when I passed the city boundary where the country opened out and I was close to home.

The Queen's Birthday parade was always a big event with lots of training, precision marching with 'old' 303 rifles with fixed bayonets. The Royal Navy uniform I was always proud of. Shining black boots with white gaiters and tropical gear with blue collar edged to represent the three great sea battles. Standing for what seemed hours was tough, and on this particular occasion one poor fellow fainted in front of me. The rifle clattered to the ground, and he fell forward and as I was at the rear rank (fortunately), it was almost funny to see his head propped between the sea cadets' boots in front, facing the crowd! He was soon carted off. But that was not all. Being a commanding officer must have been hell trying to remember the combined bellowed and barely audible orders from a distance, the presenting of arms (a relief that one could move again), standing to attention, eyes right, wheels and turns etc., whilst remaining slick must have been too much for him, for before our eyes, in his white tropical kit, his bowels opened and poured down his trousers. Now the dark kit would have been sort of OK, but in tropical kit it stood out like as they used to say, like dogs' balls! The poor guy had to march around and off the parade ground with a yellow glow to his stride whilst giving verbal orders as if nothing had happened. Scary stuff I tell you. I felt very sorry for him.

One Queens Birthday Parade I had opportunity to attend, I turned down much to the huge disappointment of my mother. The reason being, not that I was not fully committed to the Royal family and the Queen, was because my friend Bruce Morrison had invited me to go with him and his dad to Kazungula on the Zambezi River on a fishing trip. As it turned out much to my mother's and my now collective but different disappointments, my trip was cancelled. I learnt a huge amount when in the sea cadets even though we had no local sea to exercise on. One of the benefits was that I learnt the Morse code, which I used later on.

Speaking of the Zambezi, I once went with my father who was on a business trip to Kamativi Tin Mine not too far from Wankie, and then we went on to the Victoria Falls. I had been to the Falls before, but this time he would treat me to a boat trip to Kandahar Island (why the name Kandahar I never figured out, I think the name belongs in India), however, it was to include a guided tour of the island. A very irritating young lady with a loud squeaky voice and with arms waving about kept on about how she would go in front to warn of elephants that often swam out to the island. I told my father that I would explore the lower end of the island instead of walking behind a line of chattering people. This I did and it was exciting and cool under the canopy of the big trees and clusters of 'vegetable ivory' palms. It could not have been too far, and I was treading quite cautiously, when the bush on my right hand side erupted. A quite big crocodile sprang out and with body high off the ground, it virtually sprinted across some open ground and shot down the bank and into the river. I was shaken by the experience and realised that I could have easily been attacked and possibly dragged off. It was not a huge croc, probably about one and a half metres long, but nonetheless, big enough to give me a monumental fright. I quickly retraced my steps and followed up with the crowd and quietly and humbly told my father what had happened.

On another later occasion returning from the Victoria Falls with my parents, and when I was driving (I had obtained my driving licence by then, in 1958) my father's six cylinder Humber Super Snipe, a large and heavy vehicle (it weighed over two and a half tons), I suddenly saw a dark line across the narrow tar road. Before I realised it, I had driven over a very large python which seemed to lie right across the road. I braked and reversed, my father who was dozing, woke up and asked me what was going on. I explained that I had driven over this large snake. At the spot where I had hit it, there was no snake to be seen! We got out of the car, and the snake had definitely gone, but unfortunately would die of the injuries. My father did not quite believe me until I pointed out the distinct marks in the dust on both front fenders where it had recoiled. It was sad that it had happened, but it was very difficult to see sometimes on the undulating road which alternated from strip road to nine foot tar mat. I could swear that when the road was built during the depression in the early thirties, that they ran the road over anthills and down dips! As a matter of interest, the road warning signs of a dip ahead displayed the dip as a bowl shape – they often turned out that shape as well. It happened quite close to the Halfway Hotel (still in good order and presentable today), and I think it was in the lounge or reception that they already had a skinned python skin stretched way across the wall. It must have been over four metres long!

4

Expedition to Mateke - 1958

In 1958 I had the good fortune to be chosen from a selection of applicants from Northlea School to go on a RSES – Rhodesian Schools Exploration Society expedition. The expeditions were organised to go to various parts of the country, and members were drawn from the local schools closest to the planned area. This expedition was to go to the Mateke hills area in the south-east of the country. I had chosen to join the geology section because it was my first interest. There were also sections for botany, archaeology, anthropology and entomology, and the results of the studies were conducted correctly and reported. All of these field studies across the country contributed important scientific information to existing information already gathered. It was also extremely beneficial to the scholars who participated in them. My elder brother Tony had the previous year been with a group to the Makarikari Pan and Nata River. That particular expedition was in Bechuanaland (Botswana), but close and connected by the Nata River from Rhodesia.

It is strange how often one associates music with an event or time in life – sometimes happy – sometimes sad, but at that time, Buddy Holly, Elvis and Cliff Richard and the Shadows were the buzz not to mention many other artists and groups at the time. I particularly remember a new Buddy Holly number 'Oh Boy' replaying in my head on the long and cold trip (on the back of a lorry) down to the Lowveld.

Our bush camp was on the banks of the Bubye River. Being the month of May, the rains had passed, and the river was not running. In truth, it probably was, but underneath the sand. For our camp, we dug a deep hole in the sand from where to draw water for our daily needs. This was common to most of the Lowveld rivers in Rhodesia. Even though the drive down from Bulawayo in the back of a truck was cold, the bush was typically warm to hot because it was in the Lowveld. Route finding was not easy because there were at that time, no detailed maps and only very rough and indistinct tracks. River crossings were tricky, and at least one Landrover had the steering arm bent on a hidden tree stump, which had to be stripped in the bush and straightened with the help of handy Mopani tree trunks. On the way to our base camp, one of our lads standing on the back of the lorry, looking over the drivers' cab roof, was struck on the forehead by a low, overhanging branch. He landed next to us against the tailgate with a bleeding forehead, but no serious damage was inflicted, and it healed without stitches.

The camp was basic with tables, and seating cut from Mopani poles, with a crude tarpaulin, strung over the eating area. Our sleeping was also basic, and simply hip holes fashioned in the ground for comfort, covered with a groundsheet with a sleeping bag on top. I had rigged up a box type mosquito net over the bed.

Hearing the various night-sounds of the bush cutting through the silence, the happy chirping bird calls at day break, the distinct and penetrating francolin call – all reminded one that you were just a visitor to the bush and the creatures in it.

Excursions were made to the extinct Marungudzi Crater, which was most impressive. Especially from the south-western side where the bush was extremely dense and almost impenetrable. We battled to access the half -moon crater where a previously occupied site was supposed to exist – at times we would be climbing over the tops of branches of vines and thickets.

The area was highly mineralised and we came across watercourses that had the appearance of being 'frozen' but were, in fact, limestone deposits that had precipitated out over long periods to form unusual shapes. The eastern side had an opening in the hills to access the main crater. There was also some walling and passage of sorts that provided access to the upper half-moon crater. I did not partake in the climb up that side, but an old muzzleloader was found on the way up. The half-moon and prominent outcrop were well wooded and vegetated. The access had been previously built to provide passage for cattle and refuge for the people from skirmishing tribes – most likely, Matabele impis. Below the area of access

Marungudzi crater – near Mateke Hills

was an obvious gathering place under a large tree, presumably quite important, or perhaps a burial site. Further along was a village which was in an impeccable state of neatness, but devoid of people. Perhaps they thought us to be tax collectors as someone had suggested. The sight of a couple of Landrovers would have also convinced them of 'tax' intent! However, outside one of the huts was a perfectly formed and most beautiful drum. It was somewhat large and perhaps well over half a metre in diameter, a fine specimen.

On the subject of drums on one particularly quiet night at our Bubye River camp, we heard, a long way off, the soft beat of distant drums. The sound was a deep and steady rhythmic beat. Then from even further off, much further I could only imagine and guess to be more than five kilometres, perhaps, even more, another drumbeat could be heard. The original drum then sounded in response. We even heard another even further afield, or so it sounded. These folk were clearly communicating and very effectively. We were evidently not privy to the code of signal used, but judging by the mellow and pleasing tone drifting across the veld; it did not seem to carry a message of immediate alarm. Had we visited other villages; we would have no doubt seen other drums. What a perfect method of keeping the community connected and in touch. I have not heard of any study or analysis of such communication 'signals', and I believe we still have a lot to learn in this regard. The opportunity may well now be limited due to the rapidly changing times.

Not far from Marungudzi was Dawn Hill, an early mining site, excavated for asbestos. The significance of the hill was the early Iron Age occupied-site on the summit. Some potsherds recovered from the site revealed some unique patterns. We entered a horizontal adit shaft which went in as far as a vertical ventilation shaft bringing some light into our route down. Fallen rocks made further progress risky, so we retreated. Interestingly, at the entrance on a narrow shelf was a perfectly-woven asbestos bird nest. We also collected prospecting bags of bat guano. I filled a few which went on to produce excellent fertilizer for watering the garden back in Bulawayo.

On one of our excursions, we drove along a rough track to the northern end of the hills to explore the surrounds. There was good evidence of elephant judging by the numerous footprints in a muddy pan along the way. One of these impressions in the mud was so large, that I sat in it and had my picture taken – I suppose I was not that large, but it did seem considerable in size. There was no easy access to the hills, so we had to follow a fairly steep ascent path created by elephants. Elephants are quite good at climbing steep inclines. When we had reached the top of the hill plateau, we followed a distinctly smooth and wide path that the elephants obviously used. The path was at least one to one and a half metres wide and led into dense vegetation and trees. Time did not allow us to go too deeply, but it appeared to be a regular and lush area for feeding compared with the sparse mopani veld on the lower plains. We also found what looked like 'dolly' holes for crushing ore or perhaps grain. These were unlike the open 'pan' or narrow grinding pans and hollows that were common in the southern end of the hills. An Iron Age archaeological site was later found near the highest hill of the range. The rainfall is slightly higher and a bit cooler than the lower regions. When elephants were free to roam and migrate from one area to another, they would no doubt have frequented the Mateke Hills from the Gona re Zhou region and Buffalo Bend. This region was later declared a national park after the noble effort and perseverance of Allan Wright as early as 1958, who had declared the area around the Nuanetsi River (now called the Mwenezi River), a wildlife sanctuary.

Another important excursion required serious bundu-bashing with the vehicles to as far as we could go into the southern end of the Mateke Hills. We then had to hike with rucksacks and sleeping bags from there-on. We were fortunate to have accompany us, an elderly man called Andries that knew the route into the hills. He had lived in the area all of his life and was related to Chief Chinana. He firstly led us to an ancient water hole in the middle of a 'flattish' granite outcrop next to a small granite kopje. He pulled aside a granite slab, and lo and behold, there was a small reservoir of water below, from which we drew water. I noted two things, one that he only rinsed his mouth with the water and spat it out – on questioning him; he said that it was too hot in the day to drink water and that he would drink later. We were fortunate that we would later be following the Malumba River into the hills where there were some pools of water.

Interestingly, over forty years later when with my wife Jean – who was studying for her master's degree in archaeology at the time – and with the help of the then owners of the Malumba ranch, Cliff and Christine Langenhoven, we eventually succeeded in finding the water hole again. Up to that time, the owners of the farm did not know of its existence, though one of the African workers thought he knew more or less where it was. We located it without too much trouble, and the only change that had taken place was that the covering slab of granite was no longer in one piece.

But back to the original visit: before we left the water hole in the rock outcrop, Andries picked up what looked like a small stone and rubbed it within one of the small cupules (shallow holes) on a nearby boulder, and then continued to walk into the hills. This action was clear to me, and it made sense that perhaps persons passing that way either had their own particular cupule on the boulder or as indicated by the rubbed stone, of how recent a person had died. There were numerous cupules ground into the boulder and in no particular order. Unlike one would expect from the game 'Tsoro' which had holes honed in an orderly fashion of typically four by eight (thirty-two holes). It is a game commonly played throughout Africa and also also known as Marabaraba or Isafuba.

Under the watchful eye of baboons that followed us along a rocky outcrop, we reached a point a little way off and above the Malumba River course where we were to camp. At the entrance adjacent to the Shangwinani Hills which is at the southern end of the Mateke Hills complex, we stopped and rested, enjoying the view and late afternoon. I felt a tickling on my leg, which was like perspiration, but looking down noted that two tiny scorpions were ascending my leg. I brushed them off, a bit too tired to get excited about their intent. I must have disturbed a rock that they were nesting under.

I chose a spot in the grassy level below the rock outcrop for my night's rest. I noted that Andries our guide, when settling down to sleep simply drew a light cloth over himself and lay back against the rock. Very uncomfortable, I thought, but he had chosen a sensible position where the rock would offer warmth through the night. In the morning, my sleeping bag was wet with dew, and he was dry!

'We live and never stop learning'

We continued hiking early the next day by following the Malumba River. Under the guidance of Andries, we climbed a prominent granite hill called Chumbangula that revealed pottery and evidence of previous 'Iron Age' occupation. Cran Cooke and his archaeological team took notes of the interesting artefacts found. Andries told us that they had not lived on the hill during his early days in the Mateke Hills, but on the valley floor. Another unusual finding was a relatively large outcrop surrounded by boulders. Upon descending behind the boulders, it was found that the outcrop was, in fact, hollow underneath and would have provided excellent hidden shelter and protection. The most unique aspect of these hills was one that was called Lomolehoto (the mouth of the hornbill). It was higher than Chumbangula and had a substantial projecting nose pointing north. A very rare formation indeed.

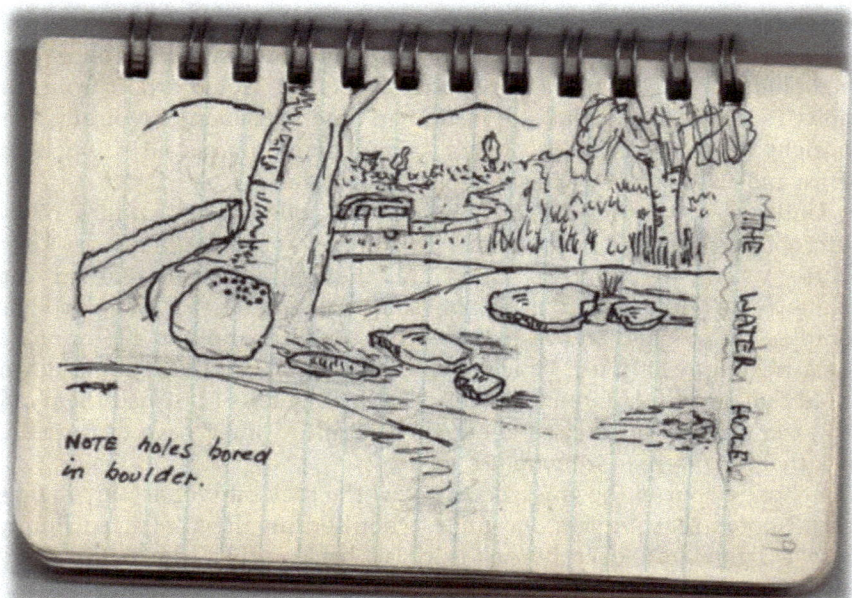

Sketch of the Zwenyambe hill water hole during RSES expedition 1958

*The water hole in the granite outcrop at Zwenyambe hill –
re-found in 1998, forty years later*

Paul at the numerous 'ground' cupules on the boulder at
Zwenyambe hill water hole – 1998 - note difference in patina wear

Picture of Andries Chinana and Cran Cooke – 1958

These hills were the scene where after re-discovering the site with my son Quintin in 1994, that my wife Jean commenced her survey and study of the Iron Age site for her master's degree in archaeology This was accomplished in conjunction with the University of Zimbabwe together with supervision by the faculty of archaeology at the University of Cape Town from 1996 to 2002. This site also proved to be an important and initial piece of the jigsaw with the early farming communities in the general, southeastern Limpopo region (see later reference Chapter 16).

Our next excursion during the expedition was planned for the Limpopo. This was not to be for me. One morning I arose feeling fuzzy in the head and headed for breakfast. As I sat down, a cloak of darkness drew across my head like a blind, and I staggered back to my bed on the ground after telling my colleagues that I was not well. Dr Strover, our expedition doctor, examined me, and he concluded that I was very ill and immediately injected me with penicillin. He said that I probably had tick-bite fever. I was desperately sick with vomiting and a thunderous headache. It was that bad, that had someone suggested that I should be put down, I might have agreed! The glands in my groin were like rods of rope under my skin. I think after a few days I managed to get up and wash but was not at all well. As we were near the end of the expedition, it was not long to wait to return to Bulawayo. I was fortunate to get a lift back with the doctor and was in bed for the rest of the month. I missed a large amount of school as a consequence. When I had recovered a bit, I discovered and removed a small tick on one of my testicles, which may very well have been the cause of the problem. I was never sure that it was solely a tick bite, or perhaps malaria, because for years after I would experience recurring bouts of shivering with a fever. This often occurred by coincidence or not, near low lying areas. Mostly by the next day, I would feel fine with no ill effects.

5

Work, Outings to Matopos

At the end of 1958, I had completed Form IV and took the long train journey down to Fish Hoek, where my parents had earlier decided to move to. I had been staying with my brother Tony at his small flat, and it was a sad and tearful departure leaving him behind. The stay in Fish Hoek was not to be for long, but I loved to surf on heavy rubber-inflatable and short 'Lilos'. These you could hire for a minimal amount of money. Though summertime, the water was often very icy, and blue lips and 'blue' bottles often occasioned the fun. My father had an old upright Ford Anglia, and where we lived in Risi View, everything was much undeveloped with lots of surrounding trees and bush. One day poor Bob, my younger brother, eventually came home somewhat late and scared out of his wits. He said a considerable-sized snake had prevented him from proceeding up our normal access road and he had to take a long deviation via a further and more distant road to get home. We believed him but did not realise the size of the snake until one day, and presuming to be the same cobra, it reared up at our car and struck at the very upright radiator grill. It was really, quite enormous.

I never enjoyed the Southeaster, and still being relatively slender, was one day blown off my feet at the back of the house on a concrete apron and into the garden fence. Yes, it did happen, in fact, often was the time that the glass milk bottles would be blown over and go clattering down the back of the house!

The stay did not last too long as my father could not make a decent living from the small number of electrical jobs or appliances that needed to be repaired, so we returned to Bulawayo.

We were not financially well off, and although I could have gone back to school, I decided to go out to work. I did not have matriculation or a Cambridge certificate, so there were not many work opportunities then. The Post Office however had openings, so I started work at the Bulawayo Central Post office. The training was excellent, and I learnt a lot but was always a bit stressed with the volume of tasks to be performed. I would often go to the toilets and retch. The family thought I had appendicitis, so I had an appendectomy, and landed up with the same stomach cramps afterwards. I knew even then that I should have been a geologist and should have worked towards that goal.

I did well at morse code, and was positioned with a few others that sent and received telegrams from outlying towns – how things have now changed! Even the teleprinters grunted away very slowly with punched tape or printed tape, which was fed through a 'tape self-wetting' handheld device and was simply glued onto blank telegram forms. The main teleprinters were huge and weighed a ton but provided the essential links with Johannesburg and Salisbury. The maintenance guys liked to work on the wiring and connections under the benches because they could peek up the ladies skirts while they were working! One declared that one of the ladies did not wear any undies... how things have changed, and maybe some things have not. I was very innocent then. Well, more innocent than I am now, but I guess the never-ending instinctive quest to find out more about the opposite sex never dies – hence the size of the world population as it is now! When at the Queens Park Post office, we had to count hundreds of sheets of stamps, postal orders or money, so on one occasion I ordered a few finger 'rubbers' from the local chemist because with the constant counting of money sheets of stamps and postal orders, they wore out. The local chemist was like a general dealer, so we would order stationery from them when required. The small parcel arrived and in front of the Postmaster and counter lady; I opened it to find that they had sent what my mother would call 'French Letters' (nothing to do with post or post offices, neither can I understand if or why the French invented the things or named them as such), now called condoms. 'I' had to send them back and ask for rubber thumbs! That could also be misconstrued these days because rubbers are rubbers, and erasers are called erasers. Anyhow, it caused a great deal of laughter in the office – principally at my expense and embarrassment!

Raylton Post Office was a bustling office, and I enjoyed it. Plenty money was sent out of the country by money orders, and these were mostly from Indians working in the country. Others, almost always Europeans, would send the local papers overseas to England. Since cigarettes were like a giveaway in Rhodesia, it was quite regular that customers would wrap a row of packets of cigarettes within the newspapers. I did not smoke, but those that did often would remove the cigarettes (but not for health reasons) from the newspapers and send them on. Obviously thinking that the Rhodesian news was more important than smoking in England! The intelligence and coding system must have reported back to the point of departure, because when one of the newspaper bundles was opened, the sender had again enclosed the packets, but had carefully put pinprick holes in all of the cigarettes.

I made a blunder one day when I was date stamping some First Day Covers, only to find after a couple of hours that I had not changed the date stamp from the previous day... oh dear. Nobody ever came back to complain, and now they may be either invalid or worth a lot of money.

The amount of letters sent by Africans to their homes in the rural areas was quite phenomenal. Asking for a 'sticky-tickey-tampa' meant almost phonetically a tickey stamp. Part of the training included postal sorting, and at the central post office sorting department, one got used to the names of far-flung villages and even kraal names. Reading some addresses phonetically also helped. There was a very high success rate of letters reaching their destination with few returns. I thereafter always held a respect for postal sorters and the shifts they had to work through the night. The volume of letters never seemed to change, and only became worse at Christmas time when thousands of cards were sent around the country and the world.

I nearly died one day or thought that I was going to when I had swallowed some tea, and at the same time, someone had told a joke, and I laughed and choked. I fell to the floor and must have been almost blue when survival kicked in and either the tea went into my lungs, or some air and tea went into my lungs. I was seriously shaken and coughed for a long time after. I tell you; it can happen. Don't try this at home!

We had an earnest chap working with us, and we always took the opportunity to have a good laugh. In busy places, this is quite common like a necessary relief from boredom or business. Our serious chap (I forget his name), used to park in front of the outside delivery gate, so I printed in bold stencil letters across a blank sticky piece of paper the letters, B S A P (British South Africa Police), and typed the date of the incident, the car registration and the constable's name with a large signature. He went out at lunchtime, we heard a yell, and we laughed, but he did not come back in. He had driven straight down to the Police Station in Fife Street some distance away and tried to explain why he had parked there. They were quite serious about the fact (though having a good chuckle) that if he could find the perpetrator, they would fine him because the ticket was a fraud. It sort of backfired but was immensely funny all the same. We did tell him sometime later what had transpired, and he saw the funny side of it.

I had bought my first car at an auction for forty pounds. It was a large beetle-shaped Standard Vanguard. I was still very short for my age but had a bad attitude about being stopped by the police for being obviously underage. After all, I was seventeen and had passed my driver's test. I was stopped no less than thirteen times but never had to show my driver's licence. I was once fined five pounds for speeding whilst overtaking an old -timer dawdling along. He was probably only forty-five or fifty! I pleaded that I did not have the money, so they agreed that I could pay a reduced amount at the end of the month, which I did. The Standard Vanguard looked grand, but the shocks were shot, and the kingpins on the front suspension were severely worn. But it did drive well, especially as the engine was the same as the Ferguson tractor engine. The column gear shift would stick occasionally and going through town in first or second gear was very stressful, both for me and the other cars. It was not long before my brother was given a new Anglia saloon, so I bought his Hillman Minx, a 1000cc side-valve engine. It was reliable but quite unable to 'pull the skin off a rice pudding' as they say. Bank robbers would never use it as a getaway car!

Going out to the Matopos and Maleme dam involved a steep descent to the dam itself. My Hillman could not go up in first gear, so I had to reverse up the bouncy twisty concrete road. I do not think my neck has been the same since... very stressful. The same happened years later when I tried to drive up Nugget Hill in Hillbrow. It did not work, and I had to reverse erratically back down the hill, also with poor brakes).

My mother was quite short and driving the broad, and heavy Humber saloon was challenging for her. She could barely see through the steering wheel even with a cushion. Our back gate had been built by my father. It looked OK, but it was really too narrow. One day my mother swept into the back driveway and scraped the offside door against the timber! Father was very particular about his cars, so this was a serious deviation from his ideals. Desperate times call for desperate measures, so my mother quickly drove into town, had it panel beaten, resprayed and returned home... It was a long time after when he looked down the side of the car and remarked that there were ripples in the bodywork and that it seemed very strange to him... She said that she could not see anything wrong, but there was, and it remained one of the great unsolved mysteries!

He also detested onions and could smell onions in food from miles away. But my mother just had to put onions in to give flavour to a meal. She always professed innocence with a remarkably straight face. But he did love curry, so we would have curry from time to time and criticised us for being sissies and would call for the curry powder and sprinkle it on the food to give it real punch. So, the next time we had curry, it was flavoured as usual, but in the kitchen, mother dosed his plate with 'extra' curry. When the plates were all served up, he called for the extra powder and sprinkled it on. We watched with twinkling eyes, while his were watering. His nose began to run as well as the sweat trickled off his forehead. He said nothing but must have suffered severe mouth burning and no doubt, again the next morning from another source, like the song relating to the 'Burning Ring of Fire'.

Tony once complained that the consommé soup tasted awful. My mothers' instant response was "that's right because there is nothing in it!" My mother always had a keen sense of humour and could see the funny side of most things. I suppose having worked in her parents' tobacconist shop in London; she met all sorts. She told me how one day a little nipper came into the shop and peering over the counter asked, "do you have any nails?", "No, my mother replied, we are a tobacconist". The nipper responded saying "well what do you scratch your arse with" and ran out of the shop!

When TV arrived, my mother was hooked. The transmission was not very good, with few 'dots per inch', or 'lines on the screen' so to speak. Only in black and white and often my eyes were so sore, that it felt like I had 'arc-eyes' from welding without a helmet! However, a few of the British programmes were quite entertaining, and she loved them to the extent that dinner was often late. "Where is dinner: my father would cry," "I am waiting for the potatoes" she would respond without moving her eyes off the TV. In a loud voice, he said, "all my life I have been waiting for the bloody potatoes" what a hoot because sometimes they would dry out in the pot!

He was very particular about the TV set and that we should be careful not to damage the screen, so one day I cut some black cotton, wet it, and strung it out across the screen into the form of a star-like crack. When he sat down for a sundowner and the TV lit up, he shot out of his chair to see the damage to the screen, only to find that it was cotton! Likewise, dogs were not really allowed in the lounge because they would pass wind silently from time to time and he could not stand that, neither could any of us as, even though the room had a high-pitched thatched roof. The gas was probably more pungent due to being fed mostly leftovers. So, one day having some various colours of plasticine on hand, I fashioned a multi-coloured number of droppings, and carefully and neatly stacked them sort of like a pyramid in the centre of the carpet, in the lounge. They appeared genuine, not huge, but in proportion to the size of our small dogs. He hit the roof (not literally because the top was at least six metres above) when he saw it, so I quickly volunteered to pick them up, and we all had a good laugh. He did have an infectious laugh, and toilet sense of humour probably gathered from the East End of London. He had a business visitor to the house, so before he arrived Tony and I placed a 'Whoopee cushion' under the couch cushion. The visitor sat down and moved from left to right while crossing his legs. Tony and I could not stand it and with suppressed deep laughter had to leave the room. It did not work, and we later discovered that the lips of the device had folded over. However, when we told the old-man, he just rocked up and down with tears streaming down his face. Half of the humour I am sure was imagining the result if it had gone off!

My mother later progressed to a new two-tone Hillman Minx, a smart and stylish looking car. One day I met her outside Meikles to get a lift home, and upon going out to where it was parked directly outside of the shop, we could not get the key to open it. We tried everything. A small crowd gathered, advice was received, bits of wire came to hand, and we tried to break-in, to no avail. After a while, peering inside, I suddenly noticed a very small St Christopher stuck to the dash. We did not have one in our car! I whispered to her, and she suddenly realised that this was an identical car to ours, but hers was parked another four cars down the street. We sheepishly mingled with the folk who had well given up trying and slunk away to the correct vehicle feeling embarrassed but relieved. We had a good laugh about it on the way home.

While waiting for my mother to finish work in Meikles, I was approached by a man who chatted about hobbies – model aircraft in fact, saying he was very interested in the hobby and if I was interested in

The Makwiro Post Office – 1961, Paul with his mother and brother Robert.

coming with and seeing what he had done ("come up and see my etchings sometime" as a Hollywood actress once said!). As I met my mother regularly, he approached me to chat again and gave me a chocolate bar. I never ate it but took it home and crushed it in the garden; and told my father. He said I should carry on as usual and he, being in the police force, would sort it out. Well, they did, at the opposite building the police set up a camera found out who he was and where he lived. They interrogated him and determined that he was a potential paedophile and warned him that he would land in jail if he ever did try and approach young folk again. Only many years later, I saw him at an auction and felt deep anger rising and felt like beating up the pathetic individual. Tony was with me that night, so we left things be.

At the tender age of 19 years, I was appointed as the Postmaster of Makwiro Post Office, a railway siding in the wealthy farming area near Norton, south of Salisbury. My father only believed that I was going, when I had packed the car and was ready to leave. He looked quite sad. However, the morning was bright, and I set off early, only to be waved down outside Cement Siding (a cement factory near Heany), by a man in a posh car. He explained that two young girls needed an urgent lift to Redcliffe, Que Que, as their mother was seriously ill, and that he could not take them further as he worked at the factory. So, without hesitation, I made room for them, and we set off. Hours later I pulled into Redcliffe and to one of the staff houses. The mother appeared at the door obviously very well, and very angry. She virtually accused me of abducting the girls from school in Bulawayo. I protested, explained, and she calmed down, but still very angry that the girls had shammed everyone. I guess they were just tired of boarding school and wanted to come home. She gave me some sandwiches, and I set off again on my journey to Makwiro.

6

Makwiro, Bush and Unrest

Makwiro was a railway-siding Post Office that I was transferred to, about fifteen kilometres from the small village of Selous which was on the main Bulawayo Salisbury road. Makwiro is an interpretation of the Shona word *makwira* — 'you have climbed' — which originates from Chief Zwimba, who long ago arrived from the Zambezi valley. I was provided with a rondavel along with a few sticks of furniture. I employed a cook who I had to provide for in terms of meat and mealie-meal. I had a staff of seven assistants to service the switchboard and as linesmen for ongoing repairs. I had one assistant in the office named Makiwa, and we got on very well. He did think that I was a bit *Tagati* (magical), because uncannily at any particular time I would tell him that my mother was going to phone, and the phone would ring for me. It was uncanny but did happen.

Party lines were always a problem as they were often down from rainstorms or animal damage and additionally, not so much because of the detailed long and short rings for each party line connection, but for the few that persisted in listening in. At times when I had to phone a farmer, I could hear when one of the regular farmer's wives would lift the receiver and listen in! No heavy breathing, she would just 'quietly' put the receiver down, or apologise nicely saying that they thought the rings were for them... Folk just like 'skinner', and still do.

I had my .22 Winchester single shot repeater 'top load' rifle which I used a number of times. Twice, I was requested by the cook to shoot snakes (identified as boomslang, and in hindsight, I should not have shot them as they are not aggressive even though venomous) in the tree next to the kitchen. And again upon urgent request by the kraal residents situated behind the Post Office to shoot a bush baby. It was not the little quaint 'nagaapie' or small and 'large-eyed night ape'. This big fellow was consuming the local chickens. It had taken refuge in the high branches of a blue-gum tree alongside the railway. Thinking I had missed with a few shots, I turned to leave, and with the locals' exclamation, it thumped to the ground.

En-route to Selous, I had the opportunity to shoot a guinea-fowl which I was lucky to shoot in the head. I retrieved it thinking it would make a good meal, however, it smelt unpleasant, so I traded it at the local garage at Selous for petrol from the attendant. He was happy, and so was I. I was surprised how heavy the bird was, so there must have been a fair bit of meat on it.

Night shooting is not fair hunting, but an easy way to kill game for the pot. I was invited by some local farmers to go on a night shoot, and after driving around for some time on the back of their Landrover, we spotted the telltale eyes of a small herd of Impala. We observed them and I chose one, and the farmer said he was going to take one fat one. I remarked that it looked like it was in foal. He disagreed and shot it. I had had a good shot and the buck looked dead. I was inexperienced in hunting and was advised to make sure by pushing a knife into the back of the skull and into the brain. Unpleasant as it was, I did it, and we gathered them up and headed back to the de Lange's farm. The two animals were to be left to the African assistants in the kitchen to skin and clean the carcasses. I insisted that if I could shoot them, then I should also clean them, and went into the kitchen. Cleaning was surprisingly easy. However, I was shocked when the 'fat' buck was opened up. There was a perfectly formed miniature animal, complete with fur and little hooves. I had been right even given my inexperience. I was disgusted with the attitude, and lack of concern for the sustainability of wildlife. It put me permanently off shooting antelope. I was allowed to keep my kill, and I hung it for some days and enjoyed fresh meat for a while which made a quite a change from ordering meat from Norton and having it delivered by train to Makwiro. I did go out hunting for wild pig on the Kujawy farm with John Francis. The pigs caused a lot of damage to crops and were quite dangerous to hunt.

However, with much night marching through dense bush and grass, we were unsuccessful. I did learn to ride a horse at Kujawy farm. John instructed me what to do – left foot in the stirrup, hold the reins firmly in the left hand and mount into the saddle. This I duly did, but in my effort to swing my right leg over and into the saddle, the reins loosened, and off shot the horse, almost at a gallop, while I, Roy Rogers style was still trying to swing my right leg over the horses back. Heart pounding, I brought it into check (the horse was very understanding and kind to me) and we went on a long walk through the bush and trees, and down to the Umfuli river and back again. It was a great experience, and I was grateful that he had allowed me to give it a try. Pushing through the bush, I learnt why cowboys were always seen wearing 'chaps'. It was not just for Hollywood show, and my trousers bore that out. Horses are not concerned about whether you are wearing protective longs, or whether a branch is too low for your head...

A few times, I went out alone to see if I could bag a hare or two but was also unsuccessful. However, I found out that there was a slight problem with my Winchester! After moving one night from one location to a new location in my Hillman Minx, I would pull the safety back to ensure that the weapon would not go off accidentally. I duly did this, pulled back the safety in the dark, held the rifle upright and pulled the trigger before placing it on the back seat. BANG! I felt such a fool alone in the middle of nowhere with a smoking hole in the roof of the car. I found out that if one pulled the safety back without much pressure, it would be fine, but, if the safety was pushed down and pulled back, it would catch on a slight ridge on the bottom of the safety slider. Lesson learned, no one hurt, a bit of hammering and the hole was sort of closed up with some putty.

Folk would from time to time ask me why I had a prominent pimple on the roof. The Hillman had a solid body, and I think that is why it was so slow to get going, however years later when I was staying at the YMCA in Johannesburg, a massive storm was brewing one Saturday afternoon. The sky was almost green, and a roaring in the distance could be heard. Then it hit us, a violent hail storm. The row of resident's cars below could be seen being pelted with the hail. Many of the cars had roofs dimpled by the impacts, apart from the bullet pimple, mine had no damage at all. It was amusing looking down after the storm had passed, to see a traffic-cop riding sideways down the hill over the layer of hail trying desperately not to fall off his motorbike.

A while back before I arrived at Makwiro, one of the local farmers had accidentally shot and killed a fellow hunter while hunting. He later married the widow. Makiwa said the locals did not think it was an accident...

Locals said that a massive python lived in a nearby outcrop of rock and boulders and that a young picannin had been taken by it when walking past there. They had stern warnings about never walking past there at night, or for children to walk nearby in the day. It would not surprise me, because pythons grow to massive proportions, and are opportunistic.

Bees invaded the Post Office one hot day, and I had to evacuate the office and close it up for business. I phoned the regional office in Salisbury and advised them what had happened. I requested that the next day a bee expert should come and remove them. Early the following day with much trepidation, I looked into the main office and did not see any swarms, so opened up only to find thousands of dead bees over everything. We swept them up into heaps and disposed of them. I never did find out why they had swarmed into the office; presumably, they had hoped to nest there, but died of heat and exhaustion instead. At occasions, when walking in the bush one might hear the sound of a swarm of bees passing by in their thousands. Clouds of them might pass overhead on their way somewhere.

Bees can be selective. On a short bush operation during the 'bush war,' I was conducting an observation of a suspected terrorist location. It was early morning when we moved to a position in a field of dried mealie stalks close to a marula tree. There were some bees around, but not a concern until a bunch of them took a disliking to just one of the three African troopies. The bees persisted, and he had to run for it crashing through the mealie stalks with enough sound to wake the dead. We retreated having bee...n compromised by them!

Back to Makwiro, I had trouble with rats in my rondavel as they would emerge when I had turned out the light and climbed into bed. They could run up and down the fibreboard walls, up to the ceiling, and down into the cavity between the corrugated iron exterior walls in a flash. So, one night I stood by the door where the light switch was located and waited. It was only a few minutes, and I heard the rat making moves. Turning on the light, it flew around the rondavel while I threw a throwing-knife at it. But it was too fast and leapt from the table over a distance of about two metres – believe me they can jump far, then it landed on my bed and burrowed under the blanket. I was nonplussed as to what to do, but grabbed the rat between blanket and the side of the bed, then visualised the mess that would take place in the bed, so released it and it shot out again. As it ran up the wall, I threw my knife, it missed and split the beading between the wallboards with the knife. Rats are smart creatures!

I developed a couple of boils, one on my back and one on my stomach. They were enormously painful, so I spoke to the station master whose wife was a nurse, and she informed me that it was caused by the blow-fly that had laid eggs in my clothes (typically in seams or folds), while they were most likely drying, and they had somehow penetrated my skin. She managed to extract the one on my back, and I eventually extracted the worm-like grub from a small crater shaped hole on my stomach. It was a painful exercise, and it required patience to avoid the head breaking off while pulling the offensive thing out. This was because the head was bulbous and larger than the body which anchored into the wound. The removal led to quick healing. I had never suffered from boils before and was pleased that it was problem solved. Hot ironing along seams was recommended to kill off such creatures' eggs.

One of my linesmen complained about a boil on his backside which was very painful. He even took some sick-days off because of it. I said it should be fixed and that he should go through to Norton to the clinic to have it looked at, but he refused. I sort of threatened him that, unless he had it fixed, he could not take time off. He said that he was terrified of needles being put in his body. I tried to reassure him, and he eventually went, but unhappily. It was over Christmas, and I took off a few days and drove down to Bulawayo. Sadly I received a call from Makiwa to say that he had died at the clinic. I was really shocked as he could not have been more than twenty -two years of age. I never received a report, but always suspected that he may have died of fear. The doctor would have no doubt given him an antibiotic with a needle. Oh dear, I was really upset at the loss.

Late one night (probably about no later than nine o'clock), Makiwa was knocking on my door to say that I must come quickly and help his wife who was about to give birth! I got up and was faced with the probability that I would have to deliver something only previously known to storks! I was really ignorant in those things but reasoned with him that if she could hang on until the early train pulled in, she could catch it to Norton and the clinic. He said I should take her by car. There was no local help available at the time, and I protested saying that the corrugations were so bad that she would probably give birth in the car which would have complicated things. Honestly, I meant it, because you really could hide a beer bottle lying sideways within the corrugations. My car had broken shock absorbers on these roads, and especially the road to Norton, where my car would drive along sideways over the bumps. Driving fast was equally as hazardous and hammered the car unmercifully. There was no happy medium. Either you drove slowly and went sideways or drove fast and tried to bounce along the crests of the corrugations. Anyway, she hung in until morning and duly caught the train, and all was well, and I was relieved of the prospect of having to deliver a child. After all, I had not even seen a woman naked let alone highly pregnant – heaven forbid!

Makiwa got into trouble one weekend when he arrived to work with an evident swollen black-eye. He confessed to me that he had a girlfriend at a distant kraal and with the promise of marriage, she had consented to his advances. The elders of the village kraal had found out that he was in fact married, so roughed him up a bit. I asked him why he had done it, and his reply was 'boss you cannot live by rice alone'...

Early one Sunday morning, I awoke to the sound of gunfire. It did not sound like heavy shots, but after hearing seven shots, I got out of bed to investigate and found that a railway ganger, a Portuguese fellow was firing a .22 rifle from some distance, at a cow that was standing next to the railway line. I asked him what he was doing as the poor beast was just standing with blood trickling from various wounds. The stupid idiot thought that the beast would just die from the various gunshot wounds. The scene was too far gone to save the poor animal, so I told him to come up close and shoot it in the brain. This he did, and the poor thing eventually fell to the ground after sustaining fourteen gunshots. He had bought the animal and was going to slaughter it for meat. I did not wait to see how he cut it up.

The Kutama mission was not far from Makwiro, and they ran a school there. A couple with two small children arrived at Makwiro and introduced themselves. The gentleman informed me that he was a newly appointed teacher to the mission, and they were from England. It was not long after that, perhaps a month or so that they rushed in to me, quite late one night in a frantic state. Individuals at the school had thrown petrol bombs through their bedroom window while they were sleeping. They were very fortunate that the bombs had failed to ignite. They were a lovely couple, and entirely non-aggressive, in fact, they were a bit naïve I felt at times, inviting all sorts in for tea etc., as they had told me previously. I had suggested to them that I did not think it very wise, as being culturally quite different, it could have been perceived as a weakness rather than kindness. But in truth, why would anyone want to harm innocent people unless there was incitement to do so. The police were phoned, and they made alternate arrangements of where to sleep. I did not find out what the police did about it, but soon after the event, one Saturday afternoon a cluster of African individuals gathered within the Post Office property and an apparent leader was giving a political speech. I instructed him to leave the property, but he was clearly trying to incite folk, argued back at me and said that he would 'kill' me. There was an African constable with them that did nothing. I was angry about it, especially the threat to kill me. I phoned the Police Station at Selous; however, no one on duty could come out. I would quite happily have shot the troublemaker had he come in to pursue his threat.

I phoned my brother Tony in Bulawayo and explained the situation, and he calmed me down, saying that given the current Prime Minister's attitude, I would spend a lot of time in jail. It was 1961 and only later did I realise that the Kutama Mission area was quite a hotbed of politicking, and that was the area from where Robert Mugabe had hailed. Given the later atrocities committed by Mugabe in his struggle and desire for power, it was not surprising that such stirrings and intimidation were afoot. The then prime minister was Sir Edgar Whitehead, and the atmosphere of change was not healthy given the Federation, the breakup of the Federation, and the economic implications on Southern Rhodesia. I was not deeply interested in higher levels of politics, Britain and the emerging rush of independences, and only began to understand the bigger picture later. Alas, shared respect and fairness of life are lost in the welter of intimidation, jockeying for position and 'personal' power, and mostly fuelled by greed, control and domination. It is a disease that affects and impacts on everyone, sooner or later.

It is interesting to note, that when Robert Mugabe eventually died in September 2019, that he was buried at his home village close to Kutama Mission in the district of Zvimba where he was born. He had arrived full circle, starting with his political 'activist' career that actively began in 1961 with his National Democratic Party (NDP) which supported subversive activities, intimidation and brutalities. He achieved precisely nothing except unhappiness and poverty through his ideology of Marxist dictatorship of a one-party state. Well over fifty years of misery, obsessive and vocal public hatred of white peoples and evil that ruined one of the finest countries in the world.

Perhaps it is no coincidence that it was the same year of 1961, when the political gathering event took place outside the Makwiro Post Office and with the petrol bomb attempt on the school teacher and family at Kutama Mission College – also known as the St. Francis Xavier College. Kutama Mission was not far from Makwiro.

The folk at the Martindale Mission were wonderful people, and there was never any indication that they had that sort of problem there. Whenever they came into the office, they always had an air of friendliness and peace about them. When I left, they gave me a beautifully embroidered tea tray cloth which I treasured.

The dirt road into Selous was better than the dirt road to Norton, but it could be a problem when the rains fell, and the local river was in flood. Usually, the concrete causeway had water flowing across it, which was entirely negotiable, but after heavy rain, it sometimes came down in flood. On one occasion, I was driving through to Selous to see a movie that they would have on Saturday afternoons at the hotel lounge. The river was high, but I thought I could negotiate it, so upon approach, I gently entered the water, and about halfway across I felt the vehicle being pulled towards the drop-off. There were a few stone bollards, but the water was almost over them. The downside I knew was deep enough for the vehicle to turn over perhaps or be below water level. While I felt the car being pushed by the water, the engine cut out. I was desperate and frightened, and at a 'light bulb' moment, put the car into reverse and pressed the starter button. It was a bit slow but successful, and I was back on the bank of the river, quite shaken, but safe. A lesson learned!

There was another lesson learned after that when I was invited to visit the Wasserman family about sixteen miles out into the bush. This was a farmer who had once gone out to the long-drop and found that he had company in the form of a large cobra. With his trousers down (always check for snakes in an 'outhouse' before pulling down your trousers), in a confined space the snake reared up, and would not move out. Well, obviously, because the door was shut. However, his shouts to his son were heard who duly arrived to the rescue, opened the door and shot the snake, while his dad was standing on the seat of the long drop – enough to empty anyone's bowels. He also told me that once one of his workers had been bitten by a Mamba and the corrective treatment he administered was half a cup of diesel fuel... he said the chap survived with no ill-effects. Hard to believe!

The flooded tributary of the Umfuli river on the road from Makwiro to Selous.

After a wonderful late afternoon and dinner, I realised that it was a long trek to return the way I had come, so I decided to take a shortcut. It was already dark. Not a good idea because after some distance over a fairly rough road, I came across a mini wetland with black clay mud/cotton soil. I studied it and checked out the various tracks made by previous vehicles and went for it. I made fair progress bouncing over grass tufts, hollows and the like, then sunk down! My car was not a four-wheel drive, even though the clearance was not too bad. So to shorten a long story, after finding a slab of rock for the jack base, cutting branches, (I always carried spare water, an axe and a few tools), all by headlight, and mostly underwater, I jacked the car up, packed the stuff under the wheel, lowered the jack, moved and got bogged down again, repeated the process three times before I was free of the quagmire. Fortunately for me, the rest of the journey was fine, but it was very late before I got back, very wet, muddy and tired. Another lesson learned – the shortest route is not necessarily the quickest!

There never was time to go into either Hartley or Salisbury to do any other personal chores. One important one was that I had to cut my own hair. This was a tricky exercise which I did quite well (at least I thought so but did not check with my customers) with using a mirror. I also had to work every Saturday, which also restricted any travelling to a local town. I got a bit fed up with this and formally requested through the regional office that I have a day off to carry out such chores. This was refused, so I phoned and protested, only to be told that if I did not like it, they could always get an African to do my job... So, the next week I handed over my required three months' notice and set about leaving. The conditions there, were really not that favourable even though I enjoyed the work and meeting all of the local folk. But having to pay rent for the rondavel and sticks of furniture, buying rations for the help and paying a wage for the cook, left me with very little to spare for petrol. Some vegetables were given to me to by the farmers, and the odd provisions I bought from Johanny Tumazos' store along the way. Later a stand-in fellow, 'fresh out from England' and who Makiwa did not take to; arrived from Salisbury and I headed back to Bulawayo. I learnt later that they did indeed get an African to take over, but all of the monthly accounts now had to be sent to Salisbury to be processed. It was an irksome task compiling monthly accounts, and it used to take up a lot of my time, especially at night and weekends as everything had to balance to the penny. Bearing in mind that accounting was done in Pounds Shillings and Pence, and if out by even one penny in stock or money required reworks until it balanced precisely.

It was sad to be leaving such wonderful people that had extended much kindness and friendship to me. Farming and country folk all have their own characters, but almost without exception, extend friendship and open their hearts to strangers.

I was ready for the change and looked forward to new horizons.

7

Camping, Snakes, Mashasha Cascades Accident and Climbing

Creatures go hand in hand with camping – particularly ants. In the earlier days, we did not have zip-up hermetically sealed tents, but simply a tarpaulin draped over rope between trees or propped up with sticks or branches, or perhaps at best, a tent without a sewn-in groundsheet. We were plagued by ants while camping at Maleme dam and had to place camp bed legs in cans of water to prevent their ingress. Opened condensed milk cans were the prime attraction, and apart from debris sticking to the openings, it was impossible to stop ants eventually, climbing in everywhere.

The Ncema (also called Ingnaima) river not far from Essexvale (now called Isigodini), was a great place to camp and was popular at weekends because it was a broad sand-based river where the water ran clear across the sand with deeper pools here and there. Tony and his friend Freddie Marx, Bruce Morrison and I camped on the bank of the river close to the water. However, shortly afterwards, the message got out to the ant colonies (I think they knew when campers would arrive), and we were

Sketch of early camping

plagued, so moved camp to a spit of sand, almost like a beach – perfect! Not so, the ants then trekked across the sand to our spot. Being smart, we cut a shallow channel at the back of the sand to form a sort of 'castle' type moat. This worked, but on close inspection later, I was fascinated to find (and you have to believe this), that the ants would cluster on leaves or grass to cross the little bit of water to gain access to our spot. I have learnt since, that ants are clever and have the ability to cluster on stems of grass, so they bend over and allow them access to wherever they wish to be.

Puff adders are bad news, and we were not short of them at Ncema. The first encounter I was extremely lucky, or nearly very unlucky when stalking barefoot through the veld with my pellet gun. I was looking ahead of me, then glancing down to see where to place my foot, when below me there was a coiled puff adder with its menacing, widely opened mouth. I had a pathological fear of puff adders because, at that time, it was said that you had about twenty minutes to live after a snake bite piercing – that has obviously now changed with current knowledge and treatment. Still, I did not know that at the time, and we were perhaps half an hour drive from Essexvale at best! My mind went into blank, and the next I knew, I was back on the dirt road to the river, the pellet gun had gone off, and I had somehow reversed my step and 'flown' bodily backwards. I had absolutely no memory of the sequence of sudden events. I was seriously shaken by that experience; the image of that puff adder below me on the ground is still as clear as day.

The next was to see a large puff adder swimming across some open water. It was quickly propelling forward through the water in a twisting movement, head slightly raised above the water. I followed after it with my pellet gun hoping to get a shot in, but it gained the further bank which had overhanging reeds and was gone. Wading through the water to the bank, I could not see it, but the hissing was distinct within the reeds (more like an exhaling than sharp hissing) it was the first time I had heard such a sound. I did not pursue it further. The next time was while relaxing at our camp; we heard a scream. It was coming from a young girl who had been splashing around in the water a little way off and apart from her friends. I quickly ran across some shallow water, and she pointed to a puff adder that was swimming away from her. I grabbed my pellet gun and managed to get a shot into its head as it swam away. It sank almost immediately and was gone. I did not know they sank so quickly, nor did I know that they as well as most snakes could swim so well. It had been lying on the sand when she surprised it, I guess. I later regretted my fear-driven action and ignorance in shooting snakes, but to rather let them go. Snakes do not deliberately seek out humans to bite them! Another lesson learned is to not walk through the veld without shoes on!

Bruce Morrison and I went camping at the Matopos dam and found a spot under some trees at the tail end of the dam where water flowed in. It was not all that exciting except that we were awoken quite late to heavy snorting and the sound of 'large tufts of vegetation being pulled out of the ground around us. We discovered that the resident hippo, which we thought was nowhere near our location, had thought otherwise. So we moved!

The Mashasha cascades was apparently a must-see, fall of water located quite deep in the bush in the Matopos East area off of the Fort Usher Gwanda road. So, Tony and Lorraine (his fiancé at the time), his friend Norman and his girlfriend and I all drove out to the closest parking spot which was not too far from the Brethren in Christ Mission. The walk entailed a three-mile walk through the quite attractive bush and small kopjes. The day was scorching, and the Mopani flies were a nuisance hovering around our eyes, nostrils and mouths. It took a while because we were enjoying the surrounds and also carrying rucksacks with water and food for our lunch, and it became progressively hotter. The 'Cascades' was a place where a small river ran over a granite outcrop, then tumbled down on to a lower shelf on the outcrop, then tumbled again down steeply into a cluster of boulders and rocks at the bottom. The water then ran between the rocks into a relatively large pool. The pool had a sandy bank on the one side and big rocks on the other.

I was walking in the front and immediately came up to the rounded lip of the falls but stopped and decided that it was dangerous and was about to turn back in order to descend by a safe route to the bottom. At that moment, I saw Lorraine to my right, and before I could say anything, she cried out and slipped. I saw her body impact against the lower shelf and tumble out of sight. At that moment, I was rooted to the spot but screamed out "Christ no" – I did not swear or blaspheme; it just came out automatically, like a cry of despair. By some miracle, Tony appeared on my left and ran right down the side of the fall without slipping or falling! It was astonishing. I then looked down from the far side of the falls and as far as I could and saw Lorraine lying half-submerged in a tiny pool between the rocks and boulders. She was clutching on to a rock, and there was blood pouring out from somewhere. We all rushed down through the bush to the lower bank and proceeded to cross the pool and rocks to recover her. She was conscious, but in a lot of pain and shock as we drew her across the pool to the sandbank. She had lost her glasses which were later recovered from the bottom of the pool. But we had a dilemma, and that was how we would rescue her back up to the top? Tony had a sleeping bag in his car, so I set off without delay so we could fashion a stretcher by cutting holes in the bottom of the bag and putting through

The scene of the accident - the Mashasha cascades.
For scale, note the figure at the top right hand side of the falls.
Photo credits fb Rhodesian Group

two poles fashioned from branches cut from a tree. This took some time as it was quite far, and oddly enough on my return, I came into an entire troop of baboons that were feeding in a glade surrounded by bush and trees, and it startled me. The path led through the centre of the glade, and I had been running when I spotted them, I walked through them all, and they did not even flinch! I did expect some reaction, but there was none, I then commenced running.

We rigged up the bag with the branch poles and tied them firmly with the bark stripped from the stems, and we eventually brought her up to the top – the climb up was not far, but steep and challenging. A thunderstorm hit us; no doubt it had been building up for it with the oppressive heat, so we took shelter under a rock outcrop and waited for the rain to abate. Then we set off again and went as far as we could with extreme difficulty as the sleeping bag was not suitable and it was exhausting trying to carry with only one person at the back and one at the front. We decided that we needed outside help, so I set off again to a mission station not far from where we had parked. The minister had a stretcher with proper carrying poles, so he returned with us and with two African helpers from the mission. By the time we had her more comfortably placed on the stretcher, it was getting late. The heavy downpour had abated and had made the trees and bush wet and drippy. The path led over outcrops and boulders at times, including small streams. It got dark, and we took it in turns carrying. The help we received was literally a Godsend. Crossing the little boulder-strewn stream in the dark made footholds hard to find, and because of this and fatigue, we dropped poor Lorraine half into the water. The night was not cold though, and we pressed on. One of us went ahead to switch on the car's headlights which helped in route-finding back to the vehicles. We were all quite exhausted.

Back in Bulawayo, the doctor attending her did not see anything too serious, so gave her a few aspirins for the night. It transpired after much pain and x-rays at the hospital, that apart from the obvious minor wounds, that she had a fractured pelvis and vertebrae. From 'not too serious' to having plaster from under her neck to her pelvis did indicate otherwise! She recovered fully and is married to my brother Tony. It is incredible to think that she fell into a tiny pool at the base of the falls – it was probably less than one and a half metres long by less than a metre wide and surrounded by jagged rocks and boulders!

It was not long after this and between jobs that I joined the Macdonald Club in Bulawayo. I truly enjoyed the events and friendship while there. Apart from the organised social events, I thoroughly enjoyed table tennis and outings into the Matopos. The excursions to Matopos included exploring and climbing notable hills; some close some quite distant. I quickly got drawn into the rock climbing aspect, and that is where I learned a lot about techniques and handling a climbing rope. There was no climbing equipment except a few slings and a Viking overlay rope. The leader took the full responsibility of safely leading the party. Granite climbing was strange in a way, that either it was straightforward, or quite complicated. Much of the climbing was friction climbing without using a rope and sometimes exposure to height, looking over broad sections or slabs of rock without immediate handholds or a bush to hang onto. It was a great delight to probe and explore through the valleys to attain our objective. To drive out there, see game, birds, and baboons and enjoy the sunsets over stunning landscapes was always refreshing. From time to time we would find new Bushmen rock art. On one outing to a remote peak or hill beyond Antelope mine, and not that far from the Bechuanaland (Botswana) border, I was leading a small party through a rocky divide and stopped when I heard a clear 'hishing' sound. We stopped, and the sound continued, and on walking carefully forward saw a considerable snake sliding through the dry winter carpet of leaves. We let it slither away, then continued walking and on peering down onto a rocky shelf in the early morning sun, saw a large cobra enjoying the warmth.

We never had any accidents despite the limitations on safety equipment. Still, we did have Dixie Dean freeze on a very exposed traverse on Shumbashabe hill, he could not move, and we had to help guide him very slowly off the exposed face. On another occasion, one of our stalwart girls was ascending a bulge in a long friction climb up part of the Silozwane hill, when she began to slip. She quietly spoke to us for help and two of us quickly friction climbed across the rock and halted the slipping and she recovered her footing and continued up the rock face. We were not climbing with a rope, because typically over open rock we would just friction climb. Where particularly risky, going on 'all fours' was the order of the day. Had she slipped further over the bulge she would have tumbled a long way down the rock face, even though it was not that steep, she would not have been able to stop and would undoubtedly have been injured! I admired her self-composure and calm attitude without panic.

Some of the finest friends I had met were from the Mac Club. I was on the committee, and my portfolio was climbing excursions amongst other tasks. It was such that we were informed that we were to receive a special guest – the Prime Minister of Rhodesia Ian Smith and some other distinguished guests. It was a formal occasion, and we togged out accordingly with suits and bow ties and smart evening dresses for the women. I had a snazzy bow tie that I liked, which had two tails either side of the bow. Ian Smith stopped at me at the welcoming party and quietly said that I looked just like *Maverick* – a popular figure on TV and movies then, and I guess he also enjoyed the programme. I was chuffed, and more than that, I was taken with the absolute quality of the man and his dear wife. It was a great banquet which was much appreciated by the Club especially for the fact that the Club was bequeathed by Sir James Macdonald many years before and his visit helped to cement and remind us of that generosity to young folk. Many years later, my mother and father were caretakers of the Club during the bush war, where white, black or coloured troopies could rest up and be cared for between call ups and skirmishes. I still have the visitors' book where those lads used to sign in and enjoy some rest. Many of those lads came from far and wide and did not have the time or opportunity to return home. My mother loved them all, and I have letters that bear testimony to their appreciation. Will we ever know how important even a little bit of care is to each and every soul, but I sincerely believe it does, and always will. Perhaps I should endeavour to return the book to the archives of the Club because I believe that the spirit under which the Club was bequeathed by Sir James still lives on, even though the circumstances of that time were different.

8

Shabani, Rock Band, Prospecting, Invention, More Unrest and Matopos

It was not long after leaving Makwiro that I joined the African Associated Mines and went to Shabani Mine in a clerical position in the Mine store. My father thought that I should try to get into accounting as a career. I was not so sure but started off happily and started an advanced bookkeeping course as I had done quite well at the subject at school.

I enjoyed the work; it was a vast store with every conceivable aspect to do with mining. Being in the environment of mining suited me, and I learned a lot. The other thing I liked about Shabani was that it was out in the bush even though it had a small town, so to speak. I stayed at the single quarters and made good friends with the other colleagues staying there. There was sport, and an excellent swimming pool. It was not long before with the advent of superb rock and roll bands emerging overseas, that a few of us decided to start a band. I had an acoustic guitar, and I was

The Blue Steels Band – Paul (Rhythm) Ian Kinsell (Bass), George Knott - enjoying the mellows

George Knott with Andre Du Plooy, our lead guitarist

happy playing rhythm guitarist. I later bought my first new electric guitar, a Hofner. I also had purchased a second-hand valve amplifier and a decent speaker. The combination of them was the love of my life.

Ian Kinsell built a bass guitar and played it. It was an excellent construction. Andre du Plooy played lead guitarist and was also an accomplished pianist. All stayed at the single quarters except our drummer who came from Shabani town and worked on the mine. We called ourselves the 'Blue Steels' and played almost essentially rock and roll numbers with great rhythm and beat.

The Shadows numbers formed a large part of our repertoire. Playing at the Shabani Club was quite a boost to our ability, but very soon we were asked to play at weddings! Folk did not know that our repertoire was severely limited when it came to requests for popular wedding dance numbers, but we tried our best and had a great time. A real handicap was that we were showered with drinks, and by the time things had hotted up, no one noticed if the odd note or chord was misplaced. One occasion left me very ill, a few too many beers left me with my bedroom constantly turning. I was not alone. On another occasion, a young fellow was rather too 'intrigued' with the instruments and kept trying to turn my guitar-string keys. A sharp bonk on his head stopped him from spoiling the show; however, it was also quite beneficial how many girls were also attracted I daresay to anyone who played in a band. I was taken with one young woman who had the most amazing eyes. Another one I was quite interested in eventually fell for Ian. He had great charm, and that was fine because she didn't really take to me.

We kept a large Baboon spider in a glass fishbowl and fed it with grasshoppers and other small insects. We called it Lucifer, and it lived in a small tunnel that we had built from small stones. It was a very quick spider, and it took a quicker hand to avoid being bitten when lifting the lid and putting in an insect. It would propel out of its lair and virtually leap at you. I cannot remember what happened to it, but it was probably returned to the wild.

Prospecting was a wonderful hobby that we took to with much enthusiasm. Andre du Plooy and Lindsey Thompson, George Knott and I went out a few times on outings, or to search for gold. It was the outings to

Prospecting on the Mtshingwe river – Paul and Lindsey Thompson

hills and remote areas that were so much fun. I think it was Lindsey's grandfather that he said had done a lot of prospecting and had found a deposit of Cinnabar (oxide of Mercury) somewhere in the hills. This area was where the famous Sandawana emeralds were discovered that had hit the international headlines for quality and beauty. However, the Cinnabar was never relocated. That sometimes happens. I had found some lithium bearing rock a few miles from Glengarry, and never re-located the small outcrop.

On one outing while panning for gold on the Mtshingwe river with Lindsey Thompson, George Knott and 'Jacko' Marshall (I think it was on Garfield Todd's farm, or thereabouts), it had been a sweltering day, and we were tired, so at the end of the day sat next to a pool on the river. The river was not flowing, and there was the odd pool here and there. This particular one was quite large and had a nice spit of sand going out into the pool which we sat on. So, we each opened a beer that we had brought, and although a bit warm, was tremendously wet and refreshing all the same. It must have been at least fifteen or twenty minutes later that the water suddenly erupted, and a hippo emerged, no doubt gasping for air. We ran off the spit of sand as fast as we could go. Hippos can run very fast; I believe at up to thirty kilometres per hour! Fatigue was gone, and adrenalin kicked in real quick, and we vacated the spot! I had subsequently heard that hippos could not stay submerged for such a time, but I swear that this fellow stayed down a very long time. In fact, we did not know that the pool was that deep that it would house a Hippo!

Some weekends when not on standby, I would drive the sweltering route through to Bulawayo on the Shabani and Balla Balla strip road – two narrow and parallel strips of tar. At bends, the road would typically be filled with tar between the strips and the verges of the road. Generally, the route was very stony too, so one had to drive carefully with the drop off from the strips and the sometimes steep camber. As I had earlier discovered that my car drove more 'happily' after a storm when the air was damp, so I developed a reservoir of water from a Balls Jar. Air was drawn into the jar by the suction line I had connected to the air intake. The vacuum was strong enough to cause the air to be drawn down through a tube with a sponge at the end to create hundreds of bubbles. The moisture -laden bubbles were drawn into the engine, providing some moist air. The gadget worked, and although with no increase in power, I guaranteed an improved 10% saving on fuel. This was later applied to my Anglia in Johannesburg with the same result. The Corner House Laboratories in Johannesburg ran an article on my development and countered a claim by the Australians that they had invented it. In truth, it was first developed during the jet engine era to give it extra boost, especially during takeoff!

One had to be careful that the container of water did not fall over and suck in pure water! Water is not compressible and would have resulted in damage to the engine. Between Shabani and Bulawayo, I used, on average, a pint of water.

Leaving Bulawayo, it was wise to get back to Shabani by sundown, as driving at night was hazardous, to say the least. Apart from the road hazards, were the regular incident of cattle or even game on the road. One particular weekend, on a return trip to Shabani, I had been given a lift with a buddy of mine. We had left Bulawayo in good time, but we perceived from the back of the small Morris saloon, a regular sound that was suspiciously like a wheel bearing growl. At Balla Balla, we stopped and confirmed that it was indeed the bearing. So, our driver friend stayed with the vehicle, and the two of us hitched a lift and managed to get as far as Filabusi, where the driver turned off. We hitched again and made good progress until our good Samaritan's car had a puncture (a common occurrence on the road) and he had no spare, so we set off again. It was now quite dark, getting late, and we reckoned that given the time and distance to Shabani being about twenty-five kilometres, we should arrive on foot by six or seven in the morning. It was pitch black and quite tricky to see the road ahead, and it was only the crunching of gravel underfoot or the road camber, that we knew we had strayed off of the road. We were not lonely as there were enough bush sounds as we progressed. The route was now deathly quiet as we plodded along. We did not expect to receive another lift because after a particular time at night, especially in the districts away from main centres; the roads suddenly become empty. It must have been about ten-thirty or later that we heard in the distance, an approaching vehicle. It eventually arrived, and we waved it down. It stopped, and the driver offered us a lift. The car was packed, and he had his wife and two children in the car, but notwithstanding, they made space for us, and we squeezed in. They had been on holiday to Durban (a great distance), and the reason they were so late on the road was that the cylinder head or a valve had blown, and blown it was! We limped along slowly and eventually arrived in Shabani at about midnight. We were duly dropped off at the single quarters. What a day, what a night of most unusual events, but above all, what a good Samaritan. It would have been his due to either drive straight past or make overloaded and limping-along car excuses, instead of giving us a lift! I expect we would have managed and may have even got an early morning lift, but his kindness struck me as being very much above and beyond what anyone could reasonably expect from anyone.

One of my duties was to offload the explosive trucks that came all the way from the AECI plant at Somerset West in the Cape. We never had any incidents because safety was paramount. The new explosives were not a problem, but the subterranean stacks of explosives could be a hazard when they started to weep. I had seen such cases weeping into the underground bunkers. Such 'dicky' stocks were duly identified, and one particular weekend, one of the qualified 'blasting' ticket chaps informed us that the 'dicky' stocks were to be detonated out in the open. The explosion was stupendous, and a reminder that the dangers of poor practice were fully justified. One of the miners told me that they had blown up rats underground by putting detonators into pieces of bread. I am not sure how a rat's bite could have initiated a detonator, but then again, I was not experienced to know otherwise. Other problems they had underground was pneumoconiosis or lung disease. In those early days, the full dangers of lung disease because of asbestos fibre (asbestosis) were not known. Most of the miners were smokers, so I conducted an experiment back in Bulawayo. I used a Balls Jar with a Perspex top; one I had used for one of my road experiments on the car. Inside I put long fibres of soft asbestos, a few stubs of cigarettes I had got from my mother, with a wet base, so the contents were always damp. This I put into my cupboard in a dark place. After about a month I had a look at the result and found to my surprise, that from the debris of cigarettes and asbestos, long stems of a sort of fungus had grown, each with a tiny white ball on the top! I did not take it any further but was convinced that the combination in such a damp and dark environment was definitely unhealthy.

A miner friend once told me that it was not uncommon to have thin pieces of hard asbestos to spike into your skin. He said that he had found that one such piece of asbestos had, in fact, travelled up his arm over a considerable length of time. I had no reason to disbelieve him.

Politics again raised its head in the form of smartly dressed Africans arriving in cars at the mine. They had come to intimidate the workers – and it worked! Trouble erupted immediately after. Management had detailed us into pickets, and a few of us were detailed for the Mine administration office. The noise was deafening with the smashing of roofs (they were asbestos), windows, street lighting and more. Police eventually quelled the riots and a few days later everything carried on as though nothing had happened, but countrywide the subversive stirrings continued!

A few years earlier, the same sort of thing had happened with much more dire consequences for the rioters. I recall when I worked at the Raylton Post Office in Bulawayo, seeing a light aircraft dive-bombing the rioters with a coloured dye so that the perpetrators could be picked up later. I thought that was quite a good idea!

Weekends off were vital to us, because being in the stores a standby crew always had to be available, as were doctors. This was per a preplanned schedule and allowed for forward-planning by the staff. It was one Friday I recall that it was my weekend off and I had intended to drive to Bulawayo. Mr Bosch, who was senior to me, but not my boss, informed me that "I was on standby for the weekend". He was an avid golfer and had a game on, and that was his reason for delegating me, and I knew it because the guys in the office had told me! I said I could not because I had made my own arrangements. His manner and approach were completely unacceptable and quite dictatorial, and he was furious. I went on my weekend and upon my return was called into the Store Managers office. Mr Fleishmann informed me that I was dismissed for the reason that I had not complied with Mr Bosch. It was grossly unfair because it was no emergency, but for a game of golf! Had he approached me in a different manner, I probably would have agreed. Mr Fleishmann said that I ought to get "iron in my blood" whilst hissing through his teeth (a typical and amusing trait of his). I could not argue about this issue further. I had great respect for Mr Fleishmann but felt that he had compromised his position by weakening to Mr Bosch. I had got on so well with my other colleagues, and they were sorry that it had happened, and that is life. I did, however, think about what Mr Fleishmann had said and could not agree that I had not sufficient iron in my blood, but perhaps I had too much! So much for losing your job because of a game of bloody golf – another lesson learned, stretch and wait your time, at least for a bit!

9

Johannesburg, Music, Hiking, Snow and Jean

Back in Bulawayo, I joined a mining supply company and enjoyed the work, and when my parents moved to Johannesburg, I decided to get a transfer with the company to the big city. I was staying in Benoni, and my first day with the company which was situated in Village Main, I allowed an hour to drive in along Main Reef road. Was I in for a surprise, the traffic was horrendous, and with my stomach in a knot and my blood pressure sky high, I did find the company; but still, I could not find a parking anywhere. Driving around the closest block to the company in Johannesburg involved waiting for no less than four sets of traffic lights – still no luck. In desperation, I drove into the company parking, and down the ramp, parked, and by the time I got upstairs, the public address system was blaring out about my vehicle – more stress. However, I explained the situation and a solution was arrived at.

The sales office was an absolute hive of activity, perhaps the busiest period of the Gold Mines on the Reef. Daily tenders had to be treated with a great deal of urgency, accuracy, and involving thousands and thousands of items. I got used to that, but what I could not adjust to, was the stress of driving in from Benoni every day, so I moved into the YMCA close to Braamfontein. That solved one problem, but the other I could not adjust to, was that the office in which I worked in, was an office within an office, and everyone smoked, and I did not. There was no natural light as the inner office had a few fanlights into the well of the building. Every lunchtime I would rush out into the street gasping for fresh air. I had constant headaches, my eyes burned, and although the work was acceptable, the state of my body and mind were not.

Denis Johnson also stayed at the YMCA and suggested that I apply for a job at Olivetti. The pay was better, there was a car allowance, and conditions and training were also excellent. Denis was an accomplished guitarist and had an authentic Gibson acoustic guitar. He also had a good voice and could replicate Buddy Holly songs with excellence. He had up to that point played independently. But after he had been reported for making too much noise, we got together, made less noise, and compiled a

'Music is the elixir of life'

few songs together. One of the chaps at the 'Y' worked for Gallo, so an intro was arranged, and we produced a seven single. That was good fun; it did not achieve, silver, gold or platinum, but we were proud of our achievement.

It was not really a big deal, but when I visited Bulawayo (which was as regular as I could afford in time and money), I was asked to appear on TV for an interview for my efforts. In truth, the vinyl-records of African music that played nonstop down Lobengula Street must have far exceeded my sales!

Television had not arrived in South Africa at that time, and my father had brought his TV down with him to Benoni. A local furniture store requested to loan the TV for which a small rent was paid to him per month just to put in the window. It was switched on and produced a fuzz of signal, but folk did stop by to have a taste of what the future held for them, whilst drawing attention to the furniture store!

Rob Godwin, Alan Murdoch, Mike McCullough and Len Louw were good friends at the 'Y', and it was great to share work and study experiences with them. On occasions, we went hiking into the Magaliesberg, Rustenburg Kloof and the Pilanesberg. The outings were always an adventure because we mostly did not just camp at a site but hiked into unknown territory where there were no paths. Later when I was married, I was to do a lot of rock climbing in the Magaliesberg, the hike into the Pilanesberg was exciting because it was not the usual weekend-outing venue, and definitely an unknown destination. The Pilanesberg was no longer used as farmland at the time we went out, as I think the farmers had been bought out or moved out. After enquiring at a local police station, we asked about the best route in, and settled for an eastern approach along a dirt track into the hill. I was fascinated with the range of hills because I had learnt that the Pilanesberg was the second-largest volcanic plug in the world and went very deep into the Earth's crust.

We found a deserted and quiet old farmhouse which would have been ideal for sleeping in but found that it was decidedly creepy, especially with a couple of birds legs nailed to the wall. We felt more comfortable sleeping outside. An old fashioned key was still in one of the doors, so I

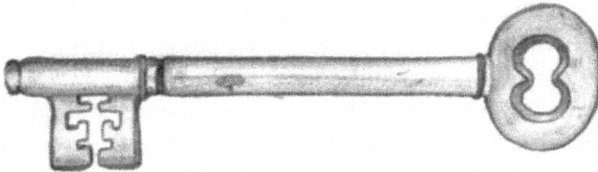

Old key from a deserted farmhouse in the Pilanesberg
Sketch: Olivia Kensley

Base camp at a deserted farmhouse – Pilanesberg Sept. 1964

kept it as a memento, which I still have, mounted on a piece of wood. Heather and Quintin have joint inscriptions on the wood for their 21st birthdays as do some of the grandchildren.

Exploring around, we found a dust-covered light horse carriage in a shelter and still in place, definitely a museum piece. It appeared to have been there for years as some of the material was torn from age. Oddly enough, when we got back from our hike, it had gone, and we saw the tracks of the wheels on a path leading away from the house. We had seen a few Africans around with cattle, and we guessed they had removed it for some reason or another. Perhaps they thought that we would take it, especially after having looked at it.

There had been good rains in the area, and the bush and grass were quite green and lush. I mention this for a reason. We set off early intending to cross the hills and attain the northwestern edge of the hills and hopefully look across towards Botswana. We made good progress even though it was hot. I was startled by a large leguaan that leapt out of the bush next to me. I was quite surprised to see it in fairly thick bush near the summit ridge of one of the hills. I thought they stayed reasonably close to water. Here there was definitely no water! Descending one of the hills, Rob Godwin took a tumble over rocks and all, but unharmed because he fell mostly on his rucksack. Some hours later it became increasingly more sweltering. We had a few welcome stops for rest in the shade where we could. On the final hill we stopped, and the only drink we had left was a beer each. This was obviously not ideal, but welcome and we had to wrap lips around the rim to prevent spillage from the erupting foam of gas and beer. We realised after descending the hill with some difficulty that if we returned via the same strenuous and exhausting route and covering that distance, we would certainly not arrive back before nightfall. We continued across a dry river bed at the base of the final hill which I am sure was solid iron ore, it was scorching, with waves of heat rising into our faces making it difficult to draw a decent breath. We agreed that we should instead head west and attempt to return through an apparent break in the hills and along a valley back to our camp. With some trepidation, we headed off and did eventually arrive at a rough path and a break in the hills. After eating our last orange each for moisture, we trudged on. It had been such a heatwave that day so that when we finally arrived back at the camp, the grass was withered and shrivelled! My cracked lips took two weeks to heal up, just from one day's hike! Not for sissies!

On another occasion, Rob and I went up Rustenburg Kloof to find the source of the stream that fed the waterfall at the Kloof. It was great walking and exploring the top of the hills. We did, we think, find the little stream almost on the summit of the mountain, and to my surprise, looking down into a small and shallow clear pool, I saw what looked like a small snake in the water. On closer inspection, I was even more surprised to see that it had a dorsal fin running the length of its back. It was just like a small eel. It was about six inches long. I was unable to get a picture of it because my camera was back at our campsite some way off. I have never found out from anyone since then if such a type of eel existed on the Magaliesberg, or in fact, South Africa. We descended via Tiger Kloof after climbing over a game fence high up on the plateau.

I woke up feeling extremely unwell and seemed to have developed flu or bronchitis overnight. We slept out in the open without cover, and it was quite cold even though we wore balaclavas. It was tough for me as I felt relatively weak and on return to Johannesburg, I was in bed for a while to recover. However, the Tiger Kloof was spectacular with tumbling clear water with large pools and the most beautiful views.

My flat, which I shared with Rob Godwin, was conveniently situated right next door to Olivetti in Braamfontein. Selling was not easy, but I managed reasonably. One particular winters day it snowed heavily, so I abandoned going into the office and headed out to Zoo Lake in the suburbs with my cine camera. I got back about lunchtime, elated with my experience, only to get bawled out in a friendly way by Mr Timmerman. I had evidently made the only sale in the team for the day in the form of an electric typewriter! I had been plugging for it prior to the sale, but it was a

The long hot hike back to camp in the Pilanesberg – with Paul,
Alan Murdoch and Rob Godwin. Len Lowe took the picture.

double treat. Besides later that day when my joy was rudely interrupted after stopping outside the Wits University red traffic lights, a student came up as the traffic light changed to green and dropped a gigantic snowball on my lap!

Calculators back then were mechanical and electrically driven with hundreds of moving parts, very heavy as well as noisy when they rattled away. Portable typewriters were relatively light. However, the electric typewriters were incredibly heavy. The real test was the book-keeping machines – they were probably the first type of computer and worked via punched-cards – these were large and weighty. Carrying these electric typewriters and 'modern' machines from your car to an office location was enough to give one a hernia!

It is certainly interesting to see how rapidly technology has changed over the years.

I had started studying for my matric with Damelin College near the station in Johannesburg. Even when I worked in Village Main, south of the city, I walked to work, walked back to Braamfontein, drank a quick glass of milk, rested for fifteen minutes then hurriedly walked back into town, and often only returned to Braamfontein at eight at night. It was about that period that one afternoon as I recall, there was a thunderous and deep explosion, and I later found out that someone had placed a bomb in the Johannesburg railway station. The perpetrator was identified as a lecturer at Damelin. He was a bit of a weedy looking guy, hardly what one would expect of a terrorist character, so you never know, but the event caused quite a stir and political concern. Apart from the occasional bomb, nothing could compare to the pie, gravy and coffee that the station restaurant served. It was tasty, filling and inexpensive!

Selling was OK, but not stimulating. I got tired of plugging the same old patter, and more than a little aggravated with having to fix typewriter ribbons and other random incidental stuff. However, one of my clients had a company from England that were providing Non-Destructive Testing services in South Africa. It involved ultrasonic testing, magnetic particle and radiography using x-ray and gamma-ray equipment. I enquired further from my contact there, and they offered me a job. I was delighted because at last, it had the relationship to elements of physics and science. It was the turning point in my career, and I resigned that month from Olivetti, although I had been well-mentored and enjoyed my time as an employee there. I must say that I never regretted any of my employment experiences, and I applied what I had learnt then in all that I did in the future.

My friends and I had joined St Martins in the Veld, and then St Columbas Church in Parkview with the primary purpose if the truth be known, to meet some girls. I had had a couple of dates, one of which I was a bit besotted over. But they passed by until I met Jean outside the Braamfontein theatre where we were introduced to one another. I had seen her before, but not been formally introduced. She had stunning features and beautiful brown eyes and we wasted no time before dating. She was still quite young, but I was struck with her. I was overwhelmed when, for the first time, I had to meet her mother and father at their house, then the extended family. They were all super folk, and I liked them all. I had perhaps previously been a bit isolated and not had too many opportunities to exercise my social skills. Therefore I was a bit shy, awkward and self-conscious. I don't think I was introverted, just a more quiet type of person. However, amongst the family, I was always made to feel comfortable and at ease. With her father, I was never totally at ease, but I was always polite and respected him. But we were just different characters, and that was that. Jean, I think in turn, also found it difficult to be completely comfortable with my folks. Parents, either way, I suppose always study the prospective partner for suitability, compliance to family traditions etc. There has to be compromise and acceptance. Anyway, when the grandchildren start to arrive, all the preconceived requirements fall away, and a new picture comes into focus!

10

Beira, Victoria Falls, Proposal, Shangani Battle Site and Prospecting

Between permanent moves, I had moved back to Bulawayo around 1965 to join my father's electrical business which he had set up after leaving Johannesburg. He had agencies for air conditioning, cold rooms, electrical switchgear, motors and furnaces. I was not long there when I was approached by a company associated with the Rank Organisation from the UK to be the chief inspector for the repair of the Beira Umtali pipeline. The pipeline fed crude oil to the Feruka refinery in Umtali, and it had become badly corroded – principally because the cathodic protection was apparently connected the wrong way, which led to accelerated corrosion. Work was tough as the trenching was through the Pungwe flats, a vast area of thick wet clay. Humidity was terrible, and the mosquitos plagued us. I used to get nasty itchy-bumps from mosquitos but became immune while in Beira.

On the job, you had to stand virtually all day in the sun. Sitting down on the piled-up mud debris offered no relief. Methane gas constantly bubbled up from shallow pools of stagnant water and decaying vegetable matter. It was nauseating and often snakes were a problem, and the Snake Park from Salisbury came down to collect snakes that had fallen into the trench overnight. It was not unusual to collect a dozen snakes overnight. We wore snake boots because we were continually in the muddy trenches, and apart from snakes, there was a real danger of being inflicted with a bite from a West African lungfish – a type of prehistoric fish that is found in swampy landscapes. I saw plenty of them, but never got bitten, fortunately. Once taking hold, the lungfish don't release their hold unless the head is removed from the body. During the dry season, the lungfish bury themselves in a moist cocoon deep in the mud, in a state of aestivation or dormancy. Incredibly they remain dormant until the next rains – up to three or four years if need be. In this state, the lungfish survive by digesting tail muscle.

Many years later on a guided 4x4 trail along the length of the Lebombo Mountains of the Kruger National park, the guide ranger took us to see a small pan. It was dry with mud similar to the clay of the Pungwe flats in Beira. He stated that it contained buried and dormant West African lungfish. Although they are known to travel overland, this particular pan was approximately 160kms from the sea and the coastal flats!

Back in Beira, mosquitos could be seen in clouds over the swamp, and they would even descend on your head if you went into the sea at night.

The monsoon brought in clouds of immense size and height; I estimated at more than over 30,000ft high. The one deluge we had, produced 15 inches of rain in two days! Unbelievable! This completely swamped our work, and we could only access with 'swamp' buggies. These buggies were constructed entirely from aluminium with large diameter tyres. The fuel was stored in the centre aluminium tube of the body, and it had a small petrol engine that drove all the wheels. It would trundle along through water, mud and grass alike. The deep treads of the tyres allowed the vehicle to propel through the water. It could not carry much but did allow access where on foot or even a standard four-wheel drive, would otherwise not have been possible. One D9 bulldozer got stuck, so we brought another D9 to pull it out, and that got stuck and sunk into a level with the top of the tracks. We had to abandon work, and the bulldozers would have to be dug out the next year after the rains had ceased, and the deep mud had dried. There were no stones over the Pungwe flats as it was all alluvial deposits from a long time past. Nearer the coastal estuary, while working in a trench in mostly sea sand, one of the welders was nearly washed away into an underground stream that suddenly appeared and opened up below him – a scary thought!

Conditions in the day used to be so bad that even the local workers struggled in the humidity and heat. It was decided that they could do 'shift' work of about three metres of trench per day, so they came in at four in the morning, and were gone by ten a.m. A very sensible and successful 'work-study' decision. Only a handful of guys that were generally employed from Salisbury, stayed the full length of time. One of the chaps just left, and did not even ask about pay, he just did not turn up for work, and reportedly had gone back to Salisbury.

I met a couple of Americans at the Estoril Hotel, who invited me along one night to help collect tropical fish. We drove out along a north-coast track through savannahs and islands of forest, interspersed with freshwater pans, filled with beautiful small, tropical and brightly-coloured fish. They caught them with a net, and then placed them in plastic bags which were charged with oxygen from a cylinder. They then flew out back to the USA with the delicate cargo. It was obviously worth it financially, but I doubt they had permits or permission to conduct the 'poaching' legally.

There are large volumes of gas in the region, on and off the Sofala Province coast. Back then, an onshore gas wellhead had ignited and could be sighted as far away as Beira, which is approximately sixty to eighty kilometres away. And, it had already been burning for a year! I was later led to believe that Red Adair and his team finally and after tremendous efforts managed to extinguish it. The resulting onshore crater was apparently at least half a kilometre in diameter.

One of the chaps I met was working for Texas Oil (as I recall), and he showed me photographs of a flare. There were two colours in the flame. He asked me what I saw, so I told him what I thought, so he said, "look carefully", and I could not guess other than gas burn-off. He informed me with a chuckle that the other flame was, in fact, crude oil! That well, as far as I know, had not yet been exploited.

With the heat, I showered in the morning, when I got back from the field, then often late at night. Only once did I have a blanket over me. For the rest of the time, I had a sheet for cover. It just never got cool enough. In the day, just shorts and open shirt was the norm. One had to drink copious amounts of liquids to offset dehydration. I was not sure that it was because of not drinking enough, that one day I had excruciating stomach cramps which came in unbelievably agonising waves. I thought that I was going to die, so I had a doctor called in. He said that I probably had Beira tummy! Indeed, it was a common complaint given the poor water quality, but it went on for hours, and I was doubled up in waves of spasm. Then just as it had reached a point where I prayed for death being an option of release, it passed! I was drained but relieved and could not understand what had happened. It was a few years later when I experienced my second of five kidney stone episodes that I realised that I had probably passed a stone back in Beira.

Two of those occasions that occurred later, I was hospitalised for, but never experienced the pain as I had in Beira. I managed to capture a stone in a sieve during a more severe episode that I experienced and was told it was a rather significant size, though looking at it, it appeared remarkably small. I figured that the body was somewhat under-designed for passing such stones.

I had had an x-ray of the kidney in Cape Town years later, and I was told that there was a stone deep in the kidney and that it would never come away – well it did! Once admitted to hospital, the stone quickly made its way back into the kidney. I was immediately fine and discharged from hospital. But with the sword of Damocles over my head! A week later it descended again, and so back to the hospital. This time in George Hospital while working in Mossel Bay, I wisely had it laser-blasted, then lost lots of blood before it settled down, and I was again fine. I can honestly sympathise with woman giving birth, pregnancy must be a scary experience, and all I can say is that giving birth is not for sissies.

Jean and her mom flew up to Beira to see me, and it was indeed a great joy to see them. I had acclimatised, but it was not pleasant for them – both the wall of heat and humidity hit them as they stepped off the plane. That

Jean and Paul at the Santa Theresa, Beira

was not all, because later they were attacked by the local mosquitos! Anyhow, they were well received by Chris and Irene Christalides who had a sort of B & B, where a few of us subsequently stayed. Jean and I went out a few times and swam in the sea. The place to eat out at was Johnnies restaurant. The prawns were prawns, not the shrimps these days that they call prawns. These were flown up from Bazaruto daily and were fresh. Grilled with lemon-butter, Portuguese rolls and wine or beer were all you required to enjoy 'fully' a night out.

I bought Jean a beautiful Chinese tailored slim dress made from the most stunning of woven fine material. She looked stunning in it. She found that it had shrunk many years later when she tried to fit it on! I had the same trouble with some of my earlier suits – sounds like an unsolved mystery! Our granddaughter tried it on a year or so ago, and she looked equally as stunning in it.

The visit was short, and I was sad to see them climb on board the Fokker Friendship aircraft and fly off back to Johannesburg.

It was on the 11th November 1965 that Rhodesia declared UDI (Unilateral Declaration of Independence). We expected it because the protracted negotiations and vacillations of Britain became frustrating and intolerable. They had handed out independence to several African countries previously under British control as colonies, in rapid succession. Rhodesia was the only economically viable country and should have been granted dominion status as was previously mooted by Britain. But an electoral change to the Labour Party changed all of that. So, with no surprises, we carried on work as usual. However, Britain decided that the UDI was illegal and sent out warships to Beira to prevent the offloading of crude oil to be pumped to the Feruka refinery. Up to that stage, the pumping of oil had not been halted, and by ingenious pipeline engineering, and even though we had to cut out lengths of corroded pipe, the pumping never stopped.

The technique of cutting into existing fuel full pipelines and bypassing the product without explosion and fire was very advanced, and a very skilled engineer was brought in from Texas to conduct and supervise the operation – expensive yes, but without incident.

The royal navy sailed into the bay off Beira and hove to, to prevent tankers from entering the port. It was later revealed that the servicemen of the Royal Navy were not happy with the task, but like the Royal Air Force and ground forces, they had always been allies with Rhodesia and had fought together through two world wars. We understood that, but it would have been bad timing for the sailors and crew had they come ashore as they still represented the political power of the time. Britain had bowed down with a weak backbone to the OAU (Organisation of African Unity) and some economically bereft African countries. This weakness allowed Russian and Chinese communism to blossom with the erosion of sound infrastructure and civilization through terrorism and intimidation. History and the record have shown that leaders that strive for position, wealth and power, do nothing for the health and welfare of their people and country that they are supposed to lead with responsibility!

Work was held in abeyance and to be continued the following year. But before packing up, Freddy Whiteman our site caretaker had found that the company accountant in Salisbury had been stealing money from employees by fraudulently signing cheques. Equipment was sold, and where it could not be sold, was divided-up amongst those remaining. It was dribs and drabs. I personally visited the company in Salisbury and proved that there had been fiddling by the accountant, and more so, I saw a cheque that had apparently been paid to me but where the signature was forged. I could not prove if the manager of the company had also had a finger in the deal. As Chief Inspector of the pipeline inspection, I felt a responsibility towards exposing it. They said they would sue me, and I said I would sue them. However, it was prudent to put it behind me, and I returned to Bulawayo to my father's business. As it turned out, the following year, I negotiated the follow-on work of inspection to be taken away from the existing company and awarded to a South African registered company.

Jean and family came on holiday to Rhodesia via Bulawayo, and then on to the Victoria Falls. Robert (Bob), my younger brother and I drove up to the falls to meet them. It was a grand reunion. Jean and I spoke seriously about things and the future under the incredible atmosphere of the falls, and a full moon. Our walk down to the falls through the forest was romantic and enhanced by our first (and only sighting), of a flying squirrel that flew or rather glided across and between trees, an extraordinary sighting, and a very special time. Then followed the more serious walkabout (hand clasped behind the back sort of stuff – perhaps like Prince Phillip) with Jean's father. He was happy with the idea of us being together though he thought Jean was still a bit young – she was in her last year of high school, matric. We had a good and friendly chat, and the atmosphere was indeed convivial.

All too soon it was time to leave them, and Bob and I set off back for Bulawayo. However, I was still keen for some bush adventure, and I had decided that I wanted to visit the site of the Shangani Battle where Alan Wilson and his men were all killed by Lobengula's fighting men. The story of that fierce battle is well known, so I will not repeat it here, but I was very

Artist depiction of Alan Wilsons last stand against Lobengula's Ndebele Impis 4th December 1893 – Artist: Richard Caton Woodville (1856 – 1927)

SHANGANI BATTLE
4TH DECEMBER 1893

The Shangani River flowing strong,
Set the scene upon that day,
For the battle in December of 1893.

Men pitched in battle fought there,
The dreadful odds were clear,
For the whites and Matabele,
The cost of lives was dear.

The regimental horns of war,
Closed in and sealed the stage,
The curtains soon nigh to draw,
On so many young of age.

Of surrender and of cowardice,
The evidence was none,
For fought they hard,
And fought they strong,
Until their final hour had come.

Perchance a song of prayer they sang,
Before they fell, succumbed,
No further shot of fire was rung,
To break the silence for the numbed.

The victory was certain,
Though of hatred there was none,
But respect for those few fallen men,
To be left and not undone.

The sons of men remember,
All the good things born of pain,
And the respect for one another,
That forever will remain.

100 Years on.   *Paul Gray© 22 November 1993* keen to experience the place where it had happened. I have included a copy of the poem I wrote of the battle at the 100th anniversary of the event.

I was then driving a Morris 1100 which had front-wheel drive, and not a lot of ground clearance. The approach was on a very sandy road that turned off the main Bulawayo road at Lupane. We managed to get to the Shangani River after much scraping of the underbody of the car on 'middlemannetjies' and thick sand. It had no causeway and was much broader than I imagined. There were some Africans gathered around a vehicle that was stuck in the middle of the river bed, in deep sand. I drove up as close as possible and stopped to survey the problem. I chatted to them, and they agreed to lift and push my car around the vehicle, past a clump of reeds, and back onto the track across the river. No water was encountered, and we ascended the opposite bank comfortably. At the stoppage in the middle of the river, was a 'madala' (old) Induna dressed in what looked like a leopard skin. When he found out where we intended to go, his expression lit up and he said that he was a boy at the time of the battle and remembered it. A surprise and privilege to meet a living link to the event. We arrived at the site where there was a simple monument to the men. I was sure that the original tree that had had an inscription carved out by Dawson "To Brave Men" was still there, though I did not see the carving. I later found out that the inscription was removed and housed in the National Museum in Bulawayo.

The Shangani Patrol battle site. We met a 'Madala' here who was a boy during the battle in December 1893.

I found a lucky bean, a sample of iron ore and an unusual seed – this I later mounted on a piece of wood marked Rhodes and Founders 1965, which I still have.

There was an extraordinary and palpable atmosphere to the place, a quiet reverence of sorts.

Being a member of a Facebook Rhodesian Group of recent times where there were references to, and a deep interest in the original Shangani battle site and happenings, I was fortunate to share experiences on this group with Doug Kriedemann, a military member of the Rhodesian Army Greys Scouts. He had carried out several patrols through the self-same area on horseback with his unit. He stated that he had an eerie experience when their horses behaved strangely and calmly as if a strange sense of security was accompanying them *in spite of the fact that this area was very active with insurgent terrorists during the bush war.* Doug related to me, as he had in the past to his fellow Greys Scouts, of the experience and his thoughts on the sacredness of the site and its surroundings...

"Being a Matabelelander, it has always held that much more significance for me...

I had the good fortune of patrolling through that area... not only once, but on many occasions... on each occasion, I was affected by the same incredible experience... hence my statement... that I sincerely believe that there was and is, a spiritual influence that presides over the battlefield... the fact that we as mounted 'Horse Soldiers' entered the zone... I felt we were all the "more recognized" for what we were..., the Reformed Regiment of Colonel Grey originally raised in 1896... We were Soldiers of Rhodesia, and therefore the common cause still remained...

Whenever we were assigned that area to patrol, I made a point of taking time out to honour out of respect, the immense privilege of visiting the battlefield...

Another point I like to reiterate is this... I have remained a horseman all my life, and to this day, having relocated to Australia from Zimbabwe in 2002 after Mugabe's madness forced us to abandon our farming business. I still earn my living from the back of a horse as I go about managing an expansive Cattle Ranching Operation... my point is, time reinforces to me just how perceptive and intelligent a horse actually is... learning to trust your mount and their instincts in the bush is wise and a considerable advantage in survival tactics, and remaining injury-free...

Going back to the Allan Wilson site and the memorial, I have little doubt our Greys Scouts horses certainly sensed and realised the 'realm' of the spiritual force that we were encountering as both friendly and comforting... their calm yet alert and tentative demeanour was absolutely evident as in the lethargic heat of Matabeleland midday they awakened back into 'fresh' mode as if it was early morning all over once again ..."

Our return to Lupane was more accessible as the stuck vehicle at the river had been pulled out with the help of cattle. Past the river and not far from a nearby mission, an African Constable (AC) waved me down, so I stopped. He asked me for a lift for him and a passenger. No problem, so they climbed in the back. I asked him where he had been, why he needed a lift. "Oh," he said, "I have been on foot to arrest this man". "Oh," I said, "what was he arrested for?" "For murder sah" he replied. We made speedy progress to the Police Station at Lupane where we dropped him, and the murder suspect off.

The trip to Bulawayo was long, and with all the activity, I had forgotten that my dear mother had given us a cooked chicken. It was in a cake-tin imperfectly sealed with wax paper around the rim. I was not certain about the condition of the contents as Bob duly began to open the tin, which was quite tight. It suddenly popped open and burst forth the foulest stench imaginable. Now you must realise that for days the tin had been in a closed car (no aircon in those days) which had been very hot even though it was July. Bob began to retch uncontrollably because it was on his lap, and I could not stop laughing even though it was not actually funny. He managed to get the window partly turned down before his stomach reacted to the signal sent to his brain! The window and the back window became dark with the outflow! We were still driving at about 100 km/h, and the picture of him propped up as far as possible to the partly open window was hilarious. We slowed and threw the offending contents and tin out the window. I swear that chicken exploded on impact with the road. Poor Bob recovered but was feeling utterly drained as he was additionally still suffering from tonsillitis. It certainly is interesting how one small event after driving along quite comfortably, can escalate into a crisis within seconds. Lesson learned; never carry cooked chicken in a closed tin in a closed hot car for days on end. So ended a memorable long weekend away.

One of the principal economies of Gwelo (now Gweru) in the early days was diamonds. They were known to be found around Somabula. One day my elder brother Tony, my younger brother Bob, Tony's friend Derek Grey, and I set off to do some prospecting not far from Somabula, but a distance west of the main road to Bulawayo. It was more a fun outing than actually digging around. However, we were pleasantly rewarded with the most amazing clear quartz stones. These were alluvial, and together with these, we also found numerous garnets. This was also a good sign. Some of the quartz stones looked like diamonds, but upon subsequent testing by Derek using hydrofluoric acid, found that they were indeed quartz, as they did dissolve. What was also fascinating, was that a long time ago, probably many thousands of years, there existed a large river probably the size of the Zambezi river that flowed south through Gwelo. This probably resulted in the alluvial deposit around Somabula. The area is fairly high, and a watershed to the north. It is common knowledge that there are kimberlite pipes along the Shangani river, which is not too far south from the area.

I had joined my father on a business trip from Bulawayo to a quarry that was not too distant from Somabula where we had prospected. They used a lot of motors and conveyors and electrical reticulation, so we met the manager in his office. Around his window-sill, he had various rock samples which interested me greatly, especially one. So, when we left, I excitedly told him that this chap had a lump of kimberlite, and yes, I did know what kimberlite looked like! This would indicate a pipe in the vicinity, perhaps where they were excavating. Not necessarily diamond-bearing, but a distinct possibility, given that diamonds were known to be around the area. He was vaguely interested, and probably deep in thought about some electrical sales. I never followed it up, but like an unsolved mystery, still lingers in the back of my mind.

One thing amused me about that trip, and although I did not laugh at the time, it was notable for telling; my father owned a really lovely low slung Jaguar. It had an excellent engine and was a bit of a gas guzzler I thought because it had two fuel tanks either side of the boot. That besides, it went very well, and we were driving comfortably at about 70 mph (over 110km/hr) when he spied from a distance, a Ford Anglia coming up in his rearview mirror. The Anglia was either a 1000cc or 1200cc at best. He thought it impertinent that such a 'piss willy' car could have the cheek to be on his tail, so he gently put foot, but the vehicle stayed on his tail. It must have been a really 'souped-up' engine because it pulled out and shot past us. He could not catch it, and it soon disappeared! There were many motor enthusiasts in those days, and this must have been one of them. Sometimes our pride gets dented, and we have to re-assess our thinking. This, I think, was one of those times.

On another occasion also driving with him to Gwelo, and I forget the type of car it was, it was extremely hot, and he was wearing KDs (khaki drill shorts), or similar. I was driving, and he decided he was going to have a G&T (gin and tonic). He asked me what I wanted, and I said I would have a cooldrink (in this case, a warm drink). It might have been a Fanta or Lemonade He pulled the cooldrink out of the wholly inadequate 'cool' bag, placed the bottle between his legs and using an opener (also known as a Rhodesian spanner) popped the cap. Now being very warm, the liquid erupted over the top of the bottle. Seats in those days were sort of bucket-shaped and sunk down below one's backside. A small pool of sticky cooldrink formed below his legs, like a little dam. Lifting himself up a fraction, the liquid continued to flow backwards between his legs and trousers and possibly inside his trousers. It was a 'crutch' twenty-two situation. He was really fed up, and I was sorry that I had asked for a drink, and I could not laugh for fear of sustaining bodily harm to myself. That would have to wait for when I was alone. We pulled over, and he cleaned up as best as possible. Sugary water does not wipe up easy and remains sticky as long as there is moisture or sweat. He remained in an unpleasant mood for the rest of the trip. What a hoot! Another lesson learned.

Years later, when Jean and I were driving to Cape Town from Johannesburg, our little daughter decided that she wanted a pee. So of course, being smart and super-efficient, out came the plastic potty, and when finished, I, trying to save time on the long journey by not having to stop, so slowing slightly, opened the window and tilted the potty out of the window. The gush of air-filled the potty and the contents flew out, or sort of scooped out and directly into my face... oh dear, another lesson learned, or perhaps revenge for events long past!

While on the subject, and I suspect that it presents as difficult a situation today as it does then, but when travelling in the Kruger National Park, you must NOT leave your car for any reason whatsoever. Even if you question why a game scout was seen riding past on a bicycle! Obviously, there are predators like prides of lions and other hostile creatures in wait all over the park waiting for people to alight from their vehicles. I once was chatting to a colleague-friend of mine, John from Koeberg Nuclear Power Station, about the problem of folk needing to relieve themselves in the game reserve, and the total lack of facilities over fairly long distances and between stops, especially when you cannot speed. Often the answer is to wait for a period when there is no traffic, or drive down an ompad, open one door and feel better. Well, my colleague-friend (full name withheld to protect innocent persons) said his wife had an absolute fear of being outside the car in the bush but was desperate for a 'number two'. This was a serious situation and called for a special procedure and tactics. By the way, this is absolutely true; so braving attack from wild animals, he got out of the car, removed one hubcap and gave it to his wife, which she had to use. In close confines, you can only be 'so' private. This situation denies one this privilege of even coming close to it. Anyhow they drove on until they crossed a causeway with running water. Husband braving attack by wild animals yet again got out of the car and commenced washing the hubcap. At that moment, a park ranger pulled over the rise in his vehicle and caught him in the act. Explaining that he was cleaning the hubcap would not sell in such a situation. The air apparently was filled with laughter on the explanation given. His wife did not think it funny, though. He certainly was not panning for gold! The old hubcaps could be quite useful at times. Most of such events are almost literally funnier in 'hindsight!

Once when in the Wankie (now called Hwange) National Park with our young children Heather and Quintin, we came across a pride of lion that was in the process of creeping up on some impala. It was an exciting moment because the lion were on our right, and the impala some way off on our left. In front of us was a couple in a Volkswagen beetle. Quintin suddenly wanted a pee, and it was desperate and could not wait. We could not open the door because of the apparent danger, so we grabbed a towel and told him to pee into it. At that moment, while Quintin was peeing into the towel, the chap in the Volkswagen in front of us opened his left side door and got out to get a picture of the stalking lions on the right-hand side! The roof height of his car sort of protected him; however, one of the lioness from quite some distance charged at him, and he only just made it back into the vehicle before the lioness furiously charged around his side. Had he been on the driver's side of the car, from the distance of probably twenty to thirty metres, he more than likely would not have made it! A charging lion could cover that distance in seconds. You can drive for hours and not see anything so one never knows where you may be surprised by nature.

11

Marriage and Bush Trip to Gona Re Zhou and Limpopo

Jean and I were married in St Columbas Church in Johannesburg in 1967 and set off for Rhodesia where we had a very happy and wonderful holiday. It was not easy to find a place where we could rent in the northern suburbs of Johannesburg, and rentals were costly for what was available. Jean's mom kindly helped with some money that allowed us a deposit for a house. We settled in Blairgowrie, a suburb in Randburg north of Johannesburg and had two beautiful children Heather and Quintin.

Johannesburg had an excellent climate and was the place to be for a business career. As a qualified Non-Destructive Testing (NDT) Inspector, I travelled quite extensively around the country to engineering construction sites, power stations, pipelines and other engineering manufacturing organisations. My deeper interest and broadening of my career really took off when I joined the Corner House Laboratories (Rand Mines) and became more closely linked to mining, the mines, metallurgy, welding technology, and fracture and failure analysis of engineering components.

Paul and Jean's wedding day – 15th April 1967

I conducted some very interesting studies underground on the Witwatersrand gold reef mines regarding 'support packs', drilling techniques, including some accident investigations. Product testing was a regular task, and it was most interesting and informative at times, to cut through supplier and manufacturer 'bull' if I have to term it that way, where they would advertise a product as complying with international or national standards such a SABS. Then upon testing the item to the given standard, to find that it fails (some dismally), to meet the basic minimum requirements. This was very important when it came to safety equipment, and men's lives depended on the item or product to perform satisfactorily. Mining always carried a risk without the possibility of safety equipment failing in service. I had done a lot of testing of critical safety and production equipment both above and below ground. There were no shortcuts, and the mine and its employees depended on the inspector to do his job and do it well. Once when I was working deep underground testing brake rods for a large subsurface winding drum, I was tempted to assume the condition of the last of the rods. I had been working for hours under challenging conditions and had tested all of the rod threads. This entailed thorough cleaning of the sticky tar and grease and muck, then doing the crack detection. It was the last rod; I was tired, and there was clearly nothing wrong with all the others – I was tempted! I stopped and thought about it. I would not compromise the good work I had already completed because of one remaining rod. So I soldiered on and somewhat bored found to my horror, that that last rod thread was severely cracked, and would have failed and could well have resulted in a skip plummeting into the depths to be crushed flat with its occupants, or ore, or both. A severe lesson learned and never forgotten. While I managed the branch office of the company in Cape Town, primarily conducting serious inspection work; I briefed our inspectors that they worked for themselves, and we happened to pay them – in that their reputation hinged on what they did, or did not do. Notwithstanding this, we did have two individuals who were tempted with reward from contracting companies to turn a blind eye to defects, thereby saving themselves money in conducting repairs. Both were 'found out' and had to leave the company. Quality of work in the manufacturing and engineering field is a vast subject and would justify the publication of a separate book.

As a family, we went into the bush as often as we could. Sometimes with the larger Caithness and Semple families to the Kruger National Park, and at other times up to Bulawayo to see my parents or to Gona Re Zhou in south-east Rhodesia. Going to Gona Re Zhou, was always an adventure and we went there a number of times. We owned a Toyota saloon, so driving on some of the roads was tricky with the limited clearance under the chassis. After crossing the Limpopo at Beit Bridge and completing border formalities (which in the sixties and seventies, was always a pleasure with the efficiency, cleanliness and politeness of border officials), I would feel the stress of driving and past pressures of work begin to lift almost immediately. Whenever I crossed the border, I felt like I was coming home, but that was then – how things have changed – unfortunately for the worse, and that is putting it mildly! The exception is Panda ma Tenga which is still as of 2012 a pleasure to complete formalities into Zimbabwe.

The Gateway to Adventure' "I just wanted to stand and look down the Chikombedzi road, you never knew what you were going to run into once you set off down it"

– A quote by Allan Wright – 'The Valley of the Ironwoods' 1972

The next stop was the Lion and Elephant motel for a pit stop and fuel, then further, turning off towards Chikombedzi and to the camp called Swimuwini at Buffalo Bend. A special place for us, not teeming with game, but you do see buffalo, elephant, and antelope but rarely see lion. They can be heard at night, though. Most occasions we were there, we were alone in the camp – one room with an open stoep with a kitchen and a long walk to the ablutions. There was a fireplace under a baobab tree – each hut had an imposing and impressive baobab tree. The lion would, we were informed, sometimes came up to the small pond next to the ablution block to drink. The Nuanetsi River (now called the Mwenezi River) was always a river of sand below the bend. The exception was up river where there were large rock outcrops, and there were pools with fish and crocodiles. On one occasion, when Bob came on a trip with us, he bumped into some dark creatures which we were sure were lion. So, we drove him back to his hut as we would do when going up to the ablutions late at night. The camp did not have fences, and the warden was about four kilometres away. It gets eerily quiet there at night, and one can hear animals very far off. One particular night we were cooking the last of our bacon over the open fire, when a sudden and most terrifying lion roar erupted just below us! Jean dropped the pan on the fire, grabbed the kids and fled to the hut, which was a natural and sensible thing to do. Bob and I speedily retreated to the

Under the Baobab tree – Paul and his brother Bob with Paul's children, Heather and Quintin – Swimuwini, Buffalo Bend Gona-re-Zhou. Photo: Jean Gray

safety of the stoep, with the pan of bacon, not risking the loss of good nosh! The bacon aroma may have very well lured the lion.

On another occasion which was during the bush war, Jean, I and the kids were sitting on the stoep, and I heard the low intermittent grunting of a leopard. It was pacing back and forth some distance off from the hut. We then heard a vehicle approaching from way off, and the warden stopped in the bush away from us, then came on and reported that there was a leopard not far from us. I remarked that I had heard it, although I do not think he believed me, but I had had a close encounter a couple of years before and knew the sound – I will recount that story later. He had come to warn us that they were shooting an impala for the pot and that we were not to think that there was a contact with terrorists. We were after all, not very far from the Mozambique border. There was an army unit based at the wardens' house – Mabalauta, next to the Nuanetsi River. Due to the escalation of terrorist incursions, it was the last time we visited the camp. Some of the roads that we traversed due to lack of visitors and traffic had small Mopani bushes growing on them. It was not worth the risk.

It was most interesting that we discovered evidence of an Early Iron Age site at Swimuwini. Judging by the type of pottery embedded in the high bank of the river, it could very well have been Gokomere which would be more than a thousand years old. But we did not have that verified.

Years later, in the late 1990s, Jean conducted a comprehensive study of an Iron Age site as previously mentioned, a bit further south in the Mateke Hills. That study was conducted in conjunction with the University of Zimbabwe. These hills could be seen from low hills called Ntabambomvu (the Red Hills) behind Swimuwini. The Mateke Hills was an early geological volcanic/magma outpouring. They were fascinating with varying vegetation types, outcrops of granophyre and even iron ore. Even outside of the Gona Re Zhou National Park, there was still much game to be seen when hiking around.

One unforgettable sunset, with the wardens' permission, we drove up into the Red Hills and walked a little way off from the vehicle – not far from a now deserted army OP (Observation Post) position. We set up two camp chairs, poured a sundowner and watched the glorious ball of sun descend into the west. At the same time, behind us, with the distinctive curtain of darkness rising in the east, watched with awe a full yellow moon rising. It was a special moment in time and life. The bush was quite thick with what looked like Lebombo Ironwoods (Musimbiti) on the crest and in the gloom, it was quite spooky so we retreated to the vehicle, and headed back. A baboon's bark interrupted from below the ridge. Night closes in rapidly in Africa and exclusively belongs to the creatures of the night.

Sketch of our chalet 'Acacia' at Swimuwini – Gona Re-Zhou – 1973

Sundown over the Ntabambomvu Hills not far from Mabalauta, a bit spooky amongst the dense Msimbiti trees when it got dark.

> *When you become quieter,*
> *you hear and see more...*

Another unique experience we had there, and I still have the slides to prove it, was when with permission of the warden, we drove to the Manyanda Pan where we met a group from Oxford University. They were doing studies on grazing habits of elephants (in fact probably a good excuse to enjoy a wonderful paid experience in the African bush). The Manyanda pan was a fair distance south of the camp and had a perfectly placed viewing platform and hide. We settled down with a snack, a flask of coffee and quietly waited under a rising bright moon, while we waited for the elephants to arrive.

Due to poaching activities, the elephants in the reserve were very skittish, and the first small group slowly and cautiously approached the pan at about nine pm. I had set up my Olympus camera on a tripod. It was not a fancy camera by any means, but it had an automatic exposure setting that would close the shutter when enough light had fallen onto the mottled platen behind the film. Another group filed in, as another left. There must have been at least four small groups that came quietly up to the pan, drank, and splashed around a bit, then left. It was a very stirring experience. When all was eventually quiet, we climbed down and returned for the drive back to the camp.

Night time full moon photographs of elephants at Manyanda Pan. Amazing long exposure results with ghostly images. Note blue sky, green trees and bushes!

Now the surprising result of the pictures was that the exposures revealed a blue sky, green trees with shadows (from the moon), and the ghostly images of 'see-through' or transparent elephants in various positions and densities – the longer they stayed in one position, the more solid they appeared. I have not seen any picture similar to this, and it only goes to show, that animals and particularly predators with keenly sharp eyes in low light can no doubt clearly see any potential victim!

One other picture I had was when I had perched myself on the window sill of the car looking over the roof and took a picture of a herd of buffalo that had just crossed the road. I turned around to look behind me and saw a very mature buffalo bull with only one horn. He was watching me very intently, so I took a picture of it and retreated into the cabin

I later read Allan Wright's book – *Grey Ghosts at Buffalo Bend,* so I was excited to read that a young buffalo in the company of old Chikami had joined forces with the old chap. Old Chikami was a senior buffalo that had years before been shot by a poacher and after a long recovery time, had been left lame. This was around 1971. The young buffalo had one night, fought off three lions that tried to kill him, this went on for some time, and locals at Malipati had heard the din and thought the buffalo dead. In the battle, he lost a horn, the bloodied remains of which was found on the stony river bed. The buffalo recovered and remained a companion to

Could this be Old Chikami's companion - One Horn? – 1973

Chikami for some time – it was obviously a powerful and brave animal. We were in Gona re Zhou in 1973, and I feel certain that this was the brave young buffalo that Allan Wright wrote about in his book. I felt honoured to see such a proud looking animal; standing on one side of the road quite confidently while the rest of the herd had already crossed. Most buffalo gaze at you with an 'as if you owed them money' look, but this one did not.

My brother Bob and his friend Jovan Lazarevic were planning a trip north to the bush and wanted me to join them from Johannesburg. We were going to rough it, so Jean and the kids stayed at home. It was an Easter weekend, so tagging on a few days gave us enough time to drive north. We had decided to go into the Mopani veld just south of the Limpopo on the South African side. As suggested by the local police, we headed west onto a large tract of government land. It had some nice granite kopjes and a few tracks winding through the extensive Mopani veld. We met the caretaker of the land who was a most interesting chap. He had lived in the veld probably for most of his life. He had a pet dassie, and the two of them got on really well, but the animal would not tolerate being near anyone else but him. He had very weathered, knarled and tough-looking hands. It was perhaps no surprise, but puzzled us, when he sketched out on the hard earth the route we should follow towards the Limpopo, by pushing his fingernail upside down so to speak like a bulldozer into the hard soil. After parking our car, a long-distance back, we set off. Route finding was quite difficult through the scrub Mopani as one could not gain view for any distance. However, we eventually approached the bank of the river only to find that it was in flood. Muddy floodwaters never did smell fresh, and what with the deposit of silty mud on the bank, and the danger of crocodiles coming into our camp spot, we decided to retreat away from the river more or less back from where we had come. We had crossed a small dry river bed and decided on a spot under some small trees. It was already getting dark, so I set about getting a fire started while Bob and Jovan collected some wood. I was suddenly aware of a low sort of cough growl. It moved back and forth a little way off. When Bob got back, I told him that I thought we had company, and by the sound, it was probably not friendly. We remained still, and then distinctly heard the repeated intermittent cough growl. We had already set down our gear, and the small fire was already quietly burning and aflame. We had a couple of torches, including a strong four-cell Eveready torch which we used to try and spot the intruder. I was fearful that it was a lion (and I still have a fear of bumping into a lion or worse into lions in the bush, though I have been told that it is not the worst type of encounter you can have in the wild, other creatures such as buffalo can be far worse). Anyhow, we could clearly see the eyes reflecting in the torchlight. I moved slightly to one side and played the light on the body, which was crouched in the grass. It had spots, and we decided that it was not a lion or a hyaena, but in fact a leopard! In an attempt to frighten it off, we threw stones at it, and it did not budge! The eyes were riveted on us. It was not more than ten to fifteen metres from us, and because we were sleeping in the open with no protection except for a sheath knife, clearly, we were encroaching on its territory. We packed up our gear, retreated into the small dry river bed and decided to head for a windmill and little pump house that was still under construction – it was close to where we had planned to camp and probably not more than fifty or more metres away. We found it, and now a little unnerved settled down 'unnaturally' I might add, onto a hard concrete floor. It was fearfully hot inside, so had the steel door open. At the rear of the little shelter was a large opening slot presumably to accommodate a pipe to an engine in the future. The opening was large enough for a leopard to enter with ease. Over the opening was propped a sheet of corrugated iron. The moon had risen, you could have read a newspaper it was so bright. It was very quiet, and then we heard the unmistakable sound of bones and meat being crunched and eaten. The reason the leopard was touchy was because it had made a kill – no doubt an impala. Despite the heat, we pulled the door slightly closed and lay back waiting for the night to pass. The next thing was that the corrugated sheet of iron propped against the opening at the back of us suddenly fell forward and inwards. Crisis! I flung myself against the sheet and pushed with all my might to close the opening. Obviously, the leopard was coming in. Pandemonium, heavy panting, hearts pounding, then silence. Cautiously I pulled back the iron and looked outside into the bright moonlight expecting to see a leopard, but there was nothing, looking down, and over the top of the sheet was a mouse! Heavens above, a flaming mouse had caused us to panic. Now slightly amused by our nervousness by it all we again settled down. It was not long after that while lying back, there was a light thump just below my chin! I shot up, heart pounding yet again, snapped on the torch, and found a large gecko to the side of my sleeping bag. So ended the night of absurd horrors.

The next morning, I found that I was missing my binoculars, so we set off back to where we had intended to camp the night before and found them still hanging from a branch where I had left them. The leopard had gone.

The following night after an interesting day, we again had a weird experience, but not like the leopard encounter. We had chosen a perfect camping spot under a circle of small trees. It was ideal having the backing of trees protecting us, and once again collected some sticks for the fire. I noted with great interest a firefly or glow-worm on the bark of a branch. It was different in that it appeared to be like a caterpillar about an inch long with a number of glowing spots on its back. I have never figured that one out. Additionally, on scooping out our hip holes for more comfortable sleeping, we came across two scorpions that popped out of the sandy soil. This was not as disturbing as the ominous and foreboding feeling that there was something wrong with the site. I mentioned this to Bob, who confirmed that there was something very eerie, even sinister about the spot. Jovan never felt that happy about camping in the open and in such a wild place, so we all agreed once again, to move. We repositioned in not so favourable a spot, but the 'ominous feeling' left immediately. Nothing is more evident, especially away from the city, and deep in the bush, to sense when things are not comfortable. There is absolutely no doubt, and it has been recorded, that some ancient or early human-occupied archaeological sites have an atmosphere or presence about them.

The full moon rose, and with our little fire, we settled down. A little later, baboons started barking in the distance from one of the kopjes, then from far off, other families of baboon started barking. Louder and more desperate became the barking from the closer kopje, then a terrible screaming and commotion, then silence. We figured that perhaps a leopard had made a kill, and then, at last, we could all settle down for the night. Such is the food chain in nature, mostly an unfortunate event – for some.

There were a lot of baobab trees around, and we found one that still had the bushmen pegs up the trunk to either access water or perhaps honey.

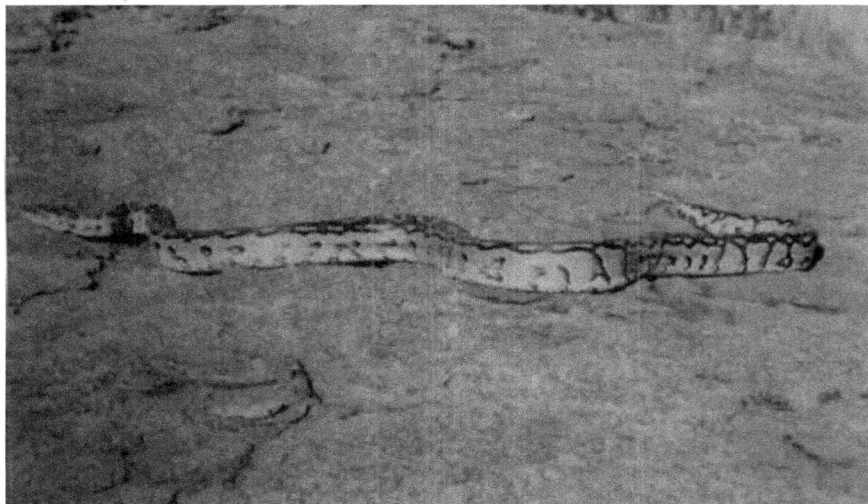

The healthy and active python that John caught.

The Capricorn kopje - rainmaking site.

Pottery and copper ring found at the rainmaking site – Capricorn – spanning occupation periods and cultures

Though Jovan did not enjoy the bush, he had no fear of snakes. Climbing a kopje, we came across a young python that was sunning itself on the rock. It was about one to one and a half metres long, but quite fat. Jovan immediately tried to catch it, but the snake was not keen, so Jovan borrowed my hat, and as the snake went for the hat, he caught it behind the head. What was interesting was that the python coiled back, then struck out almost its full length, then with a whack, hit the ground. It did this twice before Jovan caught it. Though quite short for a python, it was quite strong and had to be uncoiled from Jovan's arm from time to time. He wanted to keep it and take it back to Cape Town, but we dissuaded him because it firstly did not belong in Cape Town, and besides, when in captivity, they developed a sort of canker of the mouth. Setting it down on the granite, it happily slid away – where it belonged.

On the way back to Johannesburg, we stopped and camped not too far from the geographical Capricorn location. The camp was next to several large granite kopjes. One large one had displayed some interesting cracks on the north face that also had some hollows higher up. On the way around the lower kopje, the bush was quite dense but contained hundreds of spider webs literally. It was not pleasant walking into them, because one never quite knew where the spider was at the time. Hopefully, they would move off, but urgent brushing around the face was necessary to remove the webs. The webs were inordinately strong, almost like twine. There were lots of euphorbia about, and it was on the way up when we climbed up one of the granite slabs, that I foolishly sliced through one of the overhanging branches with my large sheath-knife. Had it cut with the first stroke, it would have been fine, but repeating the process resulted in some of the 'milk' latex spraying onto my cheek. I wiped it off, but over the following three days, the skin exfoliated dramatically, almost like layers of paper or cardboard. I was quite worried, but it did clear up.

Back to the climb, we climbed up successfully using a rope. On the summit, I was surprised to find the most incredible assortment of patterned potsherds and rims. I collected a few of them and carefully wrapped and put them in my rucksack. I also found a crude copper finger ring on the descent. These artefacts I later carefully drew with all the notes of the find, and a few years later had them identified by Professor Tom Huffman of the University of the Witwatersrand. The different samples revealed different pottery types of different cultures spanning an extended period. It was more than likely a rainmaking site that had been used for hundreds of years. The artefacts with copies of the drawings were left for storage at the university. There are now stringent laws about collecting artefacts, and disturbing any archaeological site without proper permits, procedures by qualified professional persons.

12

Rock Climbing, Army Bush Stint and Strange Happenings

Back in Johannesburg, I had continued to go out rock climbing to the Magaliesberg as often as I could. Northcliff was a good training ground, but places like Tonquani in the Magaliesberg were more remote and had much longer climbing routes. One could tackle reasonably easy or challenging routes. Going further afield to the Kransberg in the Waterberg Mountains not far from Thabazimbi, presented even longer and more difficult climbing routes. It was always refreshing to be out in the hills.

Bob was in the Rhodesian army for at least three years, so I took the opportunity to fly up to see him. We drove out to the Matopos which was an area quite deserted at the time as it was an active military area. So to all intents and purposes we were alone and enjoyed the experience and adventure of climbing together again. Bobs' faithful little dog 'Sally' would sit patiently at the start of the climb awaiting our return. The real risk when securely back in our concealed 'camo' vehicle, was the 'pepper ticks' (named as such due to the numbers of them on the skin, resembling pepper). One could hardly see them, but brushing through the long grass, all ticks are happy to see you. The same applied to the dog that would have to be checked out on a return to the house.

In the Matopos with Bob – Inungu in the distance.

We also climbed on some ironstone outcrop on a high hill on a range east of the Ncema river. The climbing was quite different from the granite or sandstone rock because it was very smooth and only broken by small ledges, rills and cracks. That was also categorised as a prohibited zone, which was essentially free of people and quiet, but added another facet to the grading of the climb!

I must add that extreme caution was always exercised. We were vigilant with ground and bush observations and protected ourselves accordingly.

Speaking of that, Jean and I went on a Flame Lily holiday to Kariba in July 1978 while the kids were cared for by Jean's mother. It was a welcome break, and we even flew out to Fothergill Island on a single-engine floatplane. The vastness of Kariba was a joy to see, and after a few days, we returned to Kariba. It was during the bush war, and as we slowly climbed out of Kariba and gaining altitude to clear the Matusadona Hills, I remarked to Jean that flying so slowly to gain altitude; I was surprised that the Viscount had not previously been a target. Despite proper flying take-off procedures, a Viscount aircraft was indeed shot down over Urungwe a few months later in September 1978 by terrorists using a Strela Sam7 missile. Joshua Nkomo of ZIPRA and backed by the Russians boasted and apparently laughed to the press including the international media that he was responsible for the shooting. The cowardly terrorists followed up to where the aircraft had crashed and after saying that they would not harm the injured, then promptly gunned them down. Those that had left earlier to retrieve emergency help, and three of the survivors that had managed to flee into the bush, survived. This was civilian aircraft, so much for the bravery of communist terrorists. The odds became increasingly stacked against the peoples of Rhodesia by Britain and other countries that preferred appeasement than standing firm in support of true free-world democracy and justice.

We had been planning to return to Rhodesia and being confident that I would be called up; I completed two years of part-time training over 1973/74 with the Hunter Group, which was a Citizen Force South African unit. The idea of a specially trained group of men was a new concept for South Africa and was promoted by Commandant van Kerckhoven of the South African Irish regiment as far back as 1966, and it was during 1968 that the Hunter Group was formed. Training began at the Doornkop Military Base (previously called Diepkloof). It was extremely tough training which was carried out on Saturdays and sometimes during the week, all on a voluntary basis; being almost essentially unconventional armed training, it was both interesting and stimulating. Coming home after a gruelling day with bruises and worn out, it took about a week to

Top: Caricature of Paul in the Hunter Group
Above left: First year qualification decal – Hunter Group 1973
Above right: Junior Instructor decal – Hunter Group - 1974

recover in readiness for the forthcoming Saturday's training. I qualified for my basic training and gained my much treasured Green Scorpion badge. After the second year, I attained the Orange Scorpion badge to qualify as an assistant instructor.

They were great guys to work with, and hardship was always shared. I recall Staff Sergeant Willie Ward, a much respected Senior instructor, would encourage us after field training with words like 'we are together as a team' and to 'climb aboard an imaginary bus' while we jogged back to our base as a unit.

Paul and Bob – RDU Bulawayo 1977

He went on to serve in Recce 2 and received the Honoris Crux Silver in 1976 for bravery in Angola (see Willie Ward's personal account in *We Fear Naught but God* by Paul J Els). He showed exemplary bravery during a brutal contact, when a fellow troopie was severely wounded during a brutal contact. Alone and under fire, Willie successfully carried the troopie for approximately 4 kilometres, back to safety and pick–up. The troopie was successfully casevaced for hospitalisation and recovery. No one was ever abandoned or left to struggle. Such was his nature, as were his fellow instructors such as Capt. Botten, Maj Sybie van de Spuy, Brian Wall, Mike Tippet and others. At the start of the year, we had about 120 intakes and landed up at the year-end with about 29 or 30! Quite a heavy drop out! During the hectic 1974 selection course in Oudtshoorn (it even snowed), where out of 29 volunteers, 9 passed the selection. The successful candidates became the first members/operators of Recce 2. I doubt very much if I would have successfully completed the extremely tough physical course (let alone the mental strain). The Hunter Group was then disbanded when Recce 2 Regiment was formed. Before I was eligible to go for parachute training, I was transferred to Cape Town and so ended my valuable training. We had intended to move back to Rhodesia, but uncertainty in the situation there had led us to put that on hold. We were not to know how bad it would become.

I soon received a work transfer to Cape Town. Jean was a Johannesburger and not keen to leave for the Cape. The broader family were not that keen on Cape Town either and had a fixation about the weather being constantly overcast and terrible for weeks on-end. From time to time it was overcast, but never to the extent to which the rumours had become 'gospel'. It was often said that the Transvaalers loved two things about the Cape: the wine, and the road north! But they still make the annual holiday trip to Cape Town. Jean did settle down, and frequent visits to family in Johannesburg helped.

The situation in Rhodesia had become more complicated and in 1977 my elder brother Tony, who had spent a lot of time in the Rhodesian Air force Volunteer Reserve when in Gwelo, and I who had some good basic training, now both residing in Cape Town; volunteered to do a stint in Rhodesia. Bob was still in the army, and my folks were again living in Bulawayo so that it would be a good reunion in any event. This decision, although agreed to by Jean, was not well received by her mother because our children were still quite young, and it was considered a risk. She was right, but we felt a strong conviction about going ahead with our decision. A difficult subject all around.

After the formalities were sorted out, I flew up to Bulawayo and on recommendation for RLI I was finally attached to 2 Platoon the Rhodesia Defence Unit – Rhodesia Regiment. After completing battle camp outside

Above left: Rhodesian Defence Unit plaque
Above right: The Rhodesia Regiment – The Depot – presentation plaque

Great troopies - 2 Platoon – RDU

of Bulawayo, I was deployed into the area of Wankie, Victoria Falls and surrounds under Op Tangent. Our convoy was delayed in leaving Bulawayo. Proceeding slowly we would have arrived late afternoon or early evening in the hilly area south of Wankie and would have been vulnerable to ambush. We left early the next day, and arriving in the hilly section before Wankie, we found the remains of an ambushed army Landrover. The driver was unfortunately shot through the head. The passenger after disembarking and taking shelter, had bravely held off the terrorists, believed to be as much as eighteen in number, returning enough fire to induce the terrorists to flee. I thought the Wankie area would be relatively quiet, but I was entirely wrong. The ops room displayed activity over a wide area. Incursions were coming in across the Zambezi from Zambia and Botswana.

I was involved with covert observations, follow-ups, stops, curfew breakers. The troopies were all African, and a fine bunch of men to have in a 'stick' or platoon. They were completely reliable troopies, extremely dedicated and sharp. Amongst our men, we had a sergeant that had served in Burma during the last war. What a great chap to chat with. He was crystal clear with his views of the communist incursions and their intention. It could probably be summed up as a relentless drive for personal power under the guise of 'freedom for the people' driven and supported by Russia and China.

*A relaxed briefing with members
of SB at DC camp Mbimba*

Members of No. 2 Platoon RDU posing at a scene of CT murder.

One of our African sergeants went home for R&R to the north-east and discovered that his brother had been bayoneted to death because they knew he was in the army. He came back to duty with no whingeing but very focused and determined. Another two of our unit died in action, one shot and another bayoneted. The latter two after I had completed my stint. When I heard about it, I wept. They were young men and knew right from wrong and were prepared to fight for it.

Oddly enough in my work in Cape Town, the pressures were onerous, and I had frequent migraines. While in the bush, up at six, in bed by eight-thirty pm and with mostly physical activities, I never suffered from one headache.

An area around the Matetsi River, we tried to intercept some fleeing terrorists who had been followed for two days by another unit. They bomb shelled before the railway line over stony ground and were lost. They had been towing a light-wheeled cannon (apart from assisting a bleeding colleague), back into Botswana. We were not allowed to follow up into Botswana even though we knew they had support bases there. In that area conducting a follow-up, I found some excellent Late Stone Age implements.

On another occasion, after a serious land mine explosion, the occupants of a lorry were killed. With a tracker, our stick followed for many miles through the typical forest of the area. Our tracker was sharp, and I was impressed when he quietly informed me that the terrorists were getting tired and would rest soon. We were prepared for action, but they had moved on from an open glade. Our tracker simply went across to where the terrorists had stopped, and he uncovered some buried mealie-cobs they had eaten. I had learnt some tracking in SA, but the experience these chaps had even when traversing soft sand was remarkable. I think they had a constantly changing display in their heads of what signs they saw around them. Also, gut-feel and common-sense plays a great part. Also, on that follow up, our tracker indicated that I should approach cautiously, and the remainder of the stick stay behind. I approached an ant-heap very quietly that he had pointed out, it had a large cavity on the side. Cautiously looking in that direction, I saw a snake which appeared to be a black mamba with about one-metre of body slowly inching into the hole. Peering down the hole, there was at least another two-metres of body slithering around the bend at the bottom of the hole. I hate to think what the overall length was. It did not hear or sense our presence, so we left it to its business and moved on. It was late afternoon when the tracks led out of the forest and scrub area into Community Lands, and we lost the advantage of tracks due to cattle and numerous other tracks. Special Branch would have to follow that one up.

You can get easily lost in the bush, especially at night. Skills at map-reading and direction-finding even using stars were essential. I had fortunately learnt a lot during my training in South Africa which included 'inter-alia' pacing uphill, downhill, walking bias, backtracking, compass work, contouring, natural signs, paths and river courses. However the risk of getting lost is still there. Route finding was also vital to avoid the possibility of accidental encounters with other army and police units working the same general area. One particular night four of us had been dropped a long way off, with the purpose of clandestine surveillance of a rural school. Walking through bush without a path or track requires careful observation, even in the day. This is because you have to constantly walk around bushes or trees or outcrops, and then re-adjust direction after the obstacle is passed. Our stick had walked for well over an hour, and I had observed a set of stars to my left-hand side. I was suddenly aware that the stars had moved across to my right-hand side. Knowing (but never entirely being sure), that the heavens do not change that rapidly, I stopped and indicated to the others that we were 180 degrees out. I can tell you that it required a great deal of persuasion to do an about-turn. I did not have to quite pull rank (as sergeant), but I could feel the aura of doubt. After about another half hour of walking, we finally intersected a small track which confirmed our position for the intended observation, and they were finally satisfied.

Wheel failure at Tjolotjo – 'premonition' – note scour mark on the road

It is sometimes strange how one can sense things in the bush. In one location, I had the strong sense that terrs had been there but had left and the direction away from the location they had headed. This was confirmed with local inhabitants. Most local peoples were caught up in the 'damned if we do and damned if we don't' situation. They did not want the violence as their lives were hard enough. Just coming into a village and seeing the paltry collection of food gathered for either consumption or storage must have been difficult for them. Then the tough terrs would go in, rough up a few of the elders, demand food and women, intimidation speeches then move on. The branding of collaborators is an easy stamp to put on folk, but a lot more difficult to fully understand the dilemma they face. I was being driven in a 'four-five' Bedford back to base when I had a presentment of something about to happen. The driver was going at a reasonable speed, but I demanded that he slow down immediately – he did so almost to a snail's pace, and the front left wheel fell off!

On another occasion, I had arranged a lift with another sandbagged truck to Bulawayo. I was strapped onto the rear. There was no immediate danger of a landmine now being on narrow tar. The soldier next to me (there was only the two of us), was sitting beside me unstrapped. We had travelled some distance and were just outside of Tjolotjo when I had another light-bulb moment and insisted that he put on his lap-belt immediately. He did so, and it could not have been another fifty metres when the left-front wheel of the truck fell-off, and we slewed across the road to a halt. He could not believe it. I heard that some of the troopies in our unit thought that I was 'Tagati' (magic) I did not think it that special, because it just happened.

Speaking of that sort of thing, it was back in Johannesburg some time before, that late one night, I was awakened by someone gripping both of my hands. In my semi-conscious state, I thought that it might be Jean, or that I was lying on my hands. I was suddenly aware of an image of a person next to the bed. It was not entirely clear and was flickering in a shell-like outline of a person. It was the head and upper torso, and while I stared at it, it slowly melted away. I was wide awake then and woke Jean. I told her that I had just seen a ghost. She was taken aback and somewhat frightened I think, but I assured her that it was not at all scary. I told her that it was either my father or my brother Tony. I was wide awake, and my brain was crystal clear and sharp as if it had been charged with electricity. I was awake until at least three am. It puzzled me the whole of the next week, and then daily events eventually took over. It was about a month later when I received a letter with a photograph of the vehicle from Tony who said that he had had a serious road accident while driving back to Gwelo late one night. He had dozed off and the Peugeot had left the road

Paul Gray

100 BUTTERFLIES OR MORE

One hundred butterflies or more,
Fluttered around the sweetened floor.

In contrast with so grim a scene,
They settled about, so white, so clean.

The explosion had blown the traders lorry,
Now silent, misshapen, sad and ugly.

The cabin and engine blown with the thunder,
That tore into metal and lives, asunder.

The lifeless bodies, damaged we found,
Not far from the site on dusty ground.

The terrorists long had flown,
To leave their landmine, buried, alone,
To wait the weary travellers wheel,
To set in motion, an act unreal.

The innocent trader plied his fare,
To distant villagers their joy to share,
But came it to naught, their simple lives,
Affecting family, friends and wives.

Lost in the crossfire of power and war,
The love of life they would see no more,
And yet,
The cargo on the back remained,
Some crates still full, some broken, drained,
The bakkie and soil awash, around,
From sweetened soft drinks on the ground.

So harsh a sight with muffled sigh!
We ask ourselves Oh why, Oh why!

Into action following boot and spoor,
To leave the wreck, and life unsure,
We left one hundred butterflies or more.

By 'Serge' Paul Gray ©

Poem from the scene of a landmine explosion on a dirt road
north off of the Wankie Victoria Falls road – 1977

and rolled-over, flattering the roof. He was then trapped over the back of the seat and pinned down by the roof. In the early morning, someone had seen the vehicle in the bush and stopped. Tony was alive and had to be cut out of the vehicle. The picture of the vehicle was frightening. It suddenly dawned on me, and I asked Jean to recall the event that I had experienced. She said "you don't have to tell me", it was the same date and time that I had had the visitation. The spiritual world is real, if anyone is in any doubt! From a more scientific point of view, in my work, I had done a lot of industrial x-ray work or more commonly called radiography. The image or outline of a very hollow object was how the vision had appeared, except that around the outline shell of the image, it was like a myriad of tiny blinking electrons dancing around. Chatting to Tony about this much later, he said that he was not aware of leaving his body, or any presence.

The final outcome of Rhodesia resulted in the beginning of the demise of a once-thriving country with a buoyant economy and happy people. Sadly, so many good people have left that were the backbone of everything good about the country. To be a leader of people is a God-given right and a privilege to serve your people, not for the people to serve the leader. Millions of Rhodesians or as now called Zimbabweans have left the country. There are very few Zimbabweans that would not love to return without having to suffer unemployment, gag on free speech, hunger, money without value, oppressive over-controlled laws, and skewed justice. But nature has a way of repairing the wounds of the past. To re-visit the Matopos and sense the energy and enduring peace that still lives in the hills, seems to shed the cloak of pervasive darkness that still lurks the corridors of government. But not just the Matopos and I use that because it is still very special to me, but elsewhere in the districts and deep in the bush, no matter how poor the locals are, they still have broad happy smiles and still live in the hope of a better future.

It was during a visit to the Matopos after the war that a young worker at Maleme Camp told us that his brother, who was a teenager at the time, was bayoneted to death by Mugabe's North Korean fifth brigade. He had done nothing except that he was a Ndebele and was born in Matabeleland. Tens of thousands of the Matabele were executed. (Reputedly to be well over twenty thousand Ndebele, all were citizens of the new Zimbabwe). They were conveniently all named 'dissidents'. There were some dissidents in the region, but it gave Mugabe the licence to conveniently carry out genocide. The genocide he 'exercised' was carried out between 1980

Matopos – Worlds View and Inungu in the distance – 1977

Rock climbing and rain in the Matopos with Bob

to 1988. They were executed by various heinous means including being shot, bayoneted, beatings and death from torture. The book called Gukurahundi contains probably thousands of accounts and reports of those beaten, abducted and missing or murdered execution-style makes for horrific reading. Beating children to death, rape, opening up pregnant women to kill the child, then letting the mother die later, beating older people, it just goes on and on. – that horror will never go away, even though the free world did not care to hear it! Mugabe had never been brought to book for it – but he will...

I have seen him virtually face to face, and if you wish to see darkness and evil, then look into his eyes, because I have, and that is what I saw.

On our last visit to Hwange, one of the park workers when asked that he must be happy that he had work, and without hesitation and with a smile from ear to ear, burst out into laughter with a couple of his buddies as said that "we all have jobs, but we do not have money". They managed to laugh about it. Pay was is in limited US Dollars, but better than the daily inflation that used to be with the Zimbabwean Dollar. It is challenging to get one's head around a trillion-dollar note. How anyone was able to figure how many noughts there were in a trillion-dollar note boggles the mind. There was a time I had heard where, for example, a petrol attendant would not count money, but just throw so many bundles of notes into a box for payment without counting them. Weighing the paper may have been more useful, I suppose. Barring Germany during the last war and perhaps a couple of despot countries, President Robert Mugabe deserves the Guinness book of records for the worst inflation in the world. But even now where South African Rands and US dollars are accepted, the sting in the cost of living is getting higher and higher, and even costly for visitors from South Africa.

But that will change in time, and by the nature of life it will eventually bounce back, but the scars will remain, even if only in the history books.

*'Special moments locked in time...the beauty
and wonder of the Matopos wilderness...
to pause and enjoy'*

13

UFOs, More Climbing and Sea Epic

Before we left for Cape Town, I had taken an interest in UFO's, and I still do, because I have a firm belief that practically and statistically there must be life, and in many forms elsewhere in our galaxy The Milky Way, notwithstanding the billions of galaxies that are around us in the universe.

Elizabeth Klarer was a most interesting person who I met in the seventies. She ran a small group called 'Contact'. She had claimed to have been taken on a trip to Proxima Centauri, and that her son Ayling was born there. No one much believed her, and I am still not certain I do either, because it is in this present-day understanding of physics, that even if one were travelling at the speed of light (300,000 km/second), it would take over four and a half years just to get there, including perhaps a holiday without the time taken for the return journey. Travelling at say 300,000 km/hour it would take over 15,000 years just to get there! That is indeed a tough challenge. There has to be another way yet to be devised.

She, like her son and husband, was as normal as anyone else one would meet. She was a bit eccentric, and perhaps folk were a bit cautious of her claims. I did see the ring that she wore that was apparently given to her by Akon. The stone looked quite normal as did the mounting.

Most ordinary people have little understanding of the cosmos, but that is changing, and rapidly so. Potential planets that may contain life that have already been identified run into the hundreds, and this will increase in number. However, they are extremely distant from us. Alpha Centauri, which is two stars about four light hours apart, are so close together that they appear as one to the normal eye from Earth. Alpha Centauri and Alpha Proxima are the pointers to the Southern Cross. Alpha Proxima, which is two light months from Alpha Centauri, are still our closest neighbours. Indeed, there are three suns within a reasonable distance from one another, but whether there are habitable planets is still an unanswered question for me.

Elizabeth had written and published a book called 'Beyond the Light Barrier', which related to her extraterrestrial visitation to a planet called Meton of Proxima Centauri, and relationship with Akon. I had the privilege to read only a part of her second book (in manuscript form) which dealt more with the science and technology of propulsion and space flight. A friend and I were allowed to have the manuscript overnight. This was very limiting, but from what I saw and read, her knowledge and descriptions made good sense today as it did in the late sixties. I do believe that there is an intention to publish the book, but discussions still revolve about the complete manuscript. I should have made a copy, because David her son a few years ago had asked me whether I had a copy of the manuscript, and I had unhappily had to tell him that I did not.

What is interesting though was that she did have direct links with the South African authorities and even had an invitation from Russia as an adviser (I saw the letter). Even in those early days to have a copy of the USAF Project Blue Book was a breakthrough. The close association with our group became limited due to the agreement (of secrecy) with the SA Authorities and no doubt, the SA air force. I had met her husband and son on a few occasions and spoken with their son David many years later. They were just ordinary folk.

I have never seen a UFO, but I have absolutely no doubt that they exist. But yes, I do recognise that like some environmental groups, there is often a 'fringe' element. One must cut through all of that, which in itself is very damaging to the acceptance and understanding of their existence.

There was a time when there was a number of serious and notable UFO observations in South Africa. The Fort Beaufort event recorded repeated sightings whereby on one occasion the SA Police took aim at a craft; the landing of a craft, and alien persons that were sighted up in the hills above Uitenhage. Regarding the latter, I had the chance to see the site and interview a couple of the rangers (also interviewed by the press). Also, the boys that had witnessed the silver-clad men that had seemingly floated across the dense scrub.

There was one particular sighting by many people at a drive-in cinema of the West Rand not far from Luipaardsvlei, where the craft had hovered above them, then moved across and above the trees. It proceeded to hover above a farmhouse. The occupants within enduring the frightful experience of their outside storage-garage roof being torn off its bolts and dropped onto the main farmhouse roof. An object, later described as a canister, was seen falling from the craft, which set the grass alight, which the fire brigade extinguished shortly afterwards.

My friend and I, later went out to speak to the owners of the smallholding. They were simple farm folk and had no motive to embellish anything, except to relate the events as they happened. There was no wind that night, and they had been alerted to the bright light shining into their house. Their children were upset, especially after hearing the great crashing noise above them. Apparently, a corner of the galvanised IBR roofing had been burned away. I was keen to see this piece of the roof as I was doing metallurgical work at the Rand Mines Corner House laboratory where I worked in Cottesloe, Johannesburg. I asked them if I could see the roofing. It was unfortunate that by the time I was able to get out to see them, that as they said, a contractor had removed all of the sheeting. I followed that aspect up to a contractor who lived in the Randburg area of Johannesburg North – Fontainbleau as I remember. It was over a weekend, and the contractor was happy to see me as at the time even though I had interrupted a family braai, and sure enough, the pile of sheeting was in his yard. I enquired about the burnt section, and he laughed saying that it had already been taken away by the CSIR. That was a dead end. We had placed some pocket dosimeters at the location where the damage had occurred, but there was no residual radiation detected. While I had been following up on the roofing, my buddy had followed up on the canister which had been observed as falling from the craft onto an open patch of ground next to the farmhouse. The canister had been taken away by the Fire Brigade. Upon his questioning, he was told that the observatory in Johannesburg had collected it. Following up on it, he was told that it had been taken to Pretoria, presumably the CSIR. He then drove to Pretoria and was informed that they did not know anything about it! I had had the opportunity to hear an actual pilot transcript (yes it could have been faked, but I had no reason to doubt it) of a major sighting above Krugersdorp, where air force jets were scrambled to investigate the craft. They could not reach it because it was so high, and it was concluded that it was a mothercraft of massive proportions.

When I had examined the roofing sheets, I had found that the roof had been pulled laterally and that the roofing bolts had torn through the sheets as much as up to six inches long! Farmers usually are quite economical with materials, so the roof being on the outbuilding did not have roofing eves and only just protruded over the brickwork. The flat roof had more than the required roofing rafters and timbers to support the roofing sheets. It indeed must have been a supernatural force to be able to tear such a roof of at least six by six metres (I actually think it was larger than that, but cannot remember exactly), laterally across the hundreds of roofing bolts, then lift it off and dump it a short distance off on to the farmhouse. And to repeat, there was no wind that night.

I visited the site where the grass had burnt which was not extensive, because the fire brigade had been very prompt. What I did find, was that there was a certain number of small circles less than four inches in diameter, and not in any particular order. They had burnt at least an inch into the soil. They were evident against the general burnt area. I collected samples from them which I studied under the microscope but could not find anything unusual such as vitreous burning of sand particles. I still have the samples.

There is more and more evidence statistically even at an extremely low percentage of certainty amongst all of the reports, that give adequate credence to their existence. I do not have to be convinced otherwise by anyone of the existence of extraterrestrial life – in any form.

Before I was married, I was on contract in Cape Town working on the construction of the new Caltex Refinery. It was a perfect opportunity to expand my knowledge and interest in rock climbing and mountaineering. It was not long before I got to know a few lads that I would team up with to do some of the classical routes on Table Mountain. But prior to embarking on some serious climbing, I had to get fit, and also to believe it or not, conquer my fear of heights. I eventually achieved both by walking up from the hotel where I was staying near Three Anchor Bay to the top of Lions Head. It was a long but steady walk with some scrambling to the top of the mountain. On the western edge, there was some serious exposure, but safe. Initially it freaked me until I became used to the perspective and focused on close features instead of the vast distance and fall off towards the ocean. I still suffer from exposure, particularly looking over the edge of buildings. The more you climb, the less of an effect it has on your psyche.

I had not yet climbed Table Mountain, and one of the chaps I had met at the hotel named Rob, had said he knew the mountain well and could rock climb. I had a Viking rope and a couple of Viking slings with steel carabiners. We examined the west face of the mountain and decided that the buttress and gulley to the right of Platteklip gorge looked feasible because one could scramble much of the way through grass and rock bands before the final rock face. From a distance, what we guessed was Jacksons Chimney would provide a good access to the upper rock face. We duly set off one weekend and attained the upper grass band without difficulty. I led the first pitch, which was not too difficult but lacked suitable handholds. Near the top of the pitch, the rock was rounded and with no grips. It was a few feet from a ledge, and as I eased myself up over the rounded rock, I found it was a bit sandy, and I suddenly lost grip with my foot and slid down. I must have only slid about six inches but managed with a desperate move to clutch a bush. It had prickly leaves, but it had saved me from a serious fall. I had no belays, or protection on the way up to have prevented a fall to the ledge below. In those days there was not the climbing aids to limit or reduce the distance fallen except pitons, or the odd sling here and there over a projection of rock or around a bush or tree. The little bush that saved me that day was a 'Climbers friend', no doubt named for similar reasons.

Anyhow, I gained the large ledge above, which was below the chimney. Now distance can be deceiving! The base of the chimney we had spied from way below Table Mountain was at least three metres or more wider at the base and impossible to bridge or climb on either wall because it was tapering up to a height where it pinched out. With a dry mouth and feeling desperate, I looked around and relief, there was a very shallow roof like a horizontal crack leading off. Peering through I could see that there was a potential route around or rather through the obstacle. I brought Rob up, and crawled through the tight gap to a wide ledge the other side. The next obstacle was a rock face, and above that, one could see an exit line to the top of the mountain. The short rock face, however, was not so simple, because it entailed a chimney with a boulder jammed in it which had to negotiate. It was tricky and involved hanging on with both arms around it to gain the upper ledge. Rob could not do it and fell on the rope time and again until I could not hold him dangling, so he retreated to the base. Both my hands were cramped, and I was worried as it was getting late. We could not reverse the route easily without danger, so I told him that I would continue up to the top of the mountain and seek a rescue party. The upper face which I had already visually scouted, appeared to be straight forward face-climbing and would not be too difficult. He protested so much with the thought that others would have to rescue him that he finally agreed to come up the rock face on a tight rope. It was a real struggle for us, him scrabbling on the rock without leverage, and me trying to haul him up on a tight rope and take in the slack when he gained a hand or foothold here and there. Finally, he emerged over the lip, and we both collapsed to recover our breath. I had to undo my cramped fingers around the rope. Tired and worn out, we gained the top and descended safely, and so ended my first and only poorly planned climb on a mountain. In truth I was totally taken in by his over confidence in all the climbing he said he had done on the mountain. He would not lead and was no support as a team member should be. True characters are readily revealed when on the mountain... or in the bush.

It is interesting to note how things of nature have changed on Table Mountain. I had met some other climbers and one of them, Bo Olsen who had completed many routes on Table Mountain, had suggested that we climb the full Right Face route from the contour path to the top. My friend Colin Budworth who had climbed in England, also joined our small team. It would be a long day, so we decided to climb up to the contour path, and sleep in one of the overhangs close to the path. It had started to drizzle from a mild North West front, but we were not concerned because we had shelter. We had no sooner settled down and eaten a meagre meal and a warm mug of tea when a troop of baboon tried to enter into the overhang, which was already a bit cramped. They were within a few meters of us and quite determined to come in, so we had to hurl climbing slings with steel carabiners (no aluminium in those days) and pitons attached at them, to scare them off. After some on and off encounters which were quite unnerving, they finally gave up, but then perched above the overhang all night. They had no doubt often used the overhang for shelter, especially when the weather was a bit inclement. In the morning, the drizzle had stopped, and then we heard a gentle thudding outside of the shelter, and as if by insult, they had defecated in front of us They were entirely finished with us or more precisely me, as I'd been ravaged by sand fleas, the live detritus of the baboon shelter, which were incredibly itchy. Once the bites healed up, they left purple marks for months to come. These days' baboons are not seen on the front of Table Mountain.

It was a successful and enjoyable climb, and we finally got to the top after a long traverse near the top which took time because we were four in number and had to pull back a safety rope for each member before the next set off across the traverse.

Shortly after moving down to Cape Town permanently, I joined the SA Navy as a volunteer reservist and was attached to SA Yselstein. It was enjoyable and interesting, but interestingly, much of what I had learnt in the Sea Cadets with TS Matabele, was repeated at the navy lectures. Because of my background with the army unit on the Reef, I was appointed as a 'terrorist' during a couple of major exercises to break into the Simonstown harbour and the Cape Town harbour. There were a couple of chaps captured, but overall our side of the operation went well. All I can say was that my experience at being a reasonable climber did help a lot!

However, our unit went on a sea exercise, and we sailed as far as Port Elizabeth in our rather small coastal patrol vessel. It was going well, and I learnt a lot about navigation, coastal signals, being at the helm and much more. However, I got very seasick and believed I was very close to death! And as a result, when I was called on watch, I mumbled that I would not be able to manage it. I was summarily ordered to the bridge and to be told that a navy could not function just because someone was feeling sick! The captain was quite right, of course, but at the time I could not agree, well at least my body did not agree with him.

The exercise went off well with the other vessels in Algoa bay off of Port Elizabeth. The next morning was calm and beautiful; I even saw a couple of hammerhead sharks cruising next to our vessel. I then went below after completing my shift. I had perhaps been dozing a couple of hours when a seaman jolted me and informed me that we were turning about as there was a gale blowing, and we were going to try and make it for Port Elizabeth. Up on deck, I could not believe my eyes. The wind was shrieking, and at first glance, the sea looked flat, but on second glance, could see that it was sea-water and foam flying across deep troughs of water. It would have been impossible for all the seamen to stay up on the bridge, and it was highly dangerous for anyone to cross the deck to the quarters in the fo'c'sle. The captain radioed through to our sister ship, the SAS Gelderland that we were going to try for Port Elizabeth, and that they held a very brief prayer for all the crew on both vessels. We left the bridge and hurried below and closed the hatch above us – we were now isolated from the rest of the ship. The impact of the sea spray was like small stones hitting one on the face. The wind speed was 130km/hour, blowing offshore and head on to us. It was not long before we could not steady ourselves below, the vessel would labour into the oncoming waves, rise up, then plummet down into the hollow, and with a thundering of water slowly rise up again. I jammed myself behind an electrical distribution board where there was a small deadlight of about four inches in diameter. All deadlights had to be closed for fear of leaking, but I opened mine to be able to see the intermittent 'horizon' to maintain balance and prevent sea-sickness. I could have closed it and secured it very quickly if necessary. The guys below were all sick and had buckets between their legs while they were hanging on. Eventually, they gave up, and the buckets rolled around the floor. Water was getting in from the hatch and was also swilling around. The cupboards broke off the walls, as did fire extinguishers and they were rolling around. Between each wave, the bows slowly rose and it looked like a waterfall outside, there was a brief view of the next wall of water approaching, and down we went again, the vessel came to a virtual shuddering stop, and all I could see through the small deadlight was green water – the bows must have been completely underwater. This went on for nearly three hours, and I, like the other chaps, were quite exhausted. I saw a fishing vessel being blown out to sea in a circular fashion past us.

We eventually made it into harbour and surveyed the damage. We were lucky to be alive because the small ship did not have a thick shell. I figured that even with a lifejacket on, I would not have been able to survive the pounding of those waves for more than a few minutes without drowning.

All paint on the port bow and superstructure had been removed down to the metal by the force of the high-speed water spray, our radio mast and communications had also been lost, as was I believe, the radar. I was told that the force of wind and water crashing over the bows and bridge had at times stopped the clear view (a revolving disc fixed to the bridge window to allow vision ahead without wipers). The canopies over our hatchways and gun cover had all gone. I still have a piece of one of the bronze bolts that had sheared off with the force of the water and wind. By some miracle, I had not been sick. But hats off to the skipper and crew who managed to keep the vessel on course. They had all been violently ill and it was so bad that it was apparently running down the cat ladder from the bridge.

We staggered ashore in our weakened state. One of the seamen who had been with the navy for decades left the ship, and said that he would never go back to sea again. One other joined him, and apparently, they flew back to Cape Town. The minesweepers fared better than our ship. But at the same time, there was a yacht race from Durban that I think was heading for Cape Town. Dozens of yachts were missing, but most were eventually found. One really smart looking yacht had been dismasted, and the owner must have been swept overboard; whether he was eventually found or not, I do not know. It was being towed back into port by one of the mine-sweepers.

The storm was a very unusual one, being a gale-force blowing offshore, and the more shallow waters had caused the waves to be both short and vertical. In hindsight (we are always smart in hindsight), perhaps we should have run with the wind like the fishermen did, until it blew itself out.

The voyage back to Cape Town was in calmer waters, and because of the damage to our ship, most of the crew were housed in one of the mine-sweepers. I did quite a lot of navigating on sea charts and taking the helm for spells. It was the last sea exercise I went on. I think it was safer climbing mountains.

14

Climbing and Expeditions and Stunt

I was never a main-stream rock climber, work rarely allowed a day in the week to dash off and do a quick route, but I did enjoy many of the classical routes on Table Mountain. The Cape rock generally was different to the 'Transvaal' rock because being sandstone it allowed so much more purchase and friction as well as weathered surfaces that provided knobs and what we termed 'juggies' to hang onto. In the early sixties, apart from pitons as previously mentioned, one could fashion your own different sized nuts (engineering nuts) and strung on wire rope, so you had an option of what size to use for a particular belay. Abseiling was still practised using the classical rope over the shoulder method and perhaps assisted by the use of a carabiner at the waist. Harnesses were made from rope and wound around the waist and tied off. Mine was made from hemp rope that gave a wonderful smell. I never did get high with it, but my climbing cupboard always smelt good when I opened it. I wore Tyresole boots (made in Wuppertal in the Cederberg from carefully shaped pieces of old tyre treads) which never wore out and always retained excellent grip on rock. Later, when climbing became a little more delicate, I bought a pair of hockey boots and sawed off the studs. Except for hiking, the overseas boots though of excellent quality, were too bulky.

Climbing, even though a great outdoor activity and highly stimulating, was time-consuming. So with a young family, we would genteelly walk along the contour paths above Kirstenbosch and occasionally up on to Table Mountain. Except for one extremely hot afternoon on the mountain and we'd descended via Blinkwater Ravine to the west, the children had become exhausted. We had run out of water, and only when we reached the lower part of the ravine, did we find shade and some water to drink. All the other escapades were fun-filled, and we often stopped and looked into ferny recesses for fairies, or where fairies were likely to have visited. Nothing beats the imagination, and a bit of 'mystery' for children to dwell on while walking.

During one trip to Rhodesia, we also went to the Chimanimani Mountains. Bob met us at the Melsetter Hotel, where he appeared from nowhere. He had apparently hitch-hiked from Bulawayo to meet us and had slept in the bush; lack of money and discomfort never bothered Bob; he was always 'bok' for some adventure.

It was a long walk up to the mountain hut, so Quintin was carried all of the way, but little Heather had walked, and even fell off the path on to a

A favourite climbing venue - Table Mountain

little slope at one stage. We were fortunate to have Bob with us to help carry some essential gear, and he looked quite the Sherpa with an additional plastic potty dangling from his rucksack. When we got to the hut, Heather took a bit poorly and was not well and showing signs of nausea so I decided to head back down to the 'Dead Cow' car park to fetch our medical kit. I wasted no time in getting back with the medicines, only to find that she was up and about and feeling once again fine. It was very far for her, and she probably suffered from some fatigue. The mountains of the Eastern Districts are exceptional, and the vistas quite remarkable. On Mount Inyangombe the vegetation is very similar to the Cape Mountains, with a type of fynbos, complete with Sugarbush and other types of proteas.

At a very young age, both Quintin and Heather with Jean and I and a few friends ascended the Brandwag Mountains to reach the snow, and we took fertilizer bags to sit on and slide down the snow slopes. We stopped at the mountain hut for the night and descended the following day. They had had a wonderful time and even got their pictures into the Burger newspaper. Apart from me banging my coccyx on a hidden rock under the snow, we were all fine. It was about a three and a half-hour walk up, so they were plucky little fellows.

We spent many happy outings into the local mountains and area, along forest paths and tracks, climbing up Vlakkenberg, Constantiaberg, Elephants eye, including the gorges above Kirstenbosch. Our border collie Beth accompanied us on many trips onto the mountain. In fact, Beth had climbed with me on a couple of occasions to ascend Table Mountain and Devils Peak, and not always by the easiest route. She later even went on some mountain rescues with the Mountain Club of South Africa to help search for missing folk. When she died, I took her up to the upper slopes of Vlakkenberg and buried her there where we would so often sit and just

Paul on a traverse on the Klein Winterhoek frontal route

look at the view. I carved her name on a slab of rock and with some of her gear placed it over her grave. I had spent a lot of time with fellow 'hackers' on Vlakkenberg to remove invasive alien plants like Hakea, Port Jackson, Wattle and Acacia Longifolia. Many years were spent on this worthwhile activity.

I had continued to climb on Table Mountain and some country routes with long routes like the Klein Winterhoek frontal with Ray Barlow (ex-member of the Mountain Club of Rhodesia). What a wonderful and classic route. Neither of us had done it before, but we had a route description. In the beginning, I was quite tired, then perked up later, but we were both very short of water, and only had one and a half litres of 'Game' between us.

Paul with climbing friend, Ray Barlow on the Klein Winterhoek frontal route

There was a bit of a heatwave at the time as well, which did not help. We went off route at some point, and I traversed out to the left, over a horrendous drop, could not find a climbable way up, reversed the pitch, and after Ray had made an attempt just above our belay position, had a fall onto a ledge just above, and out of sight of me. He was fortunately not injured; we then decided to do a 'mechanical' move or two to overcome the problem. There is no escape either left or right off of the route, so one just had to press on. It was with much joy that we got back onto the route and finally reached the top. We were badly dehydrated and on eventually returning to camp via the gully consumed copious amounts of river water. I don't think I peed for two days!

Bob and his wife Lesley and I drove up to Namibia to climb Spitzkop, a prominent 'Matterhorn' or more accurately an Inselberg of South West Africa (now Namibia). On the way, we took the opportunity of climbing up Mt Brukkaros, a very large diameter and extinct volcano, which was quite stunning with remarkable vistas, and where at the turn of the century, the Germans had set up an observatory on the top of the south rim. Little remained of that to be seen, but there was a reservoir they had carved out of solid rock to catch what little water that fell on the mountain. Spitzkop was also another classic climb, which was also a long route, and it certainly took us a long time. After leaving at five in the morning, we only got back to camp at ten that night. When the 'standard' route was originally opened up, it apparently took several attempts to find a route to the summit before the key to the route was to traverse through a tight and dark crevice to emerge on the other side on a ledge, then abseil down to another ledge, then traverse around to the West and ascend from there. It was a bit complicated, but that was the standard route that we followed. The scenery from virtually anywhere on the mountain was spectacular. The surrounding countryside is also very scenic, and we also found evidence of early Bushmen occupation in one of the shelters. We did not have the opportunity to visit the Brandberg area further north from Spitzkop, which contains thousands of stunning rock art paintings.

The wide-open spaces of Namibia have an extraordinary aura or breath of a very ancient time. It is as if man's intrusion will not change that which is so special. One of my work trips took me to Walvis Bay, and because the flights were not regular, I had to stay over a weekend. On the Sunday morning, instead of sitting bored in my hotel, I drove south-east out into the desert for quite some distance and then turned off south towards a large rocky outcrop. Everywhere was dead quiet and empty of people. I decided to climb up to the top and on an impulse, and even though it was early, it was quite hot; I stripped down naked, put on my boots, and set off. It was an incredible sense of freedom. I stopped for a while to watch a

Spitzkop - the Matterhorn of Namibia – the route to the summit
followed the recesses and columns on the right skyline

Bob ascending one of the upper pitches – Spitzkop

Bob on the summit of Spitzkop - Namibia

buck (perhaps a klipspringer), grazing around. It was not bothered by my presence. At the top, I sat down and looked across to the distant mountains; it was a beautifully clear day, no wind and utterly silent. The dirt road stretched away across the desert and was empty. I listened for anything, and the silence seemed to resonate or hum in my ears. It was if the hearing was searching for sound. Time stood still. It was a scene of profound beauty and of being totally at one with nature. It was a rare experience and marked a very special place in my memory.

In 1978, Bob and I joined an expedition with Gabriel Athiros and other team mountaineers from South Africa to climb Mt Aconcagua in South America – the highest mountain in the southern hemisphere. The expedition was successful, but unfortunately, a number of us contracted flu on the flight over. After a full year of training, it was a great disappointment because even though I recovered reasonably, it was unwise of me to ascent above 16,000 feet. Bob was worse than I, he became very ill at base camp with double pneumonia. His condition deteriorated, and he became unconscious for a few days but had been treated with antibiotics by both Dr

Robin Sandell and Dr Cecil Bloch. At the same time, a Mexican climber Fernandez Osorno had developed serious hypothermia and frostbite from being immobile in one position for a long time high up on the mountain; our team assisted in getting him down. Rolf Schwertweger and Gabriel Athiros hurried off the mountain (over forty kilometres), to get help.

Meanwhile Bob had worsened, and things did not look good for him. It was a day or so later when Bob regained consciousness and could drink some 'Game' and suck a few glucose sweets. It was very early morning when he mumbled something about choppers! I guess it must have been his years of bush fighting in Rhodesia that attuned his ear to helicopters. Straining my ears, I could just hear the faint throb of chopper blades. With a sense of urgency, I shot out in time to see not one, but two bubble choppers flying up the valley in the distance, before they circled around the lower peaks, dropped flares and then settled down on the scree slope. It was fortuitous that they sent two choppers because when Gabriel and Rolf set off, Bob's condition was not fully known. They agreed to take Fernandez and Bob off the mountain. It was a very emotional time for me, and I wept because Cecil had told me after he had flown off, that Bob was dying, and they were not sure he would have survived. It was with a sense of sadness and emptiness that I watched the two helicopters flying down the long valley, but also faith and assurance that he would be in the care of others. It was also a trying time for Rolf and Gabriel, because of the loading on the small helicopters; they had to walk the entire distance back uphill to base camp, having covered about 100kms in three days. It was a brave and sterling effort on their part, which cost them the advantage of summiting with the rest of the team.

The Argentinians were wonderful; both the air-force and the locals at the beautiful city of Mendoza. It is humbling how ordinary caring folk are to one another when in need and especially in a foreign country. However, it is sad how politics can harm shared love for one's fellow man, such as the war between Argentina and Britain that led to unnecessary loss of life. Perhaps the pilots that came on that mercy mission into the mountains of Aconcagua to help a fellow man in need died in the conflict. I hope not. Politicians so often do not feel the pain or consequences of their decisions upon ordinary folk.

I climbed part of the way up the Austrian Route on Aconcagua on a day trip, which I managed very well after having recovered from altitude sickness and flu. I was anxious to get away and find out where Bob had been taken and how he was doing. After waiting an extra day on the request of Robin, I walked out of the valley with Lynn, Robin's wife, who had a persistent cough which would not clear up. We walked the forty kilometres down the Horcones valley to Puente del Inca in one day.

Bob and Fernandez both recovered. Fernandez did not require amputations, and Bob was well enough (he had had a badly swollen heart as well), for us to trip across to Chile where we met wonderful folk both in Santiago and Vina del Mar (Valparaiso). The South Africans had used up all of their oxygen to bring Fernandez down the mountain, which I am sure helped his recovery. It was also unfortunate that Rolf and Gabriel were unable to climb to the peak. Gabriel also had to be brought down to base camp suffering with cerebral oedema, a serious and life-threatening condition. At lower altitude, he recovered. The earlier rapid walk out with Rolf no doubt limited his chances of succeeding on the Mountain. The team, however, were successful in reaching the peak – at over 22,800 ft., the highest mountain in the Southern hemisphere.

In the early seventies (1973), I had completed a traverse in the Drakensberg from the Amphitheatre in the Royal Natal National park to Cathedral Peak. My companions were Geoff Pallister and Al Goyns. It was a tough hike and a good lesson in survival because we had freezing rain for the last three days of the five-day hike. Trying to exit the top of the berg in windy, wet and completely closed in conditions, was difficult as we were not sure where we were. After careful backtracking, map-reading and compass work, we concluded that the 'void' we were looking down must be the Nceni pass. We started to descend and hoped that we could make a known cave on the upper contour pathway below. Well, that was all very good, but conditions deteriorated, and we had to hang on to bushes and plants when lowering ourselves down over several small waterfalls. Each one of us had had a fall, and I called a halt when it was getting dark because I was both exhausted and afraid that if anyone of us broke a leg, we would be utterly stymied.

We bivvied on a narrow projection, propped up with a few branches; were all cold and wet through. I had a useless and ineffective sleeping bag, made in France and termed to have excellent exothermic properties! As a result, I was almost always cold. Well, I guess I did not die of the cold, the bag was good enough for survival, but I was totally drained. After removing my wet clothes and naked, I quickly changed into a dry vest, socks and underwear and got into my bag with the survival bag (a large Karrimor plastic bag) over the top. Al Goyns was not fazed by the conditions and quickly brewed up a soup which I was terribly thankful for, and in the dark, we settled in to see out the night.

Sleep was impossible because we were jammed together, uncomfortable lying on branches and all, as well as being cold. In the morning we rose quickly and continued scrambling down the mountain. It was never easy, but better with visibility through the mist. It took one and a half hours to reach the contour path which we would have missed in the dark because it was so overgrown. We would never have found the cave either. I would never have been able to re-climb up the mountain of about 5,000 ft if we had made a mistake with the compass and map reading. I doubt, and it is the only time I have truly felt that I would not have survived another two nights in those conditions.

The Devils Tooth next to the Eastern Buttress, Drakensberg.

Heading out into the foothills toward Cathedral Peak Hotel, we simply walked through the rivers because boulder hopping was extremely dangerous with full packs; besides, the water actually felt warm – though, in reality, it was not. When we had stopped, I carefully removed my boots to examine my very white and wrinkled feet and toes and was pleasantly surprised to find there was no damage – my Tyresole boots had done me well. The 'rigor mortis' that set in after that hike was not funny, and my joints (knees) were klonking when I walked, and I could hardly get in or out of the car to drive, but it felt better after a few days. We were well equipped with the basics including an extra two days rations even though we were not carrying tents, but in harsh conditions such as that and the immense distances, nothing can be left to chance. Having two very stable and competent hiking buddies (both experienced mountaineers) is essential to survival. As a matter of interest, at one stop on the escarpment, we tried unsuccessfully to boil water for an hour, to make tea! We gave up when you could immerse your finger into the lukewarm water. The freezing rain so sucked away any warmth.

All that aside, it was a wonderful experience because we also had the pleasure of seeing Rhebok and Lammergeyer (bearded vulture). I had one Lammergeyer gliding about ten metres above me, just checking perhaps if I was still going to make it, and how much of a meal I might make – jokes aside. We also came across the most magnificent blonde and tan wild horses. Galloping across the upper plateau with streaming manes and tails was a sight to behold. Viewing the sunrise, massive clouds, and the fairly rare sight of my shadow displayed onto clouds below the mountain with a perfect rainbow type halo around my head. It was almost angelic. Countless waterfalls with crystal clear water were a delight and a privilege to behold.

On other occasions, I went to the Berg to climb the Sentinel and a special expedition to climb the Devils Tooth. The mountains of the Drakensberg are spectacular and traversing the Inner Towers to access the Tooth was a mission in itself. On that occasion, our team was Mike and Doreen Scott (Mike was one of the most accomplished climbers in South Africa and as well as other notable achievements, his successful ascent of one of the longest and most difficult walls in the world in Patagonia), Butch De Bruin (also ex Mountain Club of Rhodesia where he had accomplished some amazing routes on granite spires in Rhodesia), and myself. It was a wonderful feeling to achieve such a rock climb – the exposure and scenery were mind-blowing. Climbing on basalt rock is somewhat risky compared with sandstone and quartzite given the texture and composition of the rock. Climbing in the Berg sometimes requires long pitons that are essential for grassed ledges and more modern gear like Climbers Friend 'Cams' for belaying.

The climbing route Devils Tooth - Drakensberg

An expedition closer to home was planned in 1980 to climb Mt Kenya. The team was Bob and Lesley Gray, Mike O'Reilly, Rolf Schwerdtfeger and I.

The expedition to Mt Kenya was a wonderful experience and was quite different from the Aconcagua trip in that the logistics were not so complicated. It was a rock climb on Mt Kenya as opposed to the high altitude mountaineering on Aconcagua. It was a success for us all, as we all reached the summit of Nelion – 5188m. Bob and Mike crossed the gate of mists and climbed up to the true summit of Batian – 5199m.

Rolf and I both suffered seriously with altitude sickness, and neither of us really recovered. At our higher camp at Two Tarn Hut (4,450m), I had hoped to overcome splitting headaches and some oedema of face and arms, but to no avail. It is strange how it affects some folk and not others. My headaches continued up to the summit, and only eased off when halfway down the mountain. I had diminished sight in one eye, and orange blotches and spots in my eyes. These eventually and fortunately cleared up. Rolf had problems with his sinuses which did not help him. On a slightly funnier side and on an earlier trip into the Cape Mountains he was complaining about his head and sinuses after a very long and tiring hike into our base camp. He flopped down and said that the only solution to his condition was to 'stand on his head'. We remarked that that would be very difficult for him to do and suggested that one of us should stand on his head instead! He was not amused – sometimes buddies are not always that sympathetic.

At our hut at Two Tarn, we had a few trippers arrive from Germany; they had trekked down through Africa and looked quite dishevelled. One of the chaps was wearing a pair of lederhosen – a type of leather shorts with apron and shoulder straps. In the morning, we awoke to much cussing and exclamations. I could not understand the German swear words but knew they were significant outbursts. There was this guy holding up his Lederhosen and blurting out that rats had eaten the crutch away from the trousers. Bob blurted out that clearly the rats had a salt deficiency, and burst out laughing, then we all started laughing, such is the life at high altitude. The rats or mice were a problem, and I had some of a chocolate bar eaten away in the night, so the next night being clever, I put the choc slab in my top pocket. Generally, the temperature at night was very low, so that should not have been a problem, but it melted against my chest and soaked into my shirt, so that was that!

We then had a small team of Frenchmen stop in the hut, and they left their rucksacks on the wide upper bunk where I was sleeping, or more correctly dozing quietly. In the night I heard the rustling of rats alongside my head, so I quietly rose up and viciously punched the rucksacks to kill the creatures. All was silent thereafter until the morning when there now arose much protestation from one of the French climbers, the eggs in his rucksack were broken! It was me, and I felt terrible and apologised, but the good news was that they had all been hard-boiled. I was forgiven after I explained my dilemma. I did not see any injured rat or mouse.

Food is always an important issue on an expedition, from the aspect of nutrition, and weight. We had a few sponsors, which was a huge help. We received many packets of 'Toppers', which were dehydrated foods. Though a big help, there was a downside, that it took an inordinate amount of time to rehydrate the food, especially the veggies. Any slightly un-hydrated

The climbing team – Mt Kenya
left to right: Mike, Rolf, Lesley, Bob and Paul – 1982

veggies resulted in serious gas production in the stomach. 'High' altitude took on a new meaning, and there had to be pre-warning of any planned gas expulsion. Unplanned emissions such as when sharing a tent could be very harmful to one's health! Whether it was the (now called) 'Poppers', or not I cannot be sure, but Bob let rip (which was a loud report), at the Nairobi railway station while walking. Now I am not sure that Africans are familiar with Mlungu's (Europeans) blowing off, or whether they are ever heard, but the locals went into infectious gales of laughter. We laughed too – of course, Bob could have controlled it if he had tried, but habits away from civilization tend to degenerate quite quickly down to fundamental nature.

When we were circumventing the mountain massif of Mt Kenya, and while climbing, I had the strangest feeling that there was someone else in the team that I could not see, but was missing. I would look around and count our party number to check. It was a strong feeling or rather a presence: nothing ominous, just a tangible sense. I did have, though, a crystal clear rendition of one of the Beatles numbers playing in my head. I could recall it almost at will especially when slogging up steep scree or obstacles, and the lyrics, voices and instruments would be like an actual vinyl-record repeating itself over and over...

The descent from the summit required quite a number of abseils, and at one point we had the French team close to us. Bob had abseiled down a steep recess on the face, and suddenly there was a cry from above, one of the Frenchmen had loosened a rock, a sizeable slabby shape which slid and dropped directly below. We shouted out a warning with Bob ducking into the face for protection. The rock crashed just above him and shattered into dozens of pieces and clattered to the base of the climb far below, echoing around the mountain. It had hit the face above him and in between the two abseil ropes. It was a miracle he was not hit and judging by the scarring on the rock-face it would have certainly severed the rope if struck. He was extremely fortunate, but there was quite a lot of loose rock on the mountain, so we had to be extra cautious. It had caused such a commotion that the folk in the Austrian hut below Point Lenana and across the Glacier, fled out to see what had happened.

The whole experience of climbing Mt Kenya was incredible – the people of Kenya, the walk-in with the wildlife around. The different types of terrain and vegetation, from savannah to jungle to montane forest and giant groundsels. The flowers, the birds, and yes, even the crows that fly in and land at the summit looking for scraps of food at over 17,000 ft is quite astonishing. I had previously read of flocks of birds seen flying above the summit of Annapurna which has a summit of over 8,000 m. Also, at the summit bivouac I spotted a spider on the rock – quite a climb for a spider, but to exist up there was most surprising.

The mountain lakes or tarns, the ice-falls and formations, the most amazing sunsets and sunrises were stunning. The wildlife we saw and heard on the walk down and off the mountain were also most remarkable. Even a bit frightening at times as leopard and buffalo habituated the forested slopes. We had seen a captured mature leopard in a cage within the national park at the lower reaches of the mountain, and its size and attitude was most intimidating.

Then the travel to Mombasa and Malindi and experience the exotic fragrances of a tropical coastline. Baobabs growing out of calcrete outcrops directly over the sea, the perfume maker, and the snorkelling in the crystal clear seawater. To experience the myriads of coloured fish and corals, made the whole experience that much more fulfilling, but more so, to share with your friends.

While my brother Bob was running a camping and climbing shop in Cape Town, he was approached to help do a film stunt on Table Mountain. The scenario would involve having a fight with a person in the Cable Car, then falling out, hanging in space, then climbing back in, and that was that. They would let him know when the stunt was planned for. He phoned me about a week later to say that he had to fly to Johannesburg and asked me if I would stand in for him 'in case' they phoned. Well guess what, they did phone. Whether he flew up there just to avoid the stunt, I doubt, but doubts did occur to me... I was working at the Koeberg Nuclear Power Station at the time and had to get time off to go through to meet with them at the Lower Cable Station. I had a buddy come along with me that had done some climbing, and he would assist me.

Film folk are different from ordinary folk, and I am sure most live in a bubble. However, arriving at the Lower Cable Station, I was ushered into a room where there was much activity. I had to dress-up to look like the lead role actor (what a cop-out!), they gave me clothes to put on, and I must have looked a bit nonplussed about changing in front of everyone, they just laughed and said that everyone undresses in front of everyone else, and not to worry. So, I didn't worry and changed into the gear plus a ridiculous wig. In climbing, you have to know your limits for any particular situation, and that is where your fitness, both physically and mentally, are geared to. I knew from doing the odd pull-ups and just hanging by the arms how long one could hang in one position. My comfortable limit was one minute – now that does not sound long, but in reality, it is quite a while to hang without relief. I told them that. Not to worry they said, I would only have to fall out of the car about halfway down the mountain, because that was where they would set up the cameras. That sounded reasonable. We duly went up to the top of the mountain, whereby then it was just after sundown. I had rigged a climbing sling from a hidden waistband, up one sleeve, and my buddy would secure that to a belay for protection within the car.

I was asked by a very mellow and relaxed red-headed lady if I had done a lot of stunt work. I replied that I had not done any. She said, "do not worry because I can see that there is a protective aura around you, and you will come to no harm". Was she an angel? I was hoping she was.

The cable car usually took five minutes to descend the mountain, but they would be going more slowly to catch the scene. We had a chap hidden from view with a radio to prompt the departure time from the car. Before we set off, there was an enacted skirmish, a gun produced, dummy shots fired and a young actress (actually Sandra Prinsloo's daughter) screaming her head off very realistically. Women are so good at screaming; it was so realistic. And so, into the car we rushed, cut the filming and rearranged for the descent. We had no sooner started off when the prompt said I must fall out of the car. I protested because we were still at the top of the mountain, but he insisted, so out I fell. I had flail around with my legs, then climb back in, continue the staged fight with the aggressor, then I had to fall out again, and kick like mad, and struggle to get back in the car. Now the old cable car with the door open had a rounded sloping floor underneath with absolutely nothing to pull yourself up onto. I was left hanging on my arms, while my buddy tried in vain to pull me in. By now we were just about at the bottom, where it slowed up, and we organised ourselves properly. The film crew were delighted and said that we would not have to do a repeat. I think I was a bit rude, because I had been hanging about for about five minutes on my arms, and there was no way I was going to repeat the exercise. The tendons in my forearms had been injured, and it took about a month for them to settle down again. They paid out the princely sum of five hundred rand which I split with Bob.

It was a couple of months later that the film company wanted me to do another stunt, so I asked them what was required. "Oh," they said, "we would like you to be blackened all over and pretend you are an African" and then, and you have to believe this, "fall off of one of the bridges onto the N2" (Eastern Boulevard, the main road leading into Cape Town) "and into the back of a 'passing' bakkie". I did not have to do any serious calculation to decide that it would be highly hazardous, and that they do not always tell the whole truth, besides, I did not really want to look like Al Jolson, nor could I sing very well, and so ended my short career as a stunt artist.

15

Mountain Rescues, Strange Happenings and Accident

I had been very much involved with mountain rescue with the Mountain Club of South Africa for over thirteen years. Finer persons one could ever hope to meet and depend on when tackling difficult situations in the mountains. The dedication from the team volunteers that assisted when the call came out was exemplary. They included the callers, logistics personnel, a list of mountaineers who knew the various mountain areas well, and of course, personnel and teams that were available, or on-call over public holidays and long weekends, SAAF 22 squadron crew and pilots. Special chopper reaction teams, management and safety personnel. Each call-out was different and included searches, rescues, recoveries. Combined exercises were carried out that included police and sea rescue. There is nothing greater than a cohesive team in any walk of life, but particularly in rescue work where much personal contribution is given so willingly and without grumble, all on a voluntary basis.

It can be wretched to have to recover someone that has died on the mountain; it is much worse when it involves the recovery of children. Fortunately, it did not happen frequently. But so difficult when it did involve anxious parents, waiting in desperate hope that their child might be OK and facing the realisation that their little one might be deceased. All the more while out enjoying nature and hoping to have a fun time. It is a great joy when someone has been lost and found and returned safely home.

Quintin had joined our team to search for a chap that was missing on the back of Table Mountain. We eventually found him seriously dehydrated, well after midnight, slumped against a rock outcrop. We had tracked him along a mountain path by his boot imprints, it was clear that his steps were faltering, and he had stopped from time to time. It was about three in the morning by the time we got back to Constantia Nek; his distraught wife was waiting for him. She lashed out at him saying "I could kill you", I replied that a slight push and she might very well succeed!

Once a couple of kids had gone exploring in the mountain near Simonstown harbour, and only one had returned home reporting the incident. We searched the area where they had been, including the rock-face and found nothing. Finally, we had to give up and recommence the search in the morning. I prayed for help to be guided to where he was. I was 'driven' early the next morning to find the lad, and virtually rushed up into the gully and trees and came upon him. He'd had a horrible fall and suffered serious facial injuries. Semi-conscious, he had crawled away from the base of the cliff until an enormous boulder blocked his path. He was trapped, and his little legs had been moving back and forth all night, trying to overcome the obstacle. Bob was with us and attended to him first. He was speedily evacuated and taken to hospital.

Once two ladies from overseas had gone walking on the top of Table Mountain and had not returned. They were both elderly but apparently experienced in walking in the Alps. One of them had had two hip replacements, so teams were hurried up the mountain to find them, they split up and called out for them, but eventually had to give up and return down the mountain. The search was resumed the next day, but by late morning the two ladies appeared at the base of the mountain having walked down. When questioned about where they were, they exclaimed "yes we did hear people calling out, but thought that they were bad people", so they sat it out taking shelter until morning. They actually did the right thing in sitting it out, if many others could steel themselves to do that instead of desperately trying to get down, mostly worrying that their families were worrying about them. A night is very short on the mountain, and it is sad that many had not remained where they were until light but had desperately tried to get down even in the dark and had fallen.

Quintin had also helped on another serious recovery above fountain ledge on Table Mountain – a most unpleasant experience for him. The poor person had tragically fallen from the top and had died on impact. A policeman at the top had asked me to record any injuries that could have been inflicted in case of foul play... It was a most unpleasant task to recover the body, lower it down to a lower ledge, and carry it around to the front of Table Mountain. The cable car was halted, and the stretcher hauled up to the car and taken down the mountain.

We had many exercises and rescues in the surrounding Cape Mountains as well. The logistics of these were often daunting, and very careful planning was required. This was necessary for effective management and logistics, including back up for different scenarios. I had the utmost respect for the SAAF pilots who gave of their time and sometimes at personal risk to help others. Flying in the mountains requires special skills and training at the best of times, however flying in foul weather really pushes that boundary! One recovery of a young boy who had broken an ankle in the mountains at Waaihoek necessitated a flight for a pilot who depended on Dr Robin Sandell and me to guide him through and under inclement weather, low cloud, through gaps in the mountains and snow-covered terrain – flying almost directly by sight. The snow 'white out' was so bad that we could not land safely because the pilot could not see the ground. So he landed next to the more visible Pells mountain hut, and we walked from

The Witteberg rescue of Jill Graafland– 20th Dec 1988 – Dion Tromp and Paul

there to the Hoare hut to piggyback the boy out through snow to the waiting Alouette helicopter.

On another occasion, during a major rescue on the Witteberg in harsh winter weather, a rescue was finally achieved after one of the most prolonged and complicated stretcher lowers in Cape rescue history. After a two-day, tricky stretcher carry by the rescue team, the injured climber Jill Graafland was finally placed into a waiting helicopter on a high buttress. Due to adverse weather conditions and the chopper being extremely low on fuel, it was decided below that it could not return to pick us up. So, Dion Tromp (a very experienced rescue team member), and I said that we would be able to work our way down off the mountain. While preparing for the descent, we heard a chopper approaching. The pilot swept in, to which we quickly boarded and safely flown down. As we were the last two remaining on the mountain, the pilot said that he was not going to leave us to climb down. We would have managed safely enough, but it was the resolve of the pilot that made the difference. Many of the 22 Squadron SAAF pilots had served time during the bush war in Rhodesia. Such fine characters that they all were.

I once witnessed a Puma helicopter pilot fly into such a tight situation to recover an injured woman, that the confined area at the base of a waterfall was such, that the upthrust of the rotors actually blew the waterfall upwards. The pick-up was executed safely, the pilot with the utmost care slowly reversed the chopper up and out of the confined area, turned about and headed out into the valley below. An Alouette helicopter would have been better for the access but would not have had the necessary power. That action saved the rescue team from a massive effort to carry and winch the woman across gorges on a stretcher on suspended ropes. The whole effort would have taken about eight hours and delayed the hospitalisation of the woman. I was totally in awe of the skill and bravery demonstrated by the pilot and the flight engineer.

I was, some 20 years later, to need the services of a rescue team...

It was interesting that most rescues took place over weekends and public holidays when folk were out and about. During one multiple rescue which took place on a Sunday night involving two climbing parties in the Klein Drakenstein mountains, climbers had sustained severe injuries requiring extraordinary rescue efforts. As a result, I had to take off the Monday to continue with the rescue call out and completion. The HR or Human Resources department at Koeberg would not allow me to take special leave but had to have it taken off my annual leave. They said it was my choice to be part of a rescue team and could not allow special consideration because of that. I told the manager of HR that I hoped that he never got lost or fell on a mountain during the week! Oddly enough they would happily fly teams up-country during the week to compete in sports such as rugby, and other activities.

Soon after this, I changed my job from working for Eskom at Koeberg Nuclear Power Station to Soeker – the oil and gas business. After my transferal to the Soekor Mossgas site in Mossel Bay, I had to cease doing voluntary rescue work.

It was not much fun working in Mossel Bay because living in digs away from the family was hard, and in truth, depressing; although my work relating to the FA Platform and other offshore rigs was stimulating and interesting. Most weekends, I returned to Cape Town, a round trip of 800 kilometres. Leaving home either late on a Sunday afternoon or at four on a Monday morning was tough, and tiring.

The occasional weekend that I stayed over in Mossel bay, I would head out into the mountains. I met some fascinating folk out in the country, and climbed a few peaks which was a bit lonely, but also very stimulating to be out in the hills. I also took quite an interest in the archaeology of the area beyond Herbertsdale, and with the permission of farmers, visited some known Bushmen painted rock-shelters or caves. There were a few newly discovered sites, one of these contained images of swallows or mermaid figures. These images are reasonably scarce and were not known to exist this far west.

I also rediscovered a rare protea that was very localised and occurred on a rocky area relatively high up on the north-facing and dry Cloetesberg mountain.

It was quite funny afterwards when I took the specimen to Kirstenbosch for formal identification, and they said that I would have to pay, so I agreed and left the specimen to be scrutinised. I had no sooner done so, when the famed Professor Rourke appeared quite excitedly and asked me where I had found the specimen. I vaguely told him that I had located it in the Cloetesberg Mountains. He quickly identified it as a *Protea decurrens,* and that it had only ever been found at one location and that was at a place called Woeska. Now Woeska was a very remote and deserted place in an arid area on the northern side of the Cloetesberg, so I was pleasantly surprised, firstly by his expansive knowledge, and secondly, my unusual luck to find such a plant at all. I continued to tell him that I had found it in the same general area some kilometres west of Woeska; I disagreed with him about the identification because according to my protea book, this specimen's leaves were more curled than the one described in the book. He chuckled I think because he was mildly amused that someone should disagree with him after all, he wrote the book on proteas and was one of the world's leading botanists on proteas! Jovially, he declared that I should not have to pay for the identification of the specimen and indeed if he could keep it since the last one, collected in the fifties, was not as excellent. I was elated that while rushing down off the mountain because of a pending storm, I had slowed over a shale-band and spotted the plant which just looked different, so had despite my hurriedness carefully removed a couple of branches and put them in my rucksack. You never know your luck.

The encounter with Prof Rourke reminded me of an art exhibition in Cape Town, where several eminent guests were attending. I only knew a few people there and started talking to an elderly and distinguished gentleman and in a friendly manner, asked him where he worked. He replied, "I work at Kirstenbosch", so I asked what he did there, he replied quite seriously that, "some people think I don't do very much there". I wandered off, and I think he must have been much amused. Someone then told me that it was Professor Rycroft! I felt embarrassed, but really, I had not met him before – lesson, always introduce yourself before chatting.

Another find in the same area of Cloetesberg was a cave that the farm owner, Willem, had not known about. They had lived on the farm for generations when Bushmen were known to habit the area, never discovering the cave for themselves. It was round-roofed, spacious with a flat floor, well concealed and contained a few beautiful Bushmen paintings. Some kilometres to the north of the same location was a flat-topped hill. The farmer had told me that there was a cave where his grandfather had described a Bushmen shelter. I was keen to investigate the cave, and one weekend drove out and set off up to the top of the hill. I could not find the cave or entrance. It had to be entered from the top because the geology of the hill was that the top layer of the hill was a conglomerate of boulders (unusual for the immediate area), so the entrance would not have been obvious. I had located other very narrow hollows between the rocks, but none big enough to enter. I had measured a few, and they were deep enough that might have presented a possibility, but again, not large enough to enter. I asked him to show me the location, but he was not keen because he said that it was haunted. Not another haunted place! However, he did guide me to the site, which was not far from where I had been searching. It was not more than a couple of metres deep and branched off in a northerly direction. He would not enter, so I lowered myself down, being careful not to tread on any lurking snake. It was not safe as there appeared to be several hanging boulders, so I did not go in too deep. However firstly my torch packed up, so I thought well I would get a couple of pictures instead. I did achieve some photos before my camera refused to work! I was happy to clamber out and told the farmer what had happened; he had a wry smile on his face as if to say, "I told you so".

He also told me dead seriously that some nights you will hear an approaching vehicle on the dirt road from Van Wyksdorp, but then it would never pass the farmhouse. The farmhouse was right next to the road, and just before the Cloetes Pass. Isolated as it is and off the beaten track, there are other tales to be told of the area, of an unsolved murder, a body found in an ant bear hole and an 'evil' doing by an unscrupulous lawyer who diddled an illiterate farm lady of her farm. In places where there has been hardship and suffering, there may remain unresolved issues, and the resultant unhappiness may be palpable.

If you ever visit Die Hel (The Hell), the remote and very isolated settlement in the Swartberg Mountains, then visit the old graveyard next to the valley road. If you are sensitive enough, you may sense a presence (of spirits) and have your head tingle. It is not scary, just real. This, when Jean and I visited the place in 1993, happened to me. Jean did not sense anything. A few years later, I read the book '*The Hell*' by Sue van Waart, where she quotes that at the Esterhuizen's graves, you will 'experience' the feeling. I did not check whose graves were closest to me, but I can substantiate it by my experience.

I also had the opportunity to meet some of the local farmers at Herbertsdale and visit other rock art sites as well as do some exploring in the surrounding mountains. There were a number of forts and trenches from the Boer War period. I never got to climb Vrey se Berg which I had wanted to; it was a very prominent peak quite clearly seen from the main N2 road between Albertinia and Mossel Bay. Locals in Mossel Bay would ask me how I came to know farmers and folk in the countryside, and it was a surprise to me to know that some locals had never ventured out of Mossel Bay to visit Herbertsdale (a quaint settlement alongside the Gouritz River. I was also surprised at the existing lack of interest by local folk in the rich history and biodiversity of the area.

At one time I thought I might move permanently to George, and also having travelled so frequently along the southern Cape road, I got to know the little towns. Properties at that time were attractive both in appearance and price. I was quite interested in buying a plot in Riviersonderend. I had seen it once and suggested to Quintin that he drive out to see it. It was a Sunday late afternoon on my way back to Mossel bay when I drove into Riviersonderend and stopped outside the plot on one of the back streets south of the town. It was in a raised position with a water reservoir, fruit trees and looked promising. I was suddenly overcome with a feeling of absolute dread. It was a premonition of something or other and would not leave me. As I drove on, I was filled with the strong feeling that Quintin should not drive out to see the plot, and that something dreadful would happen. I would phone him from work to tell him. It was already dark when I had passed the turnoff to Albertinia; I was comfortable and had my coffee and sandwiches which Jean had made for me. My speed rarely exceeded 110km/hr, but on average, around 100km/hr.

I pulled over to the left within the yellow line to let a VW Golf pass me which was going quite fast. It was seconds later in the headlights appeared a small buck. It was standing towards the centre of the road but facing left. I would certainly strike the poor animal, so swerved to the right and skidded. I missed it but flew off the shoulder of the road down an embankment and struck an old cattle ramp. Poles and dust were flying about in the headlights. I had smacked my head badly against the passenger headrest, so much so, that it was bent sideways at ninety degrees to its normal position. I thought that my back was injured, as it was painful. Within minutes two chaps that were driving some way behind me, and who had seen the accident, came to my assistance. Both were from a church in Port Elizabeth and thankfully alerted the police in Albertinia who soon arrived with an ambulance. They struggled to access the crash site, but with my assistance, finally pulled me from the car window, put me on a rigid board and drove me to Mossel Bay hospital. The feeling of dread was for me. I just could not believe that the buck was standing stationary in the road just after a fast car had passed it. The good news was that I did not collide with the little bokkie, but it must have had a very close shave. I recovered despite not having a resident doctor to attend to me – bad news for a Sunday! I was eventually stitched up by a Mossgas linked doctor, and a nurse sprayed plastic skin on my head, with glass and hair still in the wound (I removed the bits and pieces over the following week). My neck (under the neck brace) and chest were still covered with broken windscreen glass. I recovered from the bang to the head, although it remained painful for years to come. However, the car did not and was considered a write-off... I did learn that it was procured by a local garage and fixed up and sold. The bits and pieces from the vehicle and the boot were never returned to me after it had been towed to the Albertinia Police station.

16

First 4x4, Bush Trips, Archaeology of Mateke Site and Mambo Hills

A few things dawned on me when I was working in Mossel Bay. One of them was that I was aware that I was getting on in years, well not that bad really when I think back, but being fifty-five years of age, I had not been feeling that well, always feeling very tired and lacking energy. At first I thought it was the fumes from the refinery that were ever-present in the air. Though that was not a healthy situation, after checking out with the clinic, I found that my cholesterol and blood-sugar levels were too high. To try and increase my energy, I had been putting extra sugar on my cereal in the morning. Producers of sugar always emblazoned their adverts with 'eat more sugar to give you energy' – wrong! Those adverts do not quote that any longer. Anyhow my levels were high, and it was having a debilitating effect on my wellbeing. So, it was at that time that I'd become more aware, as the years floated by, that I'd better start planning trips for us into the bush. I calculated that if I was to be fit enough until the age of seventy years, and that if we went into the bush every two years, it would only give us about seven trips. That seemed terribly final, and very limited, so I cashed in an insurance policy I'd had for many years and decided to buy a 4x4 bakkie which would be rugged enough for the bush trips that we might take.

The second thing was that I wanted to run my own business as a consultant in quality assurance. I knew the time was right with the extent of my experience and confidence; I now had the capability to meet the industry expectations. I accepted a package from Mossgas/Soeker because at the time they wanted to cut down on staff – and that included the quality assurance position for the FA Platform! Who decided and why I never found out. Still, it was strongly argued by the offshore team, and even though the decision was reversed, and the CEO of Mossgas had set my application aside (hidden beneath papers under in his in-basket), I decided it was the prompt I needed to leave. I was employed originally by Soeker in Parow, Cape Town and was never comfortable with my transfer to Mossel Bay. Also the drive back and forth between Cape Town and Mossel Bay to visit my family on weekends, was not suitable.

The decisions were made, and I did not regret either. The other measured decision was to immediately cut out any free sugar and other over sweet foods. This brought down the blood-sugar to a manageable level without having to take corrective medication. My cholesterol had also come down, not as low as I would have liked, but not on a dangerous level.

I bought a second-hand single cab 4x4 Nissan bakkie which was in excellent condition and fitted out the back with fold-down beds, and several other useful accessories. At the time Jean had decided to begin her master's degree in Archaeology focusing on 'Iron age' archaeology and had chosen a site in south-eastern Zimbabwe. I had originally visited the same area in 1958 with the Schools Exploration Society (RSES).

So, Quintin and I set out to try and relocate the site. This trip was to tie in on my return from presenting a paper on 'Quality and the Environment' at a conference held at Victoria Falls in 1994. It had been many years before, but by a bit of careful map-reading and contacting one of the local farmers in the area, Mike Gawler of Sheba ranch, we located the area again. It had been a long drive from Victoria Falls via Bulawayo, Beit Bridge and ultimately the turn-off at the Lion and Elephant Motel. The eighty or so kilometre drive thereafter was along a rough road, but through interesting bush and woodland; we eventually reached the Mateke Hills after crossing the Bubye river drift.

Surrounded by bush, trees and rocky hills, and thinking that I would never find the place again, we slowed and looked back into the now setting sun. With relief, we spotted the prominent and rare feature of an enormous overhanging rock – 'Lomolehoto' (the beak of the hornbill)! It was the correct location, and happily, we met Mike Gawler, the Sheba Ranch manager. He received us with open arms, and we rested well in the

A baobab at sunset behind Chumbangula hill

sprawling farmhouse. Margie, Mike's wife, was not there on that occasion but later we had the pleasure of meeting her. We became close friends for many years to come, both at Sheba and Rocky Glen ranches near West Nicholson.

The following day Quintin and I with our helper guide Sibangani from the farm, set-off into the local hills. I re-found what I called Cranium hill – principally because of the hollow-shaped dome of the outcrop which was a sizeable hollow crust of rock, so to speak, surrounded by large boulders. The access, though, did not appear to be apparent. In my mind, I somehow had a picture of animals painted on the inside northern wall of the dome, but after rushing over to that side of the dome expecting to see them there, disappointingly found nothing. I had been wrong, but everything else was as I had remembered it. Had the tick bite fever given me some hallucination way back in 1958? I had no answer for that and remained puzzled. One had to climb over the boulders, down, then emerge under a cavernous domed-roof.

Reading up later on the history of the area, I learned that it was likely that a district native commissioner named Forrestal had taken refuge in this cave during the Matabele uprising in 1893/96. Interestingly, I also recall reading of two schoolboys that had run away from Louis Trichardt and were missing for some time. They were eventually discovered in the Mateke Hills – that must have been quite an adventure over that distance including crossing the Limpopo river and surviving in the still relatively wild bush.

There was also the account by Allan Wright of the notorious criminal named Chitokwa or Mister Chitokwa. Some considered that he deserved that title for his notoriety, for robbing and thieving from stores, houses, hotels, African huts and farms in that region and wilderness for years. After an early arrest, he escaped his captors in Fort Victoria, and all efforts including intensive man-hunts with tracker dogs and policemen on horseback had failed to apprehend him. He had stolen a rifle and ammunition and was then considered dangerous after he had informed local Africans that he would use it if anyone tried to arrest him. Renewed efforts were ordered to locate and apprehend him. He traversed the country from Mateke down to, and at times, crossing the Limpopo River. He was clearly a very bush-wise and wily character, and no doubt very fit after his vast distances covered during his criminal activities. It was in 1964, and after two years on the run, he was finally caught. He'd broken into the Malumba Ranch while the owners were away, and the ranch staff had investigated after hearing noises from the house. Chitokwa dashed out, and in the dark, the farmworkers managed to grab him. They were surprised to find that it was Chitokwa that was struggling with them.

The reason he probably did not make good on his getaway was that he had found a pair of boots in the house and was in the process of putting them on when surprised. Unfortunately for him he only managed to get one boot on and had inadvertently put the left boot on the right foot! He apparently received a lengthy jail sentence. Such is the rugged and wild nature of the region that a person could be on the run for so long.

Next was the ascent of the adjoining hill called Chumbangula (also called Malumba by the name of the farm within which it is located), which required an exposed friction climb near to the top. What we saw was so much more than what I had remembered by the brief visit to the hill in 1958, it was rich in various pottery designs and types.

I was excited and enthusiastic for Jean to commence her studies. Secretly too, it was deep in the bush, quite wild and the area full of mystery and potential. As previously mentioned, Jean was happy to work the site based on the potential material it offered. It was a site and area that was little known and it would provide, and proved conclusively to do so, a valuable link in the knowledge and broader picture of the Limpopo Valley. Because the site was in Zimbabwe, Jean had to arrange the management and supervision between the University of Cape Town, and the University of Zimbabwe. That was not an easy process, and quite protracted!

One of the other hills or rather kopjes we were interested in was Guhuhu, it was across from the Malumba river bed, but was not easy to ascend. It was defined by an enormous hollow boulder on the one flank of the hill which held evidence of Iron Age material. We were fortunate to find a convenient 'key' to the ascent and descent of the hill via a 'secret' passage that followed the flank of a granite wall and allowed much easier access.

Apart from an earlier trip to Gona Re Zhou, there would be more trips with our faithful 4x4 single-cab Nissan Patrol bakkie into the Mateke Hills. Those early explorations renewed my yearning and love for the bush and everything that embraced it.

It was a challenging area to explore given the extreme heat, and sometimes dense bush. We had to be up by six in the morning and out for the hills just after seven. That gave us a good two hours of work and exploration. By nine in the morning, we'd be heading back to our parked bakkie waiting for us under some bush and shade. Even though it was winter when we visited the area, the midday-sun sapped all energy, beating down from a clear blue sky. The temperature often in the mid 30 degrees Celsius, the air seemed to stand still. All was quiet except for the monotonous high-pitched buzzing of the cicadas. So often somewhere in that stillness and heat, the sound of the Emerald-spotted Wood Dove's mournful and monotonous call came drifting across the veld as typically

Chumbangula Hill – Mateke

Boulder – grain bin cave - Chumbangula

interpreted, *'My mother is dead! My father is dead! My relations are dead! And woe, woe, woe, am I.'* I could well imagine the scene and feeling when all is dry and withered, the world is stilled, and the hope for rain is impossibly out of reach.

Early and present subsistence crop farmers, depended solely on seasonal rainfall. They'd enter into the annual ritual of 'rainmaking', and the Mateke Hills was no exception. The Sheba ranch had a 'rainmaking hill,' where present peoples came from far and wide on an annual basis to perform their ritual for the expected rain. There was also no doubt that we had discovered an early rainmaking site on Chumbangula, which was not too far from the 'rainmaking hill'.

Quintin at the waterhole hill with Lomolehoto in background

Quintin and Paul on Guhuhu Hill

We would only go out again after three-thirty in the afternoon once the sun and its ever-present heat diminished. Energy and enthusiasm returned, and by early evening, we looked forward to tea or a sundowner. The odd occasion when cooler air and overcast weather moved in from Mozambique, it was a pleasure to explore around.

The Mateke Hills area supported plentiful wild animals such as giraffe, warthog, zebra, kudu, impala, cheetah, leopard, wild dog, hyaena and the occasional lion and elephant that passed through the area. It was good to see and know that there was quite a diversity of game. Regrettably, during the late 1950s, Mateke Hills and surrounds had been divided into hunting blocks; the slaughter of game was unrelenting and devastating. Wildlife depended on isolated pools or pans in the area for water during the dry season and times of drought; as such, they became easy targets.

Between our visits, Mike had had to shoot a large lion that had killed five of his cattle, so we were surprised to see the new addition of the lion skin laid out next to the existing leopard and lion skins!

It was ideal leopard terrain, with numerous rocky outcrops, thick stands of impenetrable Msimbiti (Lebombo ironwood), Mopani, and a host of other tree and plant types. On one occasion while ascending 'Waterhole' hill, Quintin and I saw a fresh baboon kill, where only the skull remained. The leopard was still palpably close, but the bush being so dense, we saw no sign of it. Leopards are very wary, and observant, so even if we did not see any, they would certainly see us. When exploring caves, we would stand back to make a bit of noise and throw a few stones in the general direction to allow enough time for the animal to depart – hopefully. We were also cautious about snakes, though we only saw one large snake, but could not identify it.

> ## *'Exploring! The small boy dies hard in all of us'*
>
> A quote from – 'The Diary of a district officer' by Kenneth Bradley 1966

Jean was eventually granted permission and permits from the respective Mateke Hills farmers and the authorities in Harare to begin her archaeological survey. However, there was a hill called the Sheba Ridge which we were requested not to set foot upon, as it was considered 'Tagati'. As mentioned before, it is not that unusual to have hills and sites that are considered 'no go' for the same or similar reasons such as for burials, rainmaking, special gatherings or perhaps historical battle sites. I did not know what the background to Sheba Ridge was, but we respected the request. One of the early owners of the farm did not heed the warning from the locals and decided to climb and investigate the ridge himself, which was not far from the Sheba Ridge. To all accounts, as Mike Gawler retold the tale to us, the chap eventually returned in a terrified and battered state. Whether or not that was from physical attack or more likely, running through the thorny and scratchy bush, I do not know, but apparently, he would not speak about it, and shortly after the event, left the farm not to return. One cave we entered that contained an old grave also had a strange vibe to it, and several folk would not enter it, including some of the survey folk from Harare. It was challenging to find the entrance, and it was also quite dark inside. I did not experience any unhappy atmosphere to the place, neither did Jean, but Mike's wife Margie, would not descend into it because it felt 'spooky' to her.

We enjoyed another four trips to the Mateke Hills while Jean conducted her work. Having the Sheba ranch as a base from which to explore and research was a great help and privilege. It had a wide and long gauze-enclosed veranda, which was cool most of the time, with a large wooden farm table where we were able to spread out our maps, drawings and books.

*Jean pointing to grinding grooves on the valley floor below
Lomolehoto hill – Mateke*

We were able to use one of the bedrooms, which was large and fairly sparsely furnished, with an adjoining bathroom and toilet. Now the toilet was unique because it was frequented by platannas (African-clawed frog) that swam up from the septic tank into the toilet basin. You may imagine our surprise to the cacophony of noise as the platanna began its loud croaking. The shape of the toilet bowl amplified the sound. Somewhat like the old record label with the dog listening into the old-fashioned record-player speaker! We thought the problem was solved when we flushed it down, but the next night it was back, loudly announcing its presence, which echoed through our room and the passage.

Usually, Mike would shut down the generator at night, but when he was away, it was a long walk out through the yard to the back of a shed which bordered some closed bush. The old Lister diesel generator gave life to the farm, and when it was shut-down, everything became very quiet with the house in darkness except for our few candles. So, it was more than a little eerie to walk back through the pitch dark 'that closed in around you' with a small torch barely lighting up the ground at your feet.

Many of these remote and isolated farms of which Sheba was one, had been attacked by terrorists during the bush war, so it must have been very unnerving for the occupants living in them or driving along lonely dirt roads in those days. Many of which were also land-mined with disastrous effects.

Our food was very basic most of the time, so one day we negotiated with Ryno who worked in the kitchen, to buy a 'free-range' chicken – this was boom time for the seller of the chicken. It had been free-range for a long time and could have been used by Disney for a 'Road Runner' movie. In the harsh hot and dry climate, the muscles had shrunk, and I swear it was partially fossilised – in short, it was another lesson learned, it was not worth the effort of cooking and waste of good firewood! It might have been a sign that 'that' particular chicken had not yet been taken and eaten by the rock Leguaan that habited the homestead garden and regularly caught and ate chickens.

Joburg Makakani, our proud and humble guide from Battlefields Ranch – Mateke Hills

Paul and Winston Mismeke (guide support from Sheba ranch) on Lomolehoto hill.

A very large 'broken' grindstone 'Guyo' base – Valley floor

Very smooth grinding grooves – Valley floor

Jean at home working on her Master of Philosophy (Archaeology) Thesis – 'Understanding the farming community sequence from the Mateke Hills, South-East Lowveld, Zimbabwe'

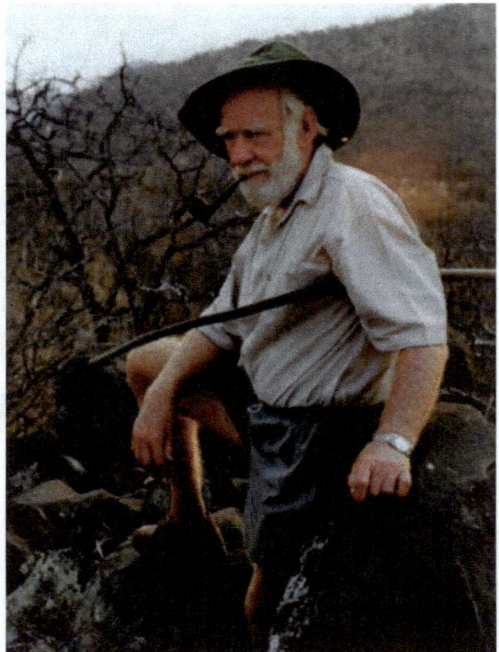

Right: Mike Gawler, a true Rhodesian and dear friend from Sheba Ranch – Mateke Hills

During our explorations within the local watershed valley area, we had the good fortune to find some sites that had never before been recorded or visited on a formal basis. These included Late Stone Age, and we suspect, a few early Iron Age sites as well. We also had the privilege to visit the Mwenezi site on the western side of the Mateke Hills, not far from the Mwenezi River, with the University Of Zimbabwe who had been doing a survey and study of the walled Iron Age site. Jean and I were assisted by a Joburg Makakani who worked for the Battlefields ranch who guided us accordingly – he had lived and worked in the area and knew the local tribal history well. Without him, we would never have found the burial site of the early and important chief Chinana's (of the Mapfumbi tribe) and that of his son Phineas, who was buried, close by. We were likewise guided by Annanius (since deceased) of Marungudzi in the location of an Iron Age site and walling close to the Bubye River, not far from Chief Matibi's kraal. All of these sites were duly recorded for the Museum and National Monuments department in Harare.

Jean successfully completed her Master of Philosophy (Archaeology) thesis *'Understanding the farming community sequence from the Mateke Hills, South-East Lowveld, Zimbabwe'* based on the Malumba (Chumbangula Hill) site of the Mateke. It was an important and valuable contribution to the otherwise limited knowledge of the area. The Malumba site was found to be quite early (around 1000 AD) and contemporary with Mapungubwe just south of the Limpopo River in South Africa.

It was a sad time while at the Sheba ranch especially for Mike, when an African drove up, wanted to see him, and 'requested' a map of the farm and in particular, the upper reaches of the farm where there was a dam, fed by the Malumba river. He was deciding which part of the farm he was going to take over. Jean and I later met up with the same fellow on the main dirt road at the entrance to the farm, where he requested help in the form of some wire, to tie up the springs on his vehicle – hardly a good business start to a farming enterprise. Mike was able to retain a small part of the farm, but cattle were stolen continuously. The other farm which Mike also managed, bordered on the Bubye river to the south, was taken over by a lawyer of Robert Mugabe who waved a piece of paper at Mike saying that he now had control over the farm. Mike had earlier been alerted by his foreman that someone had occupied the house on that farm. It turned out, that the lawyer had, and wait for it, employed a European manager from the East Rand, Johannesburg to run the spread and look after the lawyer's cattle. The farm had been originally purchased and paid for while Mugabe was already in power. The old African chap from the Battlefields ranch later told us during our last visit there, that the rampant poaching had decimated the animals. He said that the ensnared animals had been left to die 'in situ' without actually being taken for food. Such was the politics, and still is, at the time of writing, in Zimbabwe.

Mike was one of the kindest guys I ever met and was always concerned for his workers; he even requested that I bring extra mealie meal (maize meal) from South Africa to help feed his people. Food was in short supply, and government supplies were preferentially distributed to supporters of Zanu-PF. If you showed your Zanu-PF membership card, then you could stand in the queue. Many folk joined the party to obtain cards so they could feed their families. How very, very sad!

I once drove with Mike late one night through tough bush and track conditions to a far off clinic near Sengwe with a woman that was having problems with her pregnancy, seeking medical help. That was the character of Mike. We became very close friends with both Mike and his wife, Margie. When Mike died some years later on a farm near West Nicholson, the local Africans who knew him and his family well were very saddened by his passing and apparently sang with deep feeling at his funeral service at the farm.

Archaeology has always been high on our interests when travelling around the country, and on one of the trips to Zimbabwe, included visits to the Dhlo Dhlo, (Danangombe) and Nalatale ruins which were not far from Shangani. These were very interesting Iron Age sites which also dated back to the Rozwi dynasty up to around 1830. The remarkably beautiful and perhaps uniquely patterned walling of the Nalatale ruins was a sight to behold, even though they were partially reconstructed to preserve the integrity of the structure and design. At the Danangombe ruins Jean and I had planned to sleep in the bakkie, and although the sky was clear, even approaching the end of winter, the temperature was cold. It was fortuitous that we met Des Bawden and his wife, who most kindly insisted that we stay over at their nearby farm for the night. Jean was delighted because she badly needed to freshen up and have a comfortable night. We had a splendid evening and a blissfully comfortable sleep in what must have been the original 'grandma's feather bed'! Des had some great tales to tell including his fishing trips to the Deka River and Milibizi in his 1920 Plymouth truck. Des was a third-generation Rhodesian, and his 1920 truck was still running when we were there in 1996!

While in the area, we decided to venture into the Mambo Hills, which were south-west of Shangani. A most interesting area. It was a range of granite hills not unlike Matopos, though much smaller in overall area. In these hills, there were some ruins, one of which we visited was the Thabas-zi-ka-Mambo, a hill called Munyanga towards the northern end of the hills. It was believed that here, the last Rozwi king, Mambo Chirisamuru

Typical Mambo hill granite formation north of Inyati

was attacked (apparently skinned alive) and beaten by Zwangendaba
Kumalo and his marauding impis from the south-east, and south of the
Limpopo around 1834. This invasion and attack led to the demise and end
of the economically powerful Rozwi kingdom. It was in this very location
in July of 1896 that European forces beat the Matabele. Cecil Rhodes
actually attended this skirmish. The peace that followed with the Matabele
after the fighting in Matopos was initiated and driven by Rhodes.

It is strange to think and sobering as well, that in such a serene and
picturesque area of lovely kopjes with rock formations, trees and running
water, such conflict could have happened. This is no doubt true of many
historical sites around the world where nature has to some extent repaired
the 'surface' damage due to war or bloodshed from the past – upon
reflection it all seems so futile. The emotional damage is not always
repaired. The overarching sense of loss and pain can sometimes still be
felt in such places.

This area had escaped my knowledge and of course, interest all those
years before as I had no idea such a beautiful area existed. We had had
permission to camp in the hills by a local 'custodian' farm that bordered
the northern end of the hills. After we had scouted around, I set about
climbing the hill (Mambo's citadel) while Jean stayed at the vehicle. It was

quite eerie, wild, overgrown and evidently rarely visited, as there was no defined path. A large troop of baboon watched my every trepidatious step, and in fact, one large fellow followed at close range, perhaps not more than ten metres away at times. However, I did attain the ruins and noted that much of the stonewalling had fallen or was disturbed. No doubt by weather or baboons turning over stones while looking for scorpions. There were also ruins known to be on the east side of the hills, which were perhaps more impressive. However, we would not have the extra time to investigate, as well as difficult access. I did find to my surprise a grass-roofed hut in an odd depression on the upper level. Peering inside through the open entrance, I saw a drum and a couple of pots. This was more than likely a rainmaking site, so I did not venture in lest I 'disturbed' the spiritual sanctity of the place. I took some photographs and retreated down the hill. I cautiously made my way past the large baboon troop; a couple of menacing-looking males followed my descent with dark beady eyes! Years before when climbing alone in the Matopos, I was surrounded by baboons; however, they had allowed me to pass by – with my heart in my mouth!

Although the base of the hill was attractive and had many beautiful trees under which to camp, it did not feel right, and a slightly creepy. Jean expressed this feeling strongly, so and notwithstanding the late hour, we left the immediate area and camped just outside the hill perimeter also under some lovely trees. With our fold down bunks in the back of the bakkie, it was rather cramped but afforded a quick camp set up with a distinct advantage, such as not having to clear the ground and pitch a tent. It is interesting to note that this ominous mood was formally reported in the *Bulawayo – Historic Battleground of Rhodesia* by Oliver Ransford; that the location on the east of the hills and close to the Nsangu River holds an 'extraordinary uncanny atmosphere near the Mlimo's cave'. We went on to spend a comfortable night with no further forebodings at our new location. We later discovered that our new campsite was the location of *Plumer's Bivouac* during the significant skirmish in the Mambo Hills in 1896...

The following day we drove down the old 'Hunters' road towards the Inyati Mission. This road (we also saw a very old and faded road sign saying 'Hunters Road'), was the original road north taken by hunters and settlers alike. We were disappointed to see the condition of the Mission at Inyati (Emhlangeni), especially the church, and the general state of the surrounding area. However, the graveyard was historically interesting as it listed the names of the earliest Inyati missionaries – such as the Rev. Sykes who was a pioneer missionary from 1859 and died in Inyati in 1887. One grave was of an African – Makhaza Nkala, one of the two converts at the time, that had been murdered by the Matabele. Ironically, and sadly, he was put to his death for his beliefs. This was after he had returned to Inyati from carrying the missionaries to their safety in Bulawayo, where they were intercepted by a rebel impi at Elibeni but were spared because of Lobengula's words declaring that 'These vessels shall not be broken.' (The other convert Matambo Ndhlovu also at Inyati at the time was spared execution because his brother Maqamula – being a noted fighter in the rebel impi, pleaded with the Induna to be killed with his brother whom he loved, but because they could not afford to lose him, his brother was set free under cover of darkness where he fled to the hill of Ndumba)

It was Robert Moffat that originally had permission from King Mzilikazi (whom he first met in 1829 in Marico – Western Transvaal) to build a mission there. It was also paradoxically where one of Mzilikazi's best regiments was based.

We met and had lunch with the local church Minister Rev.. Denis and his wife who received us well: then we moved on via the 'Turk' and 'Queens' Mines to Bulawayo.

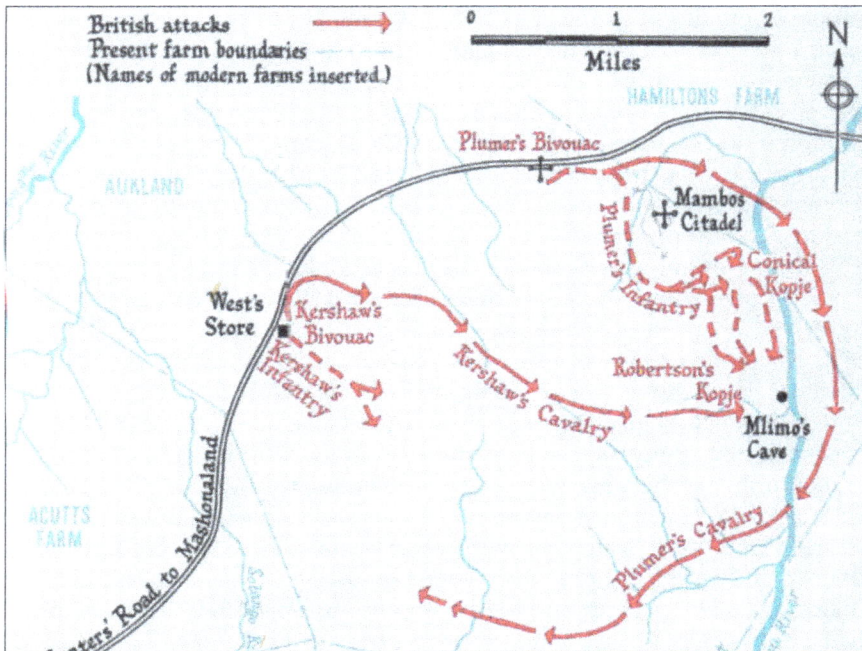

The scene of the battle engagement in the Mambo Hills in 1896. We finally camped close to Plumer's bivouac site where the Old Hunters Road to Mashonaland now passes.

17

The Singapore Experience

When I worked with Soeker, I had the opportunity to go to Singapore as the quality assurance manager for the conversion of the 'Actinia' rig from being an accommodation facility offshore which was in support of the FA Platform during construction off Mossel Bay, back to an operational drilling rig. It was a very tight schedule, as much engineering work had to be carried out in a six week period to meet contractual requirements for work in the South China Sea.

On the way in from Changi Airport, a taxi driver asked me where I was from, so I told him that I was from South Africa. He asked me why there was so much violence amongst taxi drivers there, so almost defensively I told him that it was because of the competition of taxi owner organisations that jealously guarded their taxi routes. I then asked him 'I suppose you all have set routes in Singapore' 'No he replied, we can drive anywhere we like'! The Singaporeans were very well informed of happenings in Africa, and especially the political situations.. At our shared office in town, a postman came into the office one day, and upon dropping off the post and knowing where we came from, he then wished us a happy Christmas and New Year, and at the door, paused, turned around and said 'you must never allow a poor government to run your country'... that was 1992

Two important experiences of the visit were infused in me.

During this time, I was very impressed with the work ethic in Singapore by all peoples there, nothing was too much trouble, and they would go out of their way to fully comply with the stringent standards required for 'offshore rig construction'. Their prime minister had from years back, pulled the Island back from a seedy drug and disease-ridden hole to one of the most vibrant economies and countries in the world. It was crime-free and an unbelievably clean city. Upon my enquiry, I was fortunate to meet with an environmental government representative outside of my work and after hours. I was welcomed with open arms, and they were not fussed that I could only get there after normal hours, and I was most humbled at their advanced thinking and vision for the future. Their Prime Minister had a philosophy 'inter alia' to his people that 'you are firstly Singaporeans, and secondly, Chinese, Indian, Europeans, Malaysians' and other nationalities.

Their laws, though very prescriptive, were clearly effective and working towards rapid self-regulation amongst the folk. For a country of only 600 square kilometres (just about the size of the greater Cape Peninsula and Cape Flats), they had to run a tight ship. But above all, it was the quality of the people there that struck me. Their commitment to improving all spheres of government to better serve their people was astonishing. I was shown where the last remaining shacks (there was literally a handful left, that I saw) were being removed for proper infrastructure. The death penalty existed for any drug dealing. (Bearing in mind, that Singapore was one of the worst drug trafficking zones of the world). While I was there, a couple of foreigners 'in transit' through Singapore at the Changi airport were spotted by a security man, searched and found to be carrying drugs on their bodies. They were later both executed. End of story.

Public smoking was prohibited as it was also in hotels. but happily, accepted by folk, excess drinking was discouraged by restaurant owners! It was disappointing to learn that a couple of our South African guys had argued and disregarded polite requests by hotel and restaurant owners not to smoke or over-indulge. Unhappily, I noticed some rowdy Australians doing likewise, but broadly it was wonderful to see the cheerful disposition of folk there. Being there over Christmas, and New Year (including the Chinese New Year), was an incredible experience, masses of people were celebrating without any sign of unpleasantness or bad behaviour. The feeling of being safe amongst like-minded people was overwhelming and imbued a sense of true freedom; that with mature and civilized responsibility. As I was working a long week and long hours, I was not wearing 'rose-tinted' holiday glasses either!

There was no unemployment there, and the employment percentage of the total population was way above ninety. The balance was made up of those unable to work for other reasons and for old age folk. I was told that they imported over thirty thousand Malaysians per day to help cover productivity employment needs.

Companies that were contracted to do work for us did not take short cuts with their work, were always willing and keen to comply with the numerous quality standards. Such is a country that is built, run and succeeds on the quality of their people – an excellent work ethic. I asked their environmental representatives how they would cope with overpopulation, thinking I would hit a sensitive issue. They informed me that they were limited to (then in 1991/92), an average of 2,3 children per couple. Having more children required a couple to pay more tax. That is, if you could afford them, then you could have them. In South Africa, the more children you have, the more grants are awarded. Hardly the equation for a stable population and quality of life! Notwithstanding all of that, I could never live there because it was too crowded, and there was no bush or wilderness one could getaway to, not without travelling afar; but we could learn much from their successes both in infrastructure, housing and the care for the environment.

In the conclusion of my meeting with the Singapore Environmental Management in 1992, I was honoured to be asked to review and comment on their new draft 'Singapore Green Plan' this I happily concluded and on my return to South Africa, I had the privilege of presenting extracts from the comprehensive plan to the City Of Cape Town for their information and reference. I also gave a public presentation on the same subject.

The other significant event I experienced, revolved around a spiritual occurrence: I had offered to pass on special greetings from our minister Neville Mickelthwaite of the local Methodist Church in Plumstead, Cape Town to the Fort Canning Methodist Church in Singapore. So I arranged to attend a Sunday service at the Methodist Church there. I was surprised at the size of the congregation, which apparently held up to three thousand folk. The minister duly welcomed me and passed on the message to the congregation and also asked me to return the message of greetings. It was a cheery service, and everyone was very friendly. I was invited by a couple of the church members to give them a short talk on South Africa, if I wouldn't mind, at one of their regular evening meetings the following week, to which I happily accepted. On the arranged evening, my work colleagues and I were to be invited by one of the engineering companies to go out to dinner with them. I apologised that I could not as I had already made other arrangements. They tried to persuade me to change, to which I declined, so they said that I should join them after the church meeting. I was doubtful at that happening.

I duly met with the few church members (stewards) and was introduced around. In the room, there were not more than fifteen or so persons. By some strange coincidence, there was a woman involved with the church seated in front of me who had also been seated in front of me at the previous Sunday service. Quite a coincidence considering the literally hundreds, perhaps a few thousand folk in attendance. They had a visiting minister from Malaysia who had also been invited to address the few folk present. Two rows in front of me was a young, tall but slightly built young Chinese man, who caught my attention. He looked troubled and very reserved. The visiting minister held a general prayer and then distinctly focused on this young man. He asked for blessings and the Holy Spirit to descend upon the young man and heal him. At that same time, the most amazing and unbelievable tingling, buzzing sensation descended from my head and into my body. It was indescribable and lasted for at least five minutes! I could not believe what had happened, and it felt as if I had been electrically charged. I do not doubt that others must have felt it as well. From what I thought, what might have been the usual message from a visiting minister, should then focus on that one man. It was a surprise, I think to everyone. He undoubtedly had special powers! I gave my short talk and answered some questions about South Africa, and what was happening in the country, then the visiting minister and a couple of the stewards surrounded me and also gave special blessings to me and for South Africa. We had tea, and I left – but I was still fully charged, so to speak, and on arrival at the hotel was about to go up to bed as it was about ten pm. Lo and behold, a kombi was waiting for me to take me to the function, so I agreed but not whole-heartedly.

It was a wonderful evening filled with much chat and banter. By contrast with the earlier evening experience at the church, it should not have been a success. Still, it was, and we finished off at the 'Millionaires Club' where attempts at Karaoke by some of our guys became hilarious. The Chinese hostesses tried in vain to help, but all attempts failed. My senses had not been dulled like the others, and I could only see the funny side of everything. We finally arrived back at the hotel at three am, and I was still sharp as a cricket, and not at all tired. Something profound had happened to me at that church gathering. I have since experienced similar tinglings in the head on other special occasions, but nothing like the entire five minute head to toe event.

When I first used the underground metro in Singapore, I was astonished at the cleanliness and the warnings that if you did not flush a public toilet, you were liable to be fined five hundred dollars. Littering was also a serious offence. However, I was shocked to see a racist sign on the train that said, 'No Durians Allowed.' I had visions of some poor tribe from the nearby jungles of Malaysia being prohibited from riding on trains. I enquired from our Singaporean friends, and they laughed, saying that a Durian was a highly offensive-smelling but highly nutritious and expensive fruit that was imported (like all other fruit and vegetables) from the mainland. It was not long before we had the opportunity by invitation from one of the engineering companies after hours to enjoy some special fruit. Our friends were grinning from ear to ear while offering slices of the fruit. Well, I can only describe the stench perhaps as belonging or being extracted from rotting runners socks! One could almost vomit at the smell. But the taste was good and I enjoyed it. I was not so sure about Tim Morton – one of our offshore engineers, but he did think that he should take a slice or two to Antoinette, his wife, back at the hotel. Incidentally, Durians were also banned at most hotels, including Tim's.

So, he wrapped it up carefully and took it back to Antoinette. I am quite sure she did not enjoy it, but it was within about an hour when the management came searching for the offensive fruit that had already permeated through the multi-storey building! It was rapidly disposed of – out of the building. Oddly enough, the fruit was considered a delicacy, and much sought after... and I guess to be eaten much in private!

Local fare can catch you unawares, and in Singapore, there were literally thousands of street vendors where under the most strict cleanliness conditions, one could buy many varieties of food from veggies, fish, different meats, all at a reasonable cost. In fact, it was apparent that many families with children dined out at night. A wide variety of curries could be bought at restaurants that specialised in traditional recipes and strengths. One evening we had ordered a curried shell-fish at a lovely location. The food was delicious, but a colleague was having great difficulty in eating an incredibly hot portion. I do not like overly hot curry, but mine was tolerable even though my lips felt like bicycle inner tubes they seemed to be so swollen. He, however, was taking strain biting through his portion and swallowing it. His eyes were streaming, and I think his lips and throat were also being seared! His expression was desperate, and upon examination, we found that he was trying to eat the sticks ginger sticks included for flavouring. I did break a molar, which required some dentistry because of a bag of mixed nuts that I bought as a snack. Some of the nuts, I feel, were better suited for engineering purposes and could have been made into ball-bearings!

18

Mana Pools, Chizarira and Other Bush Stories

Our trips to the bush continued whenever possible. We all have, I believe, 'in-built signals' when the seasons change. Mine emerged at the end of the rainy season and the onset of early winter when the weather was settled, the intense heat had passed, and the bush had 'paused' so to speak. I developed a deep yearning to be away into the bush at that time, and as a result, most of our trips coincided with that time.

Jean and I took a trip in our faithful 4x4 to Mana Pools and Chizarira National Park in Zimbabwe. It was a great experience being able to camp in the open with our dome tent, but quite intimidating at night with the sound of grass and vegetation being ripped out of the ground next to your ear. Something was pushing its way under the ground-sheet, so I bashed it with the base of my sheath knife, and it was silenced. Later Jean decided she needed to go outside for a pee. The walk to the long drop was too far and dangerous at night as it traversed thick reeds through a depression a few metres from the edge of the river. I would take guard with the torch while she drilled a quick hole in the sandy soil. All looked good until I spotted a bright eye in the torchlight. 'We have company,' I said, and while shining the torch to the left, announced to her that 'there are two of them.' Now I don't know if you have shone a torch close-up on an elephant's hide, but it is very difficult to see as the hide does not reflect much light. Anyhow, it was an elephant at very close quarters, and the eyes belonged to one elephant. I do not think it presented any threat, but the ablution was completed in double sharp time. Our camp setting was idyllic, and with the sun setting over the Zambian Hills, it was a sight to remember. We were a little on guard because we were quite isolated from anyone else, and at the time, poachers and thieves had been crossing the river from Zambia on a regular basis. Zimbabwean rangers had taken out some poachers a week or so before our arrival. They also told us that campers had been robbed of possessions while out and about.

I got a fright one day when Jean had gone to the 'long drop,' and there was a loud crash, and rushing out, had found that part of the river bank near the long-drop had plunged into the river. It could have been disastrous.

We collected our water from the river for washing and bathing, so we had to be extra cautious because of crocodiles.

A park requirement was that all old fire-ash had to be bagged and taken to the park camp office. This we did but reported that the previous campers had not done so. Loads, not removed by the previous campers were taken seriously, so the camp attendant looked up the booking record and declared that the previous campers would not be allowed back into Mana Pools. The same applied to folk that brought in oranges (which the elephants love). If the warning notices were ignored, and the fruit found, then the folk were there and then escorted out of the park. Anyhow, we also reported that we had heard an outboard motor very late at night, and they said that they would follow up with trackers to see if poachers had landed.

A long trek awaited us on the journey via Karoi to Chizarira along the extremely badly corrugated road. On this long journey, we only saw two vehicles, one of which had broken down in the middle of nowhere. It was a typical backpacker's vehicle all the way from Somerset West in Cape Town! We stopped and offered help, but they said that they would manage to get it fixed. The mostly stony track that led up to the summit of the Chizarira plateau was slow-going, and as a result, we arrived late and exhausted but were happily directed to our campsite. Well, if we thought Mana Pools was the penultimate in wild places, we were in for a surprise. The track to our campsite was completely overgrown, and the small site was surrounded by tall Buffalo grass and bush. We were there for five days, and the experience of the remoteness was something special. The thatched hut ablutions and wire cage to lock up kitchen goods seemed oddly out of place, but such a blessing.

We explored some of the tracks leading away from our site which was an adventure in itself. It was evident by the spoor on the sandy track close to the camp that lion were around however, we only heard a lion roar once one night. One morning we heard a loud rustling noise, but because of the dense, long grass we saw nothing; in fact, a herd of buffalo had just passed by. The scenery in the surrounding hills was staggering with Mt Tundazi standing proud towards the north of the park. Clear running streams, beautiful trees and despite the heat in the Zambezi valley, (aside from the late autumn weather) it was cooler up on the mountain plateau and frosty at night. We measured one degree Celsius one morning! Our sleeping bags were not altogether warm enough to be cosy enough.

Jean in natural fashion like most folk, especially woman, needed to have a last pee before retiring. It was downright hazardous to walk through the thick bush to the toilet which was positioned at the far side of the thatched hut, so we agreed that she go a few metres from the tent. She had no longer positioned herself for the call of nature and there was a singular deep penetrating roar of a lion! It was frightening, another hole was swiftly drilled in the sand and we decided there and then that we would sleep in the bakkie (we had not yet fitted our fold down bunks in the bakkie at that time). In the bakkie, it would be less cold, and safer.

The remarkable bastion – Mt Tundazi within Chizarira

'Wild' Bush camp – Chizarira.

Some rough tracks - Chizarira

Late one night, I heard a lone hyaena wail and then silence. In the morning we were surprised to see vultures descending into the long grass just behind the ablution. I figured there must have been a kill and ventured cautiously forward and climbed on to a small water tank structure to try and spot what was going on. The vultures were landing perhaps not more than twelve to fifteen metres away, just on the other side of a small stream. I was not prepared to take a chance, so retreated, and we drove to the ranger's office and asked if an armed ranger would come back with us to have a look at what the vultures were feasting on. Back at our camp, we all ventured forward keeping closely behind the ranger in front. We stepped over the small stream and pushed aside the long grass to reveal what remained of a waterbuck. There was the head still with horns, a spine with ribs, and the rest of the carcass was gone, pecked and eaten clean. It was obvious that a number of lion had been lying there. The ranger quietly asked us to retreat slowly away because the lions were still there! What was astonishing was that the lions were so quiet; I was not even alerted by the singular call of the hyaena. We may have become a little complacent thinking the place was safe but we were wise to be careful. With the dense bush and grass, it was by far one of the most intimidating places I have ever camped before. Just wandering around to feed the donkey boiler had me looking over my shoulder.

By arrangement, we went on a walk with two armed rangers over some kilometres and I had asked them if they knew of any caves where we might see some evidence of archaeological occupation. Again, we were more than happy to have the armed rangers with us because of the risks of traversing animal bush trails and the like. The surrounds were stunningly beautiful, and we also found some interesting Iron Age pecked stones, and pottery, these were photographed and left 'in situ'.

They took us to a shelter overlooking a lovely river that had not been occupied by early peoples, but had without doubt, and as confirmed by the rangers, been a hide-out for poachers and not that long ago! They told us that poachers would cross into Zimbabwe from Zambia, shoot elephant with tusks (and no doubt rhino as well), then cut the tusks into sections and put them into rucksacks and carry them away. They claimed quite openly that it was organised and with the knowledge of certain senior officials of the Department of National Parks! Chizarira used to be the location of the largest population of rhino in Rhodesia. We did not see any at that time but felt hopeful that there were still some there. We had seen a mature elephant limping across the track in front of us and on closer examination discovered (and photographed) that it had been snared around the lower leg above the foot and was severely injured. We reported it to the camp office, and it was followed-up the next day, and it sadly had to be shot.

A friend in Harare had asked us why we had booked to stay in Chizarira for five days! Well, it was the least amount of time one should spend there, to absorb the beauty of the place and just to relax. Certainly, the wildest place I have camped before, and in the time, we were there, we only saw one vehicle, and a couple had come to see what our camp looked like. They had come from overseas and they had hired a 4x4, and they had planned to proceed to Karoi, a great distance, and they only had half a tank of petrol left – how they got there I have no idea because there were no filling stations between where we were and their destination, but they were not fussed. They must have had to scrounge fuel from somewhere. Our tank was already showing empty, but we did have a spare 20-litre jerry can as back up to get us through to Binga

An unnerving experience we had some years later, on the banks of the Limpopo in Botswana. We had at that time sold our original bakkie in preference of a second hand 4x4 Isuzu double cab. The benefit was that it was a diesel engine, much more economical than the petrol engine of the Nissan Patrol and a much better torque for driving through sand.

We had camped close to the river in our summer weight tent which was a bit cool for the winter months; however, it was not long after we heard gunfire which I estimated was coming from the South African side of the river. It was just after this that we heard the trumpeting of elephant not too far off. They were obviously disturbed which was not a good sign for a peaceful night. Very soon after there was crashing of trees close to us, and I was sure that we might be in the path of the elephants. This went on for some time, then suddenly our vehicle alarm went off indicating that something had bumped it. We were now more than a bit unnerved. I shone our torch outside and spied an elephant not too far off, which I was presumed was browsing. More crashing of branches ensued, so I decided that with one thing and another that it would be wise to stay in the bakkie, so we grabbed our sleeping bags and with some trepidation climbed in and tried to settle down. The noise continued and around midnight, I checked outside with my torch and again spied an elephant not too far off. The elephants decided to call it a night at three a.m., so we climbed back into our tent, and so ended a fitful night. It was the gunfire that had unnerved me. Elephant are generally quite peaceful if you leave them alone but are quite sensitive to disturbance. We found this out when we had gone on the Lebombo 4x4 trail in the Kruger National park a year or so before when our group had at sunset passed through a herd of elephant quite close to our veld camp at a place called Shilowa. It was perhaps the best camp in the whole journey from the south to the north of the park at Pafuri. The herd of elephant were gathered not far from our camp and were feeding. It was most interesting to see how sensitive elephant are when we heard a light aircraft approaching and circling not far from our location, upon which, the elephant started trumpeting loudly. Perhaps expecting to be darted or culled, who knows, but they are very intelligent animals, and it is clear that they experience stress. They settled down after the aircraft departed from the area.

Some years later we went to the Khaudom National Park in Namibia with Roger Freshman (my son's father in law) and a friend of his. After stopping at Tsumkwe (where there was no fuel!), we continued onto our campsite at the Sikereti Camp. We were camped there for a few days, and the one morning we drove through to a pan that was not too far away. We followed the mostly single track through dense thickets, and on the way whilst driving quite sedately, we were charged by a huge elephant, we had to accelerate to avoid it catching us as it was charging alongside and parallel to us through the bush. We outpaced it and slowed down to our normal driving pace. Undeterred, it charged again, then again until we were far off. The pan was deserted of animals, there was a skull of an elephant there, and lots of droppings, on the way back to our camp, yet another, but different elephant charged us seemingly without reason. We outpaced it, and fortunately, in both cases, the elephants were alongside us and not in front, as it would have been impossible to reverse and turn around given the bush density. It could have been ugly. Thinking about it, we reasoned that a lot of poaching had been taking place in the reserve as it was not frequented much, and very isolated from the mainstream of tourists. Furthermore, there were various access tracks leading into the park without controls.

Also, at the Sikereti camp, we met the only other visitor and camper who stopped over with his assistant and his large dog. Chatting to the man, he told us that he was a regional vet who traversed the area widely and that his great grandmother was one of the original Dorsland trekkers who had crossed the Kalahari from South Africa to seek new beginnings away from the oppressive politics of the day. They had come in great numbers and had also died in great numbers. His great-grandmother was one of them who had died on the trek and was buried somewhere in that great wilderness. Quite a number of these early trekkers eventually reached Angola and settled and farmed there, some of the descendants are still to this day, resident in Angola, and some returned to South Africa when invited to do so years ago. We had stopped off to see the Dorsland Baobab tree which was a short way off the main track to Sikereti, where the trekkers had camped. It was astonishing to think that the vast distances that these folk travelled with little water or promise of grain and supplies to live off. Where the tree is situated, there is no visible water around that might have provided them with adequate supplies for themselves, or the few cattle they had left – really tough folk and true pioneers. I have no doubt that they did have contact with the local Bushmen, who must have helped them to locate water. The tree had huge limbs growing out of the primary base of the tree with carved names of the various party members. Some were beautifully carved in copperplate writing, complete with dates.

Anyhow, after we had all settled down in the somewhat run-down camp, and fortunately we had our own tents, it was quite late, and under a full and very bright moon, all was silent in the camp and I crossed an open area to the ablutions to have a pee and brush my teeth. On emerging, I was halted in my tracks by sight of what looked like a lioness in the moonlight crossing the open ground between me and our tent. The eyes glowed back at me from my headlamp and still unnerved, was somewhat relieved to see that it was a very large hyaena. It just stood there and stared at me; it was huge. In an automatic defence mode, I shouted at it to voetsek (basically an Afrikaans term to bugger-off), loudly. Happily, it obliged and sauntered across the open area in a typical loping manner and entered into the surrounding bush. It did not make the slightest sound. I was more than a little shaken, but that was not the end of it. During the early hours of the morning there was a commotion coming from the spot where the vet had camped, they just slept in the back of the open Toyota bakkie), and his large dog started barking. In the morning I questioned him about what had happened, and he said that 'the largest hyaena he had ever seen', had happened upon them, and his dog 'that was afraid of nothing' had hidden underneath the bakkie, and would not come out. It was quite amusing when he recounted this, as his dog was already on the back of the bakkie ready to depart! He pointed at the dog, revealing its name and how cowardly it had acted – as if the dog fully understood. It bared it's teeth and wobbled it's head back and forth in clear embarrassment, and we all had a good laugh at its expense. However, in the light of day, we can all be brave, but in the still and dark of night, the arena belongs to predators alike.

My brother Bob had a bad encounter with a hyaena late one night when he was in the Rhodesian army. He was based at a camp near Kariba, and was on watch, he told me that it was a pitch dark night, and he was fully armed with his 9mm Parabellum and FN 7,62mm rifle. When you have spent any time, and certainly as much as he had, in the bush, that your senses are heightened, especially your hearing. He was suddenly attacked from behind and had no time to use his weapon to defend himself. He had not heard a thing, and quickly realised that it was an animal, and probably a hyaena, and commenced fighting it off. It bit into his head and as he fought it off, it bit his hand, while as he said, he thinks that he almost tore its ear off before it gave up the attack. It had torn parts of his scalp and bitten through his hand. His cries for assistance were heard by the other troopies who rushed to his aid, and by early morning he had been casevaced to Salisbury by chopper, and my mother had been advised of his condition and necessary corrective surgery by the same morning – such was the efficiency of the Rhodesian army. The follow-up treatment was not pleasant given the danger of rabies. He fully recovered and was soon back in the bush but was extremely lucky it had not fastened on to his neck. The area of the camp was considered Tagati (supernatural/evil) and feared by the African troopies because of the hyaena population that lurked there at night. It is no wonder there is superstition surrounding hyaena as the silent killers in the dead of night! Their weird chuckling, giggling and eerie whooping is enough to unnerve anyone, and one could imagine them as witches gathered around a boiling witches brew, awaiting the next victim! In African folklore, it is said that evil humans can transform into a hyaena and prey upon those they wish to terrorise – usually in the dead of night...

Whilst on the subject of the Zambezi valley and animals, Bob told me of an amusing and not so amusing account that happened to one of his African troopies while on patrol. There is a lot of wildlife in the valley, particularly elephant. They were patrolling through dense 'Jessie' bush which is quite impossible to penetrate without cutting a physical path, and as a consequence, were following existing elephant trails. One of the unfortunate troopies came across an advancing elephant. The elephant charged him, and there being no escape either side of the path, barged into the poor fellow, bulldozing him for ten metres. By some miracle the tusks penetrated into the path either side of his body but left him badly pummelled so to speak, almost lifeless. The elephant now satisfied, left him for dead. Luckily he was recovered still alive, and placed into the back of an army Landrover to be rushed up to Kariba Heights (on the escarpment), for medical help. However, on the way, and in the rush the security troopie riding 'shotgun' on the back fell off the back of the Landrover after going over some bumps, without anyone noticing. The elephant victim was duly delivered to the medical centre, and upon examination was found to be badly battered, but amazingly with no broken bones. However, on finding the security troopie missing, they returned the way they had come and found the chap still lying in the road where he had fallen. He had sustained more serious injuries than the elephant victim.

19

Vic Falls, Binga, Special Characters – Peta and Paul

In July of 1996, we set off again for a round trip which also took us to the Vic Falls and beyond. We had arranged to meet up with Dr Peta Jones who was a qualified archaeologist and lived at Binga which is definitely off the beaten tourist track, but we were going to combine it with a stay at the Lokathula lodge which we had time-swapped with another resort in South Africa. This was luxury for us and since there was space, Quintin and his friend Kevin also met us there, driving in his faithful Datsun 1400 bakkie. Whilst in Vic Falls, we revisited various attractions which was very relaxing and for a change, we were like normal tourists. We had also arranged to meet one of Bob's old friends from the army Paul Connolly and his wife Marie, who lived at Vic Falls.

The unit we stayed in did not have complete closures for the front but roll down blinds, which when open gave a superb elevated view of the bush and national park beyond. The upper room had a thatched opening, and likewise, no window. Vervet monkeys and no doubt baboons could be a problem at times, but it was amusing when we returned one day after being out, to see that Quintin's special imported bag of 'pure' coffee sweets made in Germany had been raided by a monkey. There was a neat pile of wrappers, and we recovered only one sweet that had not been opened. Quintin was annoyed because they were the real deal and powerful which sort of gave you an energy boost. We guessed that the monkey would have been wide-eyed for days! What was amusing was that the monkey must have suddenly seen his reflection in a long mirror in the room, and clearly, there was the little handprint where it must have paused to check out the intruder before setting off in its heightened state. Forensics would have proved him guilty!

Speaking to one of the camp attendants one evening, we got onto the matter of malaria, which was at the time, a problem. In a serious tone in the gloom of darkness, he said, 'you see, the problem is that they are Zambian mosquitos'!

'How do you know they are Zambian; do they have markings on their wings?' I said. 'No sir, we know they are Zambian because we spray our open ponds of water, and they do not'. The seriousness of the matter was broken, and we all had a good laugh, especially visualising the squadrons of mosquitos flying across the falls in the moonlight to attack unwary Zimbabweans and visitors alike. This same chap in a very serious tone told us how he had to spend many hours in the security of a baboon proof rubbish cage when patrolling one night because a pride of lion walked into the camp, and his only safety was to stay in the baboon cage until they eventually left.

I was just having a shower one evening when Jean shouted out that there was an elephant at the back door, so I quickly put on trousers and rushed to the back to have a look and lo and behold, there was a large elephant 'at' and less than a metre from the back door. It was browsing on a tree and politely and quite tamely moved off slightly where I managed to get a picture of it.

A special breakfast treat by Paul and Marie Connolly on the Zambezi.
L to R: Kevin, Paul, Quintin, Jean and Paul Connolly
(Photo: Marie Connolly*)

When we met Paul Connolly and his wife Marie, they treated us all to a wonderful breakfast on the banks of the Zambezi, as well as a short canoe trip in the nearby waters, what a special event it was for us, for which we were very grateful. Paul, a lawyer by profession, was a champion canoeist and was one of two canoeists from Africa that had qualified for the Olympics. He was the Zimbabwean qualifier and the other was an Egyptian. Believe it or not, the Zimbabwean government told him he could not go because they had too many official delegates attending, and they could not include him...

Paul, along with his other various interests, ran wild canoe safaris up the Zambezi river and was I believe, the founder of Zimbabwe's commercial white-water rafting back in 1985. Having experienced this white-water rafting myself, under 'controlled' and 'white knuckle' conditions in 1996, I have a huge respect for those brave folk that ventured years back into the unknown rapids of the Zambezi below the falls to master and conquer those fearsome maelstroms of roaring and tumbling waters. Paul was also the first person to canoe a 350-km stretch of the Luapula River between the DRC and Zambia alone! He vowed he would never repeat it as it was *'a sinister place'*

He told us that one day on the bank of the Zambezi River he observed an unusual behaviour by a troop of baboons against one of the troop. Apparently, one of the troop was chased out into the river where it positioned itself on some rocks. Over some hours, it attempted to return to the bank of the river, but the troop would not allow it, and kept attacking it. He was unaware of what the baboon had done, but no doubt it was a serious deviation from baboon standards. Wet and exhausted, it eventually became desperate and ventured again to the bank of the river, where the dominant baboons of the troop finally attacked it and I believed killed it. Was it a stranger trying to join the troop and was ostracised or some other strange behaviour, we may never know?

Paul Connolly came into the news in October of 1998: Only two weeks after his perilous solo canoe trip down the Luapula River, he had a serious encounter with a leopard at his house in Victoria Falls. An extract from a Cape Town newspaper report that I read describes the account as follows:

He did not expect that his most dangerous adventure would be in his home. 'You come out of your kitchen on a nice sunny morning and you walk into a leopard'.

A domestic worker was hanging up the washing when a leopard jumped over the wall. The woman screamed and fled, pursued by the leopard. Connolly's Jack Russell ran in front of the leopard, distracting it. The dog escaped by jumping into the house through a window. Connolly, hearing the shouting, went to investigate. 'I ran out and saw the leopard trying to get into the house,' he said. He instinctively applied a lifetime of lessons learnt in the Zimbabwean bush – if a leopard or a lion threatens you, charge at it, make a noise and it will back off. 'I ran up to within a few metres of it, yelling at it, but it turned and leapt at me.' The leopard seized Connolly's right arm in its jaws. Connolly punched at its head with his free hand. When this had no effect, he began to throttle it. They fell to the ground and Connolly saw the cat's back feet thrashing at him.

'My shirt was being shredded. It was trying to disembowel me,' he said.

He broke free and reached the kitchen, slamming the door behind him.

'Then the most incredible thing happened. It launched itself through the big pane of glass in the kitchen window.'

Connolly punched the leopard with all his might, breaking its momentum and stopping it in the kitchen sink as it slashed at him with its front claws. His resistance made the animal flee back out of the window.

Connolly staggered into the bathroom to bathe his bleeding arms and hands. Minutes later he heard the crash of a 12-bore shotgun. His neighbour Fanie Pretorius, a big game hunter, had heard the uproar and come running. He killed the leopard with two shots to the chest.

Connolly had deep punctures and scratches on both arms and a snapped tendon in his left wrist. He had a small scratch on his chest. 'I got off amazingly lightly'

The leopard's paws are being stuffed, one for each of Connolly's daughters.

Paul has been charged three times by elephants, twice by buffalo and twice by lions. On the Zambezi, he has been rammed by hippos and crocodile.

His wife Marie said – 'Animals must like him'

There is no doubt that Paul's fitness and strength, experience and courage gave him a fighting chance!

(Marie sadly, has since passed away)

Dr Peta Jones is a remarkable woman. Although she has a doctorate in archaeology, she has devoted much of her life to the study and benefits of donkey power. There is perhaps a huge amount of information that has missed the technological headlines about donkeys that have been quietly serving man for hundreds if not thousands of years. Zimbabwe has been no exception, and we tend to zoom past donkey carts, without realising how valuable they are for carting both goods and people. Single, double, triple and even four spans are often seen on or alongside the road trotting 'inexorably' towards their destinations.

We did not learn much about archaeology, but much about her current projects. The route to her abode was along a deep sandy track out of Binga but parallel to the lake. Kevin and Quintin battled along in their 1400 bakkie, eventually getting stuck in the sand. We assisted with towing them out to find that their gearbox transmission had filled with sand, only allowing first and reverse gear to be engaged! As a result, we arrived just before dark. We could not find her house without enquiring, as it was not obvious, but set back within long grass and bush. When Peta appeared, we were shocked to see that she was almost black from head to toe and was wearing a woven conical hat which was remarkably similar to the one worn by Gandalf from the classic film – 'Lord of the Rings'. She had we found out, been creosoting poles for a new hut. Kevin was already unnerved by her appearance and began to question my interest in coming there in the

Dr Peta Jones with Paul, Quintin, Kevin and Jean,
in her humble dwelling in the bush near Binga.
L to R: Paul, Peta ,Quintin, Kevin and Jean

first place. He did not allude to a 'broom', but we sensed his concerned observation. We set up camp next to a Tilapia farm and went to her 'house'. The house was in fact a large roomed open-plan thatched mud hut. There was a low wall which was open below the eves, with no windows, no door, but a small gate which she said was to keep out chickens. Believe it or not, she had already lived in the simple mud dwelling for eight years! A remarkable existence indeed. Spiders abounded, and apparently, the white ants (termites) had already eaten some of her books and references. I doubt it ever got cold there, so the open-plan must have been necessary. She was not afraid of the bush and used to walk some distance to her lands, and other raised thatched huts where backpackers from overseas could stay overnight. She showed us around her permaculture garden which was not in good shape, and some of the young donkeys which were quite appealing in appearance. If she ever travelled to Bulawayo or even to Louis Trichardt where her mother stayed, she would catch a local bus, with all the chickens and accoutrements that are normally found on the long-distance buses. The only book I have seen on the whole background, nature and uses of donkeys, was produced by her. It was a practical and definitive textbook on donkeys.

Despite her tolerance for the discomfort and inconveniences she endured, she eventually had to leave Binga due to political pressures. She was in many ways a woman trying very hard to make things work for the betterment of local folk in a somewhat hostile environment.

It was a strange coincidence that we found that she was connected and related to our friends at the Sentinel Ranch on the Limpopo whom we had met years before. When she left, she took her remaining donkeys which she loved dearly, and walked from Binga Kariba to the Limpopo River, a distance of over 600 kilometres. And thence across the river and on to Louis Trichardt (now Makhado), where she continued her good work. Some tough lady! She now has a small place near Mopani south of Messina. The donkey-cart is a model that does not change with the times and whims of continual upgrades, such as modern four-wheeled cars that have to change to please the public and be *'in vogue'*. I firmly believe that the donkey-cart will always have a place in the basic ways of life, but more remarkably, the nature of these amazing animals that pull them.

After leaving Peta and having the sand cleaned out of the gearbox transmission, kindly helped by Enzo Rossi, the owner of the Tilapia farm, we travelled on towards Siabuwa and Gokwe. But en route, we had to stop and wait for Kevin and Quintin to catch up to us, so we pulled over to the side of the road and got out of the bakkie to stretch our legs. It was not long before an African appeared from the bush across the road and called out 'Is your car buggered', 'no it is not buggered' we replied, 'we are waiting for someone'. So, he crossed over, and by then followed by a number of piccanins, announced that he was Zebedayo Mutale, the elder at the local church. We thought his description of a broken down vehicle quite amusing, but nonetheless very descriptive. I have heard the sincere expression in the bush of a pump being 'fuk-ed', so I guess the church elder was being quite polite. The children were delighted when we gave them some lollies we had brought from Cape Town. We had earlier also handed out pencils, erasers and exercise books to local children we had seen along the way near the Mucheni School. There were absolutely no nearby shops or garages, so I am sure they found these few items quite helpful. Proceeding on, we stopped on the road to Gokwe to admire the view of Mt Tundazi in the distance to the west and the amazing surrounding country but... the Mopani flies were really bad as they kept trying to access the eyes, nose and mouth if they had the chance, so we just had to continue. Additionally, it was terribly hot and so dry that any moisture was a bonus to them. At sunset, we camped next to the road in a well treed and forested area beyond Gokwe on the edge of the Mafungabusi Plateau. One vehicle passed us in the night.

20

Kruger National Park Hikes, Maguga Farm and Knolfontein Rescue

Apart from the periodic visits to the Kruger National Park, Jean and I were also fortunate to enjoy a couple of the renowned hikes inside the park. It was a real joy to be able to walk freely without being stuck in a vehicle for hours on end. Of course, it is necessary to have a guide that knows the terrain and habits of the wildlife, as well as being armed in case of need.

The Bushman Trail in the south-west of the park was most attractive, and we shared the experience with a few friends from Cape Town. Being on foot and seeing all the signs on the ground, in the veld, and the fresh early morning scent on the air, reminded one of the amounts of information wandering animals must pick up from such signs. We are only able to register a small percentage of what they do. The same applies to hearing. As much as one becomes attuned after some time to the sounds of the bush, it is still a fraction of what animals can hear. Nonetheless, early man and hunter-gatherers must have become acutely aware of the daily signs of the wild. The vegetation, trees, insects, spoor, scats, hills and granite koppies, weather and seasons all form a part of nature's picture. Walking and hiking grants a sample of what is available to you which would otherwise generally be lost when self-driving in the park.

On that trail, we were able with the specific knowledge of the ranger guide and his assistant to view some early Bushmen rock art. At a sunset location at the end of a day, we had the privilege to witness a lone wild dog pursuing an impala. We were at some height so had a ringside seat so to speak. We watched the pursuit across the running river and into the reeded bed and beyond. We could not visually see the kill but it was clearly audible. The wild dog returned across the river, running into the distance yelping for the pack to join him in his prize catch. Indeed a special sight to behold.

Silent as we all were, I am sure we would all share the realisation of the experience that it was something that you could just not buy. Seeing a white rhino at close quarters including a tiny week old or so rhino calf, trotting unsteadily in front of its mother was also special, and particularly now where the greed for poaching horn from the far east has decimated these poor creatures. Of course, elephant and lion throughout Africa are also victims of unscrupulous poaching.

The Oliphant's Trail, which was situated next to the Oliphant's River in the centre of the park lengthways and against the eastern boundary, was also a great experience. Apart from the pod of curious hippo watching us as we went by and numerous crocodiles, we also came across a mature dead lion in a hollow next to the river. It appeared to have been deceased for quite some time and had not been scavenged either, which was a puzzle even for the guide. On close inspection, a hind leg was clearly broken. Perhaps an encounter with a hippo had caused the serious injury. We also had the opportunity to track hyaena for kilometres through the bush, and they were not too fussed at being followed, but I was surprised at what distance they cover when seemingly strolling along. We abandoned tracking a lion after hearing its low-pitched call resonating from the bush.

It was interesting to note how unobservant some folk are to route finding, recognising landmarks, basic compass points and their general whereabouts on returning to our vehicle. One afternoon we had gone reasonably far and at sundown we were alerted to a large, lone elephant with ears wide-spread intent on approaching us. We retreated into a river bed while the ranger-guide and his assistant tried to hold it off. It continued to approach us, perhaps through sheer curiosity. We backtracked behind a rock outcrop, repositioning when it came ever closer. Our guides shouted and even threw some rocks in its direction. Upon seeing us more closely it turned and loped off. Relieved, we tentatively followed in its wake as dark descended. Not far on, we then walked into a group of grazing buffalo! They were not the least concerned with us as we edged through finally reaching the vehicle in virtual darkness.

'I had a farm in Africa' is not an uncommon statement, particularly in Zimbabwe let alone Karen Blixen in Kenya, but 'True's Bob', we had a farm or rather a piece of land in Zimbabwe. In the early seventies, although we lived and were settled in Johannesburg, we (or rather selfishly I), had tentatively thought of returning to Rhodesia, and my preference would have been Bulawayo. My parents still lived there, and we thought that the situation in Rhodesia would improve and it would be a good place for the kids to grow up in.

I had purchased a coastal plot unseen near Hermanus when I was in Bulawayo. However, the Johannesburg based company that had sold me the property, went insolvent. Since I worked in Johannesburg at the time, I went into the office, where for years I had paid in monthly for the plot, and spoke to a lawyer, virtually pleading with him to make a plan. He told me that if I could pay the outstanding amount which amounted to about two hundred and fifty pounds, he would make a plan to transfer the plot.

The only asset I had was tied up in a policy, which I arranged to cash in. This I managed, through much persuasion and pressure. I was able to save my investment, and ultimately received the title deeds. I was fortunate to be able to do this, whereas my dear father who had purchased a piece of land at Gaansbaai from the same company, was not able to do so and lost everything he had paid in. In truth, the company was up to downright crookery. They must have taken a lot of unsuspecting folk for a ride.

Since the thought of returning to Rhodesia was attractive to me, I advertised in the Farmers Weekly, that I was looking to swop a piece of ground at the coast for some land in Rhodesia, particularly in the bush. I was very interested in the eastern districts around Melsetter, or around Bulawayo. I was quite surprised to find that several offers were sent to me, so I finally accepted some ground, 750 acres in fact, just off the Heany Bushtick mine road. It was not particularly good farming land as it was classified as 'forest' sandveld, but it did have some granite outcrops, scattered trees on rolling grasslands. There was also a small stream with fish that meandered down towards the south. I was delighted because it was some good open space, and undeveloped. It did have a railway siding called Maguga, of which the farm was named. The big snag was how was I going to do the transaction?

Working through a conveyancer in Bulawayo, it would have been easy enough, but the fact that no money was passing hands was a puzzle because the ownership was passing from one country to another, and Pretoria found it strange that no money was involved. I doubt whether such transactions were common, in fact far from it, but I made it clear about the written agreement back in Johannesburg. Aside from some transfer and conveyancer fees, the deal was done. My visit to Bulawayo and to the land has already been briefly alluded to, but when I had walked many miles across the veld, I was more than pleased with the decision. It was stunning, and even had sugar bush trees on it, similar to those found on the highveld areas of Transvaal. I met the adjoining neighbour and some Africans who knew the area well. The views were also a delight to behold as one could see far south to the edge of the Matopos range. I had approached the Department of Agriculture in Bulawayo, and they told me because the land was not that suitable for farming, should not carry more than sixty head of cattle.

Work took over as priority in South Africa, and I had not made any plans to develop the land at that stage. However, in the meanwhile,

Paul at the lovely stream on Maguga farm

Robert Mugabe had won the elections (by fair means and foul) and was elected the President of the new Zimbabwe. I had not heard his statement myself, but my father who was still living in Bulawayo warned me that Mugabe had stated that he would take over the land. It was early days and I naively believed that it would not happen because there was some hope after the change that all could benefit from the new situation. I was terribly wrong! My father again warned me that I would lose the piece of land, so unhappily, I decided to sell, but not without realising that a move back to the now Zimbabwe was no longer a wise option. It was too risky for my young family. Mugabe's threats, the palpable uncertainty of a communistic philosophy, hollow 'liberation and freedom' being thrust upon the people, was enough reason.

An African gentleman was keen to buy the land, and we agreed on a price – yes, wait for it, fifteen Zimbabwean dollars per acre. I asked him what he intended to do with the land, and he said that he was going to run ninety head of cattle on it, so I informed him about the recommendation by the Department of Agriculture that sixty head should be the maximum for the sustainability of grazing. He said 'I am not interested in that, I am a businessman, and I will be running ninety head of cattle on it' what could I say to such superior knowledge!

My father was 100% correct in his intuition and wisdom. Mugabe also imposed minimum wages for all workers which was not a bad thing except that there was no measure of how economical a farm or business was, or whether it could afford it or not.

My farming neighbour did pay the minimum wage, though he could not afford it, so he had to pay up. He then set up a small farm store so that his workers could buy their own provisions, like maize meal. This normally would have been included in their wage package prior to the imposition of minimum wage policies. It caused some unhappiness, but he had no option.

A United Nations representative from Denmark came to see me before I had sold the property about reaping the long grass which was quite abundant. He said it was for building extra kraals. I agreed that it could be done for twenty cents a bundle (a large bundle). He told me in his broken accent that I should understand that the rebuilding of the country and that I should be doing it for free. I politely refused, and I guess he went elsewhere, but shortly afterwards probably a week or two, my neighbours and my land were set alight which was quite devastating. Shortly after the transfer of the land went through, Mugabe announced a block on all foreign funds, so I could not even draw the paltry amount out of the country. However, Jean and I did enjoy a few holidays up into the bush and could draw some of the money to pay for park fees. I have no idea what became of the next owner or the state and condition of the land, but I put it behind me.

Interestingly, I subsequently discovered that the land had probably belonged to Colonel William Napier. His primary farm to the West of Maguga was called Duncal. The remainder land at Maguga was called Napiers and Napiers Surplus. Col. Napier who was born in Scotland in 1861. He'd had an outstanding military record including his service with the Victoria Rangers in 1892 where he was chosen by Dr Jameson, with five others, to lead and command the Victoria Column of 397 men, 397 horses, and a contingent of Cape Boys. He was second in command to Major Alan Wilson under Major Forbes in the infamous Shangani Patrol in 1893. He was also involved with Colonel Spreckley in the futile invasion of the Transvaal in March 1894. On the 11th May 1896, he was with the large force that set out again to the Shangani to meet up with the Relief Force from Salisbury. So, what does this have to do with Maguga farm? Well it is of interest to have noted that he died in Lakeside, Cape Town in 1920, and not much unlike Cecil Rhodes (who died in Muizenberg and was carried back to Rhodesia and buried in the spiritual site of Malindidzimu in the Matopos), was taken back to his farm Duncal for burial. His gravesite is a declared historical site and lies around seven kilometres from Maguga in what is *quite remote within the now Tribal Trust Land (TTL) of Esiphezini in the Mzingwane Trust Land.*

It is also of historical interest that Captain Frederick Courtney Selous (of famous hunting expeditions, exploration, mammalian, bird egg, and insect collections), was a renowned scout for the Pioneer Column. This included numerous military exploits during the rebellions of 1893 and 1896 around Bulawayo. He also served with The 25th Royal Fusiliers in the first world war in East Africa where he was shot dead by a German sniper on the 4th January 1917. He was buried close to where he died, at Chokawali on the Rufigi river in Tanzania – The Selous Game Reserve is named after him.

He and his wife managed a farm nine kilometres east of Maguga next to the Ncema river (also called Ingnaima by F.C. Selous), and I imagine he may have returned there had he not died. It is fascinating to think that both Napier and Rhodes wished to be buried thousands of kilometres away from where they last lived...back to the country they loved and what was so special. Perhaps Selous may have liked to return to the then Rhodesia to be laid to rest. With lives filled with adventure, major historical events and even grand wealth (like Rhodes), to be buried far away from all glamour and celebrated popular places of prominence, to lonely graves close to the earth, is maybe not so puzzling after all...

"The Spirit of Nature' is strong"

Roger, my son Quintin's father in law, who'd had an extremely successful farm in Matepatepa not too far from Bindura, was not so fortunate. He had bought the farm soon after the bush war, received his papers from the Mugabe government that he could own and farm it, only years later to be kicked off. He had over a hundred employees on the multi-crop and computer-controlled hydroponic flower producing farm. When we were there, they were a very happy team (I have it on film), but that all changed, when he was issued with papers, and he had to leave and was refused to re-enter the farm to collect any of his assets. His son, though threatened, and under much duress, managed to collect some gear. They were forced to pay out two severance packages over about a three month period. He and his wife after much inconvenience now live in KwaZulu-Natal. They were of course not alone, as all of the neighbouring farmers were given notice to leave their farms. They were I suppose quite fortunate that their house was not set alight, dogs beaten to death, abusive neglect of horses and cattle, all under the approval of Mugabe. Hatred and 'clean hands' cruelty must have run deep in his veins. He was still seen as a hero, and nothing is ever said about his racism or committed brutalities, atrocities and massacres of at least 20,000 Zimbabwean civilians by the North Korea trained 5th Brigade. But, perhaps he should receive the highest award for gross mismanagement of a country. A country which, all he had to do, was oil the wheels from time to time...

In 1999, I met Andy Rice, who had the idea of purchasing a farm in the Kouebokkeveld. His idea was that individually, most people could not afford to outlay the capital and manage the running costs, so if a number of interested folk got together, and had shares they could afford, then it would be possible.

Our meeting was very fruitful, and it was agreed that I would draw up the Mission statement, Environmental Management Plan and Guidelines, and receive one of the shares for my efforts. Andy had found a suitable farm which was principally undeveloped in the Swartruggens range in the Kouebokkeveld, and then the process of advertising for shareholders began. Over six hundred applicants were received and screened and taken out to the proposed property. It was surprising to find that so many folk wanted all the bells and whistles provided for the sum of R26, 000 per share. The final selection of folk had to be completely committed to conservation and protection of the environment. Time was running out for the full amount to be paid over, and twice we nearly lost the purchase. A few of us were really stretched and had to source extra money from our existing bonds to make up the balance. Finally, all was sorted out and the balance of the purchase price over the deposit was settled. Work began in cleaning up the remnants of the earlier farming attempts with domestic stock and crops. The total area was 2,400 hectare of marginal and unique veld at an altitude of over 1000 metres. It had amazing sandstone rock formations, healthy plant life, and seasonal water.

During the first year, I had met with Nik Wullschleger of Klein Cedarberg (also known as Lord's Acre), and we drafted up a Swartruggens Conservancy Management Plan and Constitution. This was well received with the many surrounding farmers and owners of wilderness terrain, much covering rocky and even mountainous areas. In all, we had twenty-six members, and we all agreed that our logo would be the quite rare *Vexatorella amoena* on our signage. The flowers of the plant are both attractive and have a delicate and pleasant fragrance. Many years of happy exploring and enjoyment has been experienced by the shareholders and their families, just being out in the environment is uplifting and exhilarating. The area weather could vary from extreme heat of over

35 degrees Celsius to heavy snowfalls and temperatures well below zero in winter.

As Jean and I have a deep interest in archaeology, we were delighted to know that there were rock shelters with both Bushmen and 'Colonial' type paintings, all of which are of great value and interest to visitors and institutions such as the University of Cape Town. Over the years the veld has revealed and yielded surprises. We decided a couple of years ago to purchase a 'camera trap' which would be placed at various strategic positions where we might expect to see some nocturnal animals. Up to that time, we had only seen the occasional baboon, jackal, rhebok, hares, tortoises and various birds, and a fair number of snakes. After ten years of general observations we were treated to our first pictures from our camera trap, activated both mainly at night, and sometimes in the day of rare animals such as aardwolf, aardvark, African wild cat, additionally others such as porcupine, jackal, steenbok, duiker, hares, rhebok, baboons, koorhaan. What was amusing was to find the curious baboon looking directly into the lens of the camera, in a most suspicious manner. Additionally, we saw the stray donkey and one of the caretaker's dogs out and about after one a.m. in the morning, no doubt hunting! We knew there were leopards in the surrounding mountains, as they had been seen by other landowners, and we had also seen the remains of buck that had no doubt fallen prey to the leopard. During 2013, a young donkey foal was taken from next to our farmhouse and dragged away. A follow up by Danie, our resident caretaker revealed no remains, so perhaps it may have been taken some distance to feed cubs. They are really quite elusive cats.

The area experience extremes in weather. We have had drought periods where our faithful spring next to the farmhouse has dried up. Torrential downpours of six inches of rain in one hour which washed away our seasonal dam close to the farmhouse. The dam typically filled up with winter rains but being sandveld, it would permeate through the sand, sandstone and drain away. During the drought period, we had to put down a borehole at great expense, which has been an enormous success. We had always been very careful about usage of water and found that the borehole level has in fact increased appreciably over the last couple of years. But we have had good rains since the drought. All watering of plants and trees is solar-driven from a small pump in the spring, and all water from our borehole is from a solar-driven submersible pump. We do use gas for cooking and only use solar-heated water for showers and washing. There is a backup gas water heater, however, the cost of gas has made it prohibitive to use. Bathing in winter is, therefore, a very brief affair with definitely no waiting required!

Blizzard conditions at Knolfontein farm, Swartruggens – 1ˢᵗ September 2008

Heavy snow conditions at Knolfontein farm, Swartruggens – 1ˢᵗ September 2008

Jean and I went out to the farm a couple of days before spring day, which was the 1st of September 2008. There was a strong north-westerly wind bringing in a cold front, and we were just ahead of it with light rain all the way to the farm. We had just about unpacked when the front hit us en-force.

By nightfall, the wind had increased dramatically, and it became increasingly colder with light snow. We were well equipped, and of course, being inside the farmhouse we were sheltered, but it did not stop the creeping intensity of the cold. Later that night, blizzard conditions prevailed with much heavier snow. The wind was probably over one hundred kilometres per hour, continuing throughout the night and into the rest of the following day. That morning I stepped outside to take some photos and video footage. Despite being clad in a down-duvet jacket and gloves, the wind chill factor was so severe, that it was impossible to stay out in the full blast for more than a few minutes without taking shelter. We were housebound most of the day while watching the snow blast up against the windows. Equally too, against the farmhouse front door. Snow drifts built up, but due to the high wind factor, most of the snow, which was blowing practically horizontally, blew away down into the Tankwa Karoo, where it would no doubt fall as icy rain. Had this not happened, we would have experienced deep snow. Snow on the Swartruggens Mountains is not unusual, and light falls are experienced almost annually, especially at the higher altitudes, but this was the heaviest and worst snowfall and blizzard in over fifty years according to the weather statistics, and we were in the middle of it!

The first of September is considered to be the onset of spring, in fact, we had a large picture of the flowers taken on the first of September a few years before, and it was hung in the lounge of the farmhouse. On Monday morning on the first of September 2008, the storm had passed, and all was quiet, and there laid a fairyland of snow around us. I quickly dressed, ventured outside and stomped around taking photos in the morning light. It was impressive. I had agreed to climb up the sandstone outcrop located behind the caretaker's cottage and take an elevated photo of the farm. It would be an unbelievable contrast to that taken a while back on the same spring day. All went well, and because of the wind, there were only sparse patches of snow on the outcrop. Skye our border collie was with me, and after taking the pictures, our dog bounded down, and I followed suit, by stepping onto a ledge below me. It all happened in a flash, as my foot slid away (as if it had been pulled) on what I could only surmise was 'black ice' or what in Europe is called 'Verglas' – a thin layer of very hard ice. Anyhow, for the first time in my climbing career, I had a serious fall and went over the edge and after hitting a rock protrusion landed on a slab of

The rescue helicopter – Knolfontein farm, Swartruggens – 1ˢᵗ September 2008
Photo credit: Jean Gray

rock, then bounced into the snow. It was not more than about four and a half to five metres vertical drop, but I had landed hard, and was most unfortunate not to land in snow. I cried out more in shock than pain and just knew instinctively that I had broken bones. It all seemed to be on the left-hand side of my body. My left arm was hanging across my chest and my shoulder was not in position. I knew too, that my leg was in trouble as I could barely move it without pain. The farm caretaker Danie had heard the thump and had come running out. He quickly called Jean who arrived to find me lying there and assisted by feeding me some coffee and pain tablets. Danie managed to slip some polystyrene sheets under me to ward off any cold from the snow. I was not cold because I was very well covered. Jean was relieved to see that I was not covered in blood because from a distance, my 'blood red' duvet jacket looked like I might be.

I was as comfortable as I could be but trying to move was painful. I propped my arm up at the shoulder with my hiking stick, while Jean tried in vain to raise communications by cell phone. Eventually Danie walked a long distance through the snow to the neighbouring farm Groenfontein, owned by our friend Volker Miros to raise help. Apparently, the phone landline was down because of the storm, so their foreman Jan bravely drove the long distance and down the hazardous Katbakkies Pass to Op Die Berg to get help. Jean had given the full details of my condition and exact location in a written note to Danie to give to the police and had also noted that I could not be transported by ambulance to Ceres because of my suspected injuries. It was not too long before the matter was reported back to Cape Town.

At the same time, there had been a rescue call out to the Matroosberg Mountains to look for some chaps who were missing but were eventually safely located. The same helicopter was alerted to my location and arrived with a paramedic at the same time as the local police arrived... The paramedic examined me and said they could take me through to Ceres, but I declined knowing that I should rather be airlifted straight through to Cape Town. The paramedic reasoned, saying that the helicopter's engine battery had already been jump-started in the Matroosberg and it was a risk to fly further than Ceres. Additionally they did not have enough fuel to fly to Cape Town! I do not know who arranged it, but instead of the normal Mountain Rescue which was organised through the Ysterplaat base with 22 Squadron, an AMS helicopter was then dispatched to come out for me. That was fine except that they could not find the farm, and the team of folk already at the farm including myself, heard the helicopter fly past in reasonably clear and stable weather, towards Calvinia! An hour or so later it returned, and eventually located our position. I was uplifted and thankfully taken directly through to the Constantiaberg Clinic in Cape Town which was not far from our house. The accident (because of my doing), occurred at about 08h30 in the morning, and I was uplifted at 15h30 pm, rather a long wait while lying on the ground amongst the now melting snow! Having been on the rescue team for many years, I was surprised that the new helicopter did not have GPS; neither did it have a ground to air radio. This seemed to be most unlikely, but apparently true as as it had not yet been fully commissioned. Jean was annoyed because one of the organisers told her that despite having the actual GPS position of the farm was told that GPS positions can be quite far out! She was fully 'au fait' with GPS workings as we had used ours frequently on our trips, and to locate archaeological positions deep in the bush.

With the help of an old friend Alan Butcher (the cave rescue specialist), who had also come out to assist, had kindly forgone a quick return to Cape Town and assisted Jean in reconnecting the battery to our bakkie (which had been removed to ensure no power loss during the intense cold) and was able to drive our bakkie back to Cape Town.

Anyhow, I was grateful for the help, and discovered that I had a badly broken femur, a fractured pelvis and a badly damaged shoulder. I did have a broken rib that seemed to grind back and forth when I breathed, and a finger that was skew, but no-one was much interested because they were not serious. I eventually strapped the finger up and it recovered well.

I never fully recovered the use of my shoulder, but after seven operations, rehabilitation and exercises and no money, I am after a decade, back to being as normal as I possibly can (ageing excluded!). My mobility improved vastly after I'd had a left hip replacement as the original operation had begun to deteriorate. My left leg was once again the same length as my right leg. Jean helped me tremendously over the initial and subsequent recovery periods and I am sure I inconvenienced her by the hassle of getting me in and out of the car and into a wheelchair, but I was very grateful for her help. Bonita Julies an outside carer, came in regularly to help me with the many daily tasks, and over the next few years through the number of operations, to assist with the muscle and movement by massage therapy.

The injuries were a reminder of how fragile we are, but it did not stop us from taking our annual trips away and into the bush.

At the farm, we had a special award ceremony to both Danie and Jan for their help and determination to get through to Op die Berg. I will be eternally grateful to them and to Volker Miros for what they did. Jean was an absolute star and kept a cool head, was well organised during the rescue and during the numerous visits to hospitals – she also deserved an award for this. We must remember as I am sure so many folk are aware, that the hospitalisation and recovery are one aspect of an injured person, but there is also a stack of administration to be done as well – proof that you can pay the hospital bill before operating, financing, checking the hospital printouts, that are probably just a little shorter than the dead sea scrolls!, discussions with doctors, inadequate hospital cover (which you only find out when lying on your back), running out of money, not being able to work and receive vital income. It pays not to have an accident...

21

Knolfontein, Stars, Fossils, Plants and Life

Nature does not always give up its secrets easily, and we are still discovering on this planet and beyond, what has always been there. As scientists, we are making new discoveries in the field of technology, and how better to do things for ourselves on planet Earth. If we care to search the internet every day, there are continual new discoveries about our Universe being reported or studied. At Knolfontein if one was to drive through it as one might through other farms in the area, you might think that it was a bit mundane, but after two decades, every trip to the farm would reveal something new, even if was a beautiful sunset or sunrise. The heavens at night are spectacular and the starlight so bright that you can clearly see the starlight shining on your hand, and it would even cast a shadow at times. Additionally, while it is quite easy to spot the constellations around Cape Town, in the mountains, the stars are so numerous in their multitude that they are generally more difficult to isolate from one another at first glance. The Milky Way is truly the Milky Way. The moonlight of course was so bright that you could read a newspaper without much trouble. If you had to walk through the veld, you would have no problem in finding a path. My friend Barry Nugent who is also a farm member, is a fundi on the stars and has a wonderful computerised telescope. He witnessed with the help of his son, the rare but not unknown occurrence of the Australis Borealis over the farm. It is obviously not as dramatic and beautiful as the Aurora Borealis in the Arctic region, but nonetheless an exciting and unusual event to behold.

To witness the path of the space station effortlessly gliding across the night sky is also a special moment to behold, not to mention the many satellites that are visible.

Pause and Observe – If we allow ourselves the time to stop and observe things around us, it is surprising what becomes evident. Sometimes an interest can be sparked by something unusual or to the enquiring mind where answers are sought. In the case of plant life, seasonal changes will reveal their beauty or not at all, and in some cases, some plants only flower every so many years, or perhaps only after fire.

Dr Ivor Jardine who is also a shareholder member of the farm, and who apart from his semi-retired profession as an ophthalmologist is a dedicated and highly enthusiastic and knowledgeable amateur botanist. He contributed much to the Protea Atlas Project some years ago and ever since he joined the farm he began collecting plant specimens. Over the 15 or so years that he and his wife Cora have walked the many kilometres across the veld and under all sorts of weather conditions, they have carefully collected hundreds of plant specimens. They were very particular in the plant storage, description, observations, and under a special consideration and approval, recovered them to the Kirstenbosch Botanical Institute for identification and classification. All in all, to date they have collected over 700 specimens of which hundreds are common or unique to the Swartruggens, and of these, *16 new species of plant have been discovered*. This is a remarkable achievement; he has with the assistance of some other members compiled a definitive record and reference catalogue. This has been a wonderful contribution to the botanical world to which he was awarded the Botanical Society of South Africa prestigious medal including the Alf Morris award. (Alf Morris was a well-loved science teacher from the Wynberg Boys High School and gave decades of his time to the eradication of invasive alien vegetation and the nurturing of seedlings and the planting and watering of many hundreds of Silver Trees on Vlakkenberg above Constantia after the devastating fire of 2000). The Cape Environmental Trust – CAPTRUST, decided to dedicate a special award to Ivor for outstanding botanical environmental achievements. His work is well advanced and continues.

While trying to find one of the farm beacons on the farm, I came across some slabs of sandstone that displayed some unusual, slightly undulating longitudinal markings. When I had the opportunity, I sent a picture through to our friend Dr John Almond and following up with a site visit to the location with him, he confirmed my suspicion that is was a glacial plate. He further expanded to explain that is was evidence of early subterranean sand glacial movement. In other words, not the typical surface scratching so common of the action of a glacier on a hard base, but on a sand base. On another occasion I was sitting next to a watercourse and noticed some strange almost worm-like impressions on the surface of a mudrock/sandstone base. It was not widespread, and perhaps easily missed. I had remembered that I had seen something similar on an adjoining farm. So once again I bounced the question off John Almond, and he said that they looked like trace fossils – horizontal burrows or grazing trails made from some sort of invertebrate such as a mollusc or arthropod. The geological horizon would probably be the Witpoort Formation (Late Devonian), or possibly the Floriskraal Formation (Early Carboniferous) and they are perhaps known as *Spirophyton or Zoophycos*. These originate between the Silurian and carboniferous periods of 400 to 350 million years ago, when the first amphibians appeared. I was to later discover slightly different fossil impressions in sandstone on the top of Grasberg. These would have been easily missed, but the fact that they looked different aroused interest and a closer examination. These samples have yet to be formally examined and identified.

One day while walking on the top of Grasberg, I had stopped to take a picture of a low growing protea that I had seen earlier, and as I stooped, below me lay a small adder. It was a light reddish colour (almost rust coloured). I was not able to entice it out of the low shrub protea but was keen to have it identified. Looking it up later, I was most surprised to learn that it was only fully identified about seven years previously as a Red Adder, and seemingly quite scarce. However, some years later, I came across one of these snakes that had been hit by a passing car on our road that passes through to the Kagga Kamma resort. I was annoyed, because motorists do not drive at a reasonable speed, and we had previously found dead jackal, and rabbits (one of these rabbits was quite unusual for the area, and I identified it as a Hewitt's Red Rock Rabbit). Anyhow, I recovered the Red Adder, photographed it, and informed the Stellenbosch University, who came and collected it, and informed me that it would be sent to Port Elizabeth to have the DNA recorded, and the snake studied. Surprises pop up when you least expect them.

There is no doubt that the dramatic geological events over the aeons of time have made their mark and left us with the landscape we see today. Early forms of life have left their imprints on our landscape, the dinosaurs have come and gone, and have left us with skeletal forms in the rock. When Quintin and I visited the Sentinel Ranch, Zimbabwe in 1994, we were privileged to be shown a newly discovered dinosaur fossil by Colin Bristow, which is still embedded in the rock. The fossil found there was an excellent example, and they have now erected a small museum to display it. The more you observe, the more you find, or realise – sometimes the dawning of realisation and confirmation of a finding can take years!

The Bushmen predate all other incursions of and movements of 'modern' peoples into southern Africa by thousands of years. The evidence of their passing has been left for us to find either in their stone implements or their rock art. The Cedarberg and the Swartruggens were no exception and on Knolfontein farm evidence of their occupation or passing through, exists today as it does on other farms in the area. The beauty and meaning (as we understand it), of their art, is remarkably widespread and spans from the Southern, Western and Northern Cape, the Drakensberg, Namibia and Botswana (where the remnants of these peoples still exist today), Zimbabwe and Mozambique. Their nomadic life did not leave much in the way of permanent structures, so they made use where possible of shelters and caves in the mountainous and rocky areas. In the Swartruggens like many other high altitude areas, there was perhaps and for obvious reasons a migration to warmer climes during the winter.

Much has been studied and written of the Bushmen. Attempts to preserve their culture have been established and are still ongoing especially for the bushmen children as well as tourist attractions to preserve their sustainable way of hunting and gathering. Regrettably, over the last two centuries, their freedom to migrate has been prevented due to the pressure of land ownership, population pressures and development. There are written records of the Bushmen that have had interaction with hunters, explorers and travellers alike within the last hundred years or so in Botswana and Rhodesia/Zimbabwe, when they still had the freedom to hunt and move across the landscape albeit diminished and controlled by others. They were gentle on the environment and never destroyed or over hunted for the sake of it. Quite often they derived meat from lion kills and were living almost literally from hand to mouth. European hunters were killing game for their hides or tusks, and apart from feeding their helpers and Bushmen guides and families, much would go to waste. This would be particularly true for elephants.

Modern man has brought about huge demands for resources, space, and the ongoing need for development to provide living needs and jobs for the exponential growth (both near and afar) of the population. By necessity, food has to come from farms and sustainable usage of the land. The migratory way of life for man and animals has now been effectively closed by boundaries and fences, so it is important for us to acknowledge and respect that which has passed. The period of man from the Early, Middle and Late Stone Age spans approximately from two and a half million years ago until as recently as two thousand years. Within the wide-open spaces certainly, throughout Africa, the evidence of early man is to be found either on the surface and open to the elements or contained within deposits of earth or debris within shelters and caves. More recently than two thousand years the nomadic Bushmen/San peoples worked stone tools or implements that can be found for us to analyse, date and study. Juxtaposed to geological events, this has all occurred, so to speak, in very recent times and has left little impact on the landscape. So, when we walk across the landscape including the wilderness, we are probably not the first to do so, nor will we be last, but when we do so, there are those signs that provide a forensic trail for past events. Humans by their number dominate all living things but are not immune from catastrophic events that can bring us to our knees in a very short time – because scientifically we know that such events have happened. We know that the era of the dinosaurs was brought to a sudden end, so if it could happen to them so rapidly, then it could do so to us. This all sounds negative, but with our knowledge from past events both of life and our living planet we may even minimise, by taking timeous corrective action, the effects of such events. With all our modern aids to survival, we really are no less vulnerable to our demise however that might occur. There is no doubt that early man may have flourished here and there, but over a million years did not expand to the extent that is happening now, he did get around but was subject to the vagaries and trials of daily life for food, shelter and security, notwithstanding fickle weather patterns and climate changes. And so, when wandering the open veld, where we are still able to do so, it is with great interest frail as we are, to absorb all that has past, and presents itself before us. Some folk explore the achievements and art of modern man in civilised countries, to meet different peoples and visit museums and historic sites, but to witness the more basic and fundamental elements of nature first hand wherever possible is a pleasure and a privilege, and an appreciation of what we have around us.

The current rate and scale of change is running ahead of us and is not currently sustainable. It is my view that there is not enough balance and harmony across the world, exploitation of natural resources is running rife. It will sort itself out one way or the other – man will do it himself, or nature might throw in a 'curved ball' – which does happen from time to time. But the measures required to take precautionary measures 'just in case', or 'just in time' might be a hard pill to swallow, or not be mutually acceptable to some of our fellow humanoids to flatten out the peaks and troughs to be beneficial to all living beings. There seems to be blindness right now in the desperate rush forward which appears unstoppable. There is enough wisdom in the world, but it is being overshadowed by over -consumption of most things. For example, what has been lying under the ground for millions of years is being consumed and will be consumed within a couple of hundred years. The present climate and environment over which we are supposed to have sensible control is being punished, and the potential harm to the quality of water and air is without question, but largely ignored in the quest for more fossil energy, mineral resources and demand for jobs. For example, how do you come to terms and understanding such as was reported in the Farmers Weekly (2013) that the recent estimation of lost arable land in South Africa to development and mining (mostly coal for export), is equal to the size of the Kruger National Park! And I have great difficulty in understanding our desperate need for more fuel when every morning and evening, tens of thousands of cars – literally sit in traffic jams for hours going to and from their destinations – the waste of fuel is phenomenal, not to mention our physical and mental energy in this mindless exercise: but money drives everything, and while I am aware and concerned about this just in South Africa, it is happening simultaneously across the world every day! – But that is a subject and story all on its own, and a very long and ongoing story at that.

22

Bumbusi Ruins, Hope Fountain Mission and Matopos

When you have a passion and deep interest for something, there is really no end date. I have mostly always enjoyed my work because it has provided a stimulus towards one's own understanding and advancement as well as providing a valuable contribution towards the community and development, no matter how small your contribution might be. The adage that 'The whole is greater than the sum of the parts' is probably true of all of us, especially in our modern world where specialisation is a natural 'part', so we must be satisfied that we are doing the best we can collectively towards a meaningful goal.

'Multum in Parvus'

However, running parallel with the demands of work and family development responsibilities, many have external passions of hobbies, some of which may develop then fade, or some which continue through life. I had chosen to deepen my interest in nature and in particular, archaeology a long way back before I even thought of retirement. A hobby can be the anchor in your life and is vitally important to your well-being. The 'pie-chart' of life's needs has to be as far as possible, in balance – 'all work and no play make Jack a dull boy' etc., is true.

To some, it might be sport, art, music (the infinitely variable elixir to all peoples), reading, or even television that nowadays contains amazing programmes and documentaries. It could be a combination of several interests. In my case, even when my work was a bit mundane, to plan the next trip away into the bush or game reserve provided a great deal of excitement in the planning and expectation of what to experience. As a family and when Heather and Quintin were still very young, we boldly set out on trips, and sometimes they had to rough it when we slept in the car 'en-route' to our destinations, though this was the exception rather than the rule. Following the event, is the recall of all those things that were important and precious. The bonus is if you can also share your knowledge and experience with others perhaps not so fortunate, then there is also benefit to others.   There is no person on this planet passed or still living that has not learnt something from others. Advancements in knowledge I believe are built on those bold enough to push the boundaries. Big steps are rarely made without the small steps of others.

With a little observation and interest, we can all contribute in some way to the library of knowledge.

So, when or where do you stop following your interests – well simply, while you have your health in every sense, you don't stop.

Of more recent times, Jean and I have been on a number of trips into the bush, a combination of camping, cottages or chalets where possible were included where we could afford it, and where you could enjoy at times, the comfort of a proper bed, facilities, and even air conditioning (or a fan!).

Jean had organised a trip to the Limpopo River region for the Archaeological Society of the Western Cape Branch, more commonly known as the Shashi Limpopo valley that is well known for archaeological sites. These include Iron Age sites such as the well-known Mapungubwe hill site (of gold beads and artefacts and the 'iconic' Golden Rhino) as well as some early Iron Age sites and Bushmen rock art shelters within the very picturesque sandstone valley close to the Limpopo River.   Venda sites were also visited towards the east which included Thulamela (which is a hill-site adjacent to the Luvuvu River and within the Kruger National Park and discovered not that long ago – also a very important reference Iron Age site), and the important Dzata site further south and within the Soutpansberg range of hills. Visiting such sites provides a tangible picture of the cultures, movements and times of such peoples. It is most likely that climates of the times dictated the rise or demise of such occupied sites. Food and water and grazing for cattle principally were vital for sustainability as of course was the availability of wood. To be able to learn more by seeing, feeling (such as climbing up the special limited and narrow access to the top of Mapungubwe), where hundreds if not thousands of feet and hands had used the same route many hundreds of years before, are brought alive. Quietly contemplating the past puts you temporarily in the shoes of those past peoples and enables you to picture and understand the trials of daily living. The same applies to the many Bushmen rock art sites as mentioned, that also occur in the valley and surrounding areas. The visual displays leave literally, a clear picture of the attire, hunting weapons of bows and arrows and associated accoutrements – no doubt contained in the carry bags so often seen slung over the shoulder or on a carry stick, and the type of animals hunted and killed for food and other useful animal parts such as bone and hides. The skilled artist was indeed a special person that could recall accurately the details that were displayed, and were I am certain proud of those skills and the events that surrounded them. We have been privileged to witness them later (and perhaps they were also mindful that other Bushmen tribes would also see them when they also visited such shelters and caves). We are often taken with the beauty of the painted sites, and how special the sites are when first seen. It is no surprise then, that if we recognise a site as being special, then so did the occupants and the artist think likewise, and of it being a place of importance. We tend to picture the Bushmen as adults (so often painted images reflect hunting and other scenes where adults are portrayed) but when you witness a painting of a small child holding the hand of a mother, or a multitude of handprints on a shelter or cave wall, and you spot some much smaller child handprints, or sometimes a small footprint amongst them you are reminded of the vulnerability, care and responsibilities of the nomadic families as they lived and moved across the landscape. I am also sure that the artists among them knew that the paint media and materials used had to be robust as well – their skill in drawing such delicate and tiny images with fine lines has always been a fascination for me – they must have had remarkably steady hands to draw such fine lines. As mentioned before, being nomadic, this was important evidence of their passing through as well as the stone tool/implements carefully worked and left behind.

Jean and I had also camped on the Botswana side of the Limpopo on a number of trips, and while enjoying the tranquil settings with huge shady riverine trees, birds and game, we were also fortunate to come across surface scatterings of worked stone implements. These were mostly of more recent (Late Stone Age) times, and we were also struck by the variety and colours of the implements – clearly a lot of these different mineral materials did not originate at the locality where we had seen them. None of these implements were removed or disturbed from their original position. We were delighted to find on a newly marked 4x4 track through the Mopani bush, an Iron Age site not far from the river. It had not been noted anywhere before, and we would have missed it had I not got out of the vehicle to negotiate a steep drop off. Looking around, there were numerous potsherds, ostrich eggshell beads, grindstones, and remains of grain bins. This was exciting to behold and was duly reported to the relevant authorities in Gaborone for reference and follow up. It is possible that the site was an early one and contemporaneous with the Shroda site not too far away 'as the crow flies' in South Africa. The owners of the land happily agreed to close this part of the route to protect the archaeological site.

It is interesting to note that most of the worked stone implements being of 'late' origin, were relatively much smaller compared with the large hand axes and cleavers we have found around the Crags and Mossel bay area – clearly, the larger implements were from a much earlier time period, Early Stone Age (ESA) and could possibly date earlier than 500,000 years old. However, Bushmen principally not being pastoralists or confined to seasonal planting of crops as farming communities, could move from place to place according to the conditions of the veld, availability of food or water resources, seasonal or climatic conditions. Their style of living though not at all easy did require shelter or protection from the elements but did not leave behind obvious permanent structures such as walling. Pastoralists and herders had by necessity to build stone kraals for the protection of their domestic sheep, and the evidence of this is found in the form of walling even in rough form, including rock art that may also display their hunting and gathering 'tools of the trade', and including 'fat' tailed sheep. The fat-tailed sheep were valuable as a source of fat as literally described, within principally, the tail.

One special trip or rather an expedition in 2013, was to travel up to Zimbabwe via Botswana where Jean was attending an archaeological conference in Gaborone, then on to Francistown, where we would meet some friends of ours from Cape Town – Phil and Gill Cohen and Cilla Williams who were travelling in their 4x4, then onwards with a memorable stop off at Elephant Sands where elephants can be observed up close and personal (but not that close!). Gill and Cilla were close friends and to pass the time between viewing, cooking or eating played a lot of Scrabble. It was here that we named the game Squabble after one of the players (shall remain nameless to protect innocent bystanders and the author) became irate and tipped the board over (it was not even a hot day!) after she found that the other player had cheated because she used a 'W' upside down to represent a letter 'M' to create a word, which she did not otherwise have. This was taken very seriously – one of the players laughed and the other did not, we did not see the importance of such an outburst, but there is nothing like a bit of humour in the bush.

We entered Pandamatenga via a pleasant and quiet border post into Zimbabwe. This small village (also a version referenced as the Mpanda Mutenga – meaning the grove of Mpanda trees (*Lonchocarpus capassa* or rain tree) that grew at the site of Mutenga's old kraal) was during early hunting and exploration days, a trading post set up by Westbeech on the original abandoned kraal site of Mutenga (son of chief Nekati of the Milima tribe) for hunters and traders as well. It was so positioned because it was just outside of the 'Fly' (tsetse) country, and at the headwaters of the Matetsi River. It additionally provided reasonable access to the favoured hunting areas, the Zambezi River and the Victoria Falls.

We were going to drive to a bush camp called Bumbusi, which was an old hunting camp in the northern more rocky sandstone area of Hwange. The route we were to take required that we go via Robin's camp where we had planned to stop and camp for a few days. Robin's camp was not new to us as we had been there several times over the years, but it is still in a 'time warp' state, where though clean, nothing much has happened since the early development and the period when not as much traffic passed through the park during the bush war. (Our present GPS noted that petrol was available at the park – but we knew that it was not, and upon our arrival checked out the dusty and rusted petrol pumps that reflected a somewhat faded petrol price of 7/6 a gallon – seven shillings and sixpence!).

Herbert Robins owned a large tract of land when Pandamatenga was still a hunting and trading post. Also, at the time when no doubt, regular trekkers passed through the Matetsi and down the Deka River to the Wankie area in the early 1900's. He was dedicated to the preservation of the game that flourished there and was totally opposed to poaching. In this regard, he built a tower (which still exists today including some artefacts and memorabilia installed therein) which had a grand view across the wilderness. At the top of the tower, he erected a large compass rose mounted on a table, and with his telescope (of which he had a deep interest in astronomy as well as looking at wild game), he would spy out any distant fires which would indicate the presence of poachers and their cooking fires. He would then take a compass reading and head out into the bush to encounter and apprehend the trespassers. As time passed, he decided to cede the land over to the Rhodesian government for the use and protection by all citizens of the country. The farms were then included into the Wankie (Hwange) Game reserve as we know it today. When he died, he was buried just outside of the entrance to the camp. The grave was neat with a simple headstone with the inscription of his full name: Herbert George Robins... died on the 27th June 1935... aged 72 years.

When we were at Robins some years ago (1993), we climbed up the tower and met with a very likeable camp ranger called 'Bagman'. He told us a tale of an experience he had during an anti-poaching radio duty on the intermediate level of the tower (which improved the radio signal to field officers on patrol). He said that late at night when all was quiet, he heard someone plodding slowly up the stairs. To his utter amazement and disbelief, the footsteps passed him by and continued up the steep steps to the open observation tower on the highest level. He was quite unperturbed about his experience in the telling. He said that this had happened on *more than one occasion*. On later visits, we asked some of the administrative staff working on the lower level of the tower if they had experienced anything, and they said they had not, and thought it quite amusing. I had no reason to disbelieve him. He also told us that (certainly at that time, and no doubt later), that it was the duty of the madala (oldest man) of the camp staff to ensure that Robin's grave was always kept clean and free of grass. If this was not done, he said, 'rain would not fall on the camp, but would elsewhere'. 'Hence he said, you will see that the gravesite is clean and well looked after'. I do not know from where the requirement originated but do not doubt the belief. We are not always privy to the deeper beliefs amongst tribal peoples and should not simply brush them off or confuse them with 'superstition' or 'curse' activities such as of witch doctors, because they may be born of respect rather than fear. I think the same may apply to graves and rainmaking sites – this is more so in the rural areas than in cross-cultural and cosmopolitan urban areas.

Because of the indistinct 'back' route and uncertain condition of the Deka river crossings, we decided to take the longer route via Sinamatella to the Bumbusi camp. The route was rough and stony, and we had to frequently pull and cut small trees and branches out of the way. Scouting ahead was also required where deep wash-aways had occurred on the track, we had to pack stones in place to prevent damage to our wheels or vehicles due to insufficient vehicle clearance. Because of the intermittent and slow travel, we used portable two-way radios to communicate conditions. This was wise because when we had progressed ahead of Phil, he radioed to say they had had a blowout. We returned to help jack up and change the wheel. Unfortunately, he only had one spare which made things riskier when we had to negotiate a very steep and rocky ascent up the final hill pass in low gear range and four-wheel drive before we could stop at the top to catch our breath! We happily arrived at the camp after travelling the distance of twenty kilometres from Sinamatella in a time of over three and a half hours!

My original intention of going to this remote place was because it featured a very special archaeological site and unique engravings. The Bumbusi ruins related to a remnant of the Rozwi peoples called the baNambya (also referred to as the Abananzwa) who had moved to the area when the central Rozwi kingdom was invaded by the aggressive Zwangendaba from the south. Whether or not the ruling chief (understood to be chief Shana Chazho the fifth Hwange that ruled in Bumbusi from 1834 to 1860) of Hwange had occupied this site before establishing his permanent 'town' on the north side and close to the Zambezi or not, I am not sure, but he would have been familiar with the surrounds. I have an old map drawn by Thomas Baines from 1877, and also noted from Barber's and Frewen's map around 1878 where Wankies Old Town is noted close to where Bumbusi is today.

Note: Hwange is often referred to Chief Hwange by travellers and hunters to the area, but it is interesting to note that Hwange is supposed to mean 'To clear and make peace', and may mean simply a kingly title – Dendelende, who changed his name from Dendelende to Sawanga, then to Whange – was the son of Mambo of the Rozwi Changamire dynasty king.

We were delighted with the camp which was situated under huge shady trees – Natal Mahogany, Jackalberry, *Kigaleria africana* (sausage tree) etc... we were greeted and welcomed at the camp by the camp manager Moses Garira and his friendly wife Abigail Sibanda. To sleep under a roof with clean and comfortable beds and excellent ablutions was a pleasure, especially after the long, hot and tiring drive. It was a splendid retreat far from other park visitors. To eventually stop after the long trip from Cape Town, and to just relax and absorb the surroundings and peace of the area, was magical. We were told by Moses that a few days before, a wild dog pack (also called painted wolves in Zimbabwe) had run through the camp in pursuit of impala, then repeated the event the following day. But we were treated to numerous elephant with many very young infant elephants that were browsing the still green trees before the dry winter fall. The elephants were not at all concerned about our presence and seemed to know that we presented no threat to them and that there was no danger in the camp area. There was no fence to provide a barrier for their wandering close to the camp, and in fact we had to wait to access our cottage one day while one elephant finished eating outside the door! The numerous baby elephants peacefully browsing around gave the place an air of being an elephant nursery. Birds were aplenty, and so were the baboons that were feasting on the fruits from the high tree branches. They were not a problem otherwise. Despite the reasonably well-wooded region, wood was not wasted on the donkey boiler, or the small glowing water kettle fire that gave hot water for tea or otherwise throughout the day. It was extremely heartening to see such conservation and sustainable practice. So often advertisements display a huge bonfire enclosed in a boma with numerous lights, a food table fit for a king, and attendants standing around – in reality, more likely than not, luxury camps actually do have such a spread. This was none of that, and it was restful for the soul and as it should be when it gets dark, and nature recovers its rightful place again. It was like stepping out of a busy and troubled world into one which is at peace with itself – a delight even if only a temporary indulgence.

Bumbusi archaeologically and historically had always been a special place through time. It is situated on the northern watershed area of the park which is cloaked in Mopani and Baobabs as well as other tree species over the open veld, and it lies alongside at least four springs – one of which we saw supplied clear clean water despite it being the winter dry season. The Bumbusi River is less than a kilometre away from the camp and feeds into the Deka River through some not too far off hills to the northwest which eventually feeds the Zambezi River to the north. It is not surprising then, to find that the area had been occupied for the later Iron Age peoples, and most certainly for the even earlier peoples which had, we believe and as we understand it, carved out the hundreds of spoor on the rocks close by to the ruins and in shelters near the top of the sandstone ridge to the south-east.

Moses guided us to a sunset spot on a low rocky rise overlooking a vast plain, and he was delighted to spot in the distance, eland that he had not seen in the area for a long, long time. The spot also revealed a lot of late Stone Age worked implements – of many different colours and geological materials. We also passed by the once dwelling of Albert Giese who had first registered the coalfields for later development. Apparently Giese had overheard a senior induna who was part of an envoy sent by chief Whange to meet with white peoples moving into Matabeleland and beyond, speaking about the 'black stones that burn' when he was in the Tati area around 1893, and later followed it up to find and register claims for the deposits of coal which Wankie Colliery is now, and has now been mined for over a hundred years. (It is interesting archaeologically speaking to note that Basil Fuller's book *Bid Time Return*, makes mention of many surface workings, apparently of ancient origin, and probably the Abananzwa, and perhaps, others before them, that had worked and used the surface coal in the neighbourhood of the Matetsi River). Strangely enough despite the many millions of tons of coal already mined, it is of present interest to know that serious attempts have been made to mine coal within the Hwange National Park. Certainly not too distant from Bumbusi, serious exploration and preparatory development had been conducted – but that is another story of positional exploitation... et al.

When we were at Robin's camp, we met Jane Hunt of the Hwange Lion Research who had just been to Bumbusi doing lion research, and knowing that we were headed there, recommended that we contact Roger Ngwenya who was a Hwange Parks bush anti-poaching ranger and guide, and knew the history of the Bumbusi ruins well. We failed to contact him when we passed through the Sinamatella camp but were very fortunate when at Bumbusi to find that the changeover of rangers for the area included Roger Ngwenya. Roger had worked in the area since the seventies including part of the bush war and was a fount of knowledge as well as an expert tracker. We had firstly visited the ruins with our friends from Cape Town with two of the earlier guides allocated to us. They were really helpful and absolutely necessary because the surrounding bush was a popular place for elephants, and their paths and droppings were everywhere. Apart from this, I had heard lion in this general area one night, so was grateful for the armed guides. What we saw was stunning to say the least with the hundreds of engravings (unique in this extent amongst the few engraved sites found in Zimbabwe), and to be able to wander around the ruins and see what remained of the well-structured dry-packed walling. Much had collapsed, mostly due to animals that frequented the place, and especially baboons that have the habit of turning over stones to find and eat scorpions. They may have also climbed up the walls and caused damage. Notwithstanding that, the site had a special atmosphere about it, and once again when quietly looking out north and west to the rolling veld, the mood was contemplative and most rewarding. I amusingly (but not without some reason), nicknamed the ruins as the Bumbusi 'Casino'. The reason being was that I counted at least twenty 'Tsoro' games (carved hollows or cupules four by eight) in the surrounding boulders and surfaces in and around the ruins. Some even had white pebbles still lying in the hollows. I had seen these game 'boards' before in and around other iron age sites, but never this many, and could only conclude that they must have been sufficiently sustained to be able to spend that amount of time carving and using the game 'boards'. It was interesting to note that some of the 'boards' looked very much older than others, but that may very well have been because of the grain structure of the sandstone. We also found a few grinding hollows, both large and small (named Huyo and Guyo i.e. pestle and mortar). The larger ones were likely to have been for grinding grain. The surrounds were dotted with Baobab trees and sandstone outcrops and it was very picturesque.

When our friends had left early in order to try and purchase a spare tyre before the weekend 'en route' back to South Africa, we remained and were fortunate to go back to the ruins with Roger Ngwenya and his fellow ranger and to spend a little more time absorbing the atmosphere of the ruins and surrounds. Additionally, it gave us a second opportunity to photograph more of the walling and features of the site. Roger had many years before, been able to speak with a descendent of one of the chiefs who gave him much detail of the area. There were two special aspects that he brought to our attention, the one being a distinct but well-hidden recess in the rock, where the chief had kept his muzzle-loader rifle for his own use, most likely for hunting opportunities. The other interesting spot that he pointed out was a position within an enclosure where a well had existed but had since been filled in with debris and stones over time. One might ask why there was a well there because the springs were not that far away, but it would have given them the security of precious water when they depended on it. Interestingly, when we were down in the Mateke Hills close to the Bubye River, we were shown the remains of a well that had been dug close to a walled enclosure. The well or what remained of it was quite close to the river where water could have been drawn from. However, during the dry season, they would have had to dig under the river sand to find water, much the same as elephants have to do to create a seep from which to drink, so it would not be unreasonable to guess that they could dig a well down to the existing water table, but secure within their living area. The peoples of this era would have had cattle, which would have probably been kraaled, so they would have had water if necessary, at night, and without the danger of being taken by predators out in the open.

The real bonus was to be shown the deeply carved spoor above an existing shelter near and within the perimeter of the ruins. The carvings included those of human feet and cat spoor which we had not seen before. Detailed archaeological findings from excavations carried out in 2008 revealed dates from deposit samples taken from within various surrounding shelters of a few hundred years old (being the Later Iron Age occupation) to as far back as over 3500 years BP - Before Present (being the late Stone Age). The earlier dates were from the Late Stone Age (LSA) peoples. I do not doubt that it was the bushmen that had occupied this area and as a *'permanent'* site over these thousands of years – I suggest that this site is an exception to the more nomadic bushmen lifestyle conducted over wider regions. Apart from climatic and periodic changes in weather patterns, the area would have been ideal for ongoing and sustainable use. This is perhaps not surprising because the location is reasonably high, with good vegetation, trees, well-watered with two rivers (the Deka and the Bumbusi) not far off, and a number of perennial springs. The sandstone outcrops also provided shelters that were few and far between, further south across the span of the existing Hwange National Park. Generally, they faced north and the watershed towards the Zambezi. The area has a special and appealing vibe – one could sense it.

We were also fortunate to be shown large sections of fossilised wood that were outcropped near the sandstone ridge. What a wonderful experience to be able to see these on foot obviously with armed rangers, but within a terrain that is as wild now as it probably was then – in truth though, it was most likely wilder then! The elephant trails criss-cross the different outcrops and walled enclosures, and have, clearly with the help of baboon as mentioned, caused a great deal of damage to the structures. But that is the course of nature when man moves out, nature in its slow but certain way, takes it back.

A superb engraving of a footprint at Bumbusi

Grinding 'Dolly' holes with other Tsoro game boards

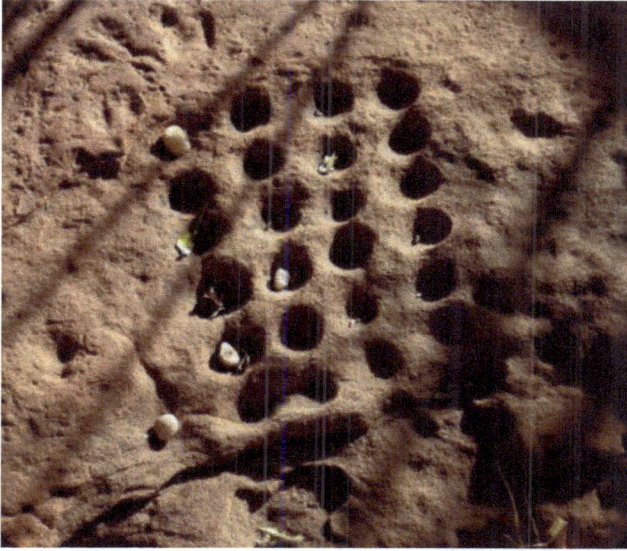

An example of one of the many Tsoro Game boards

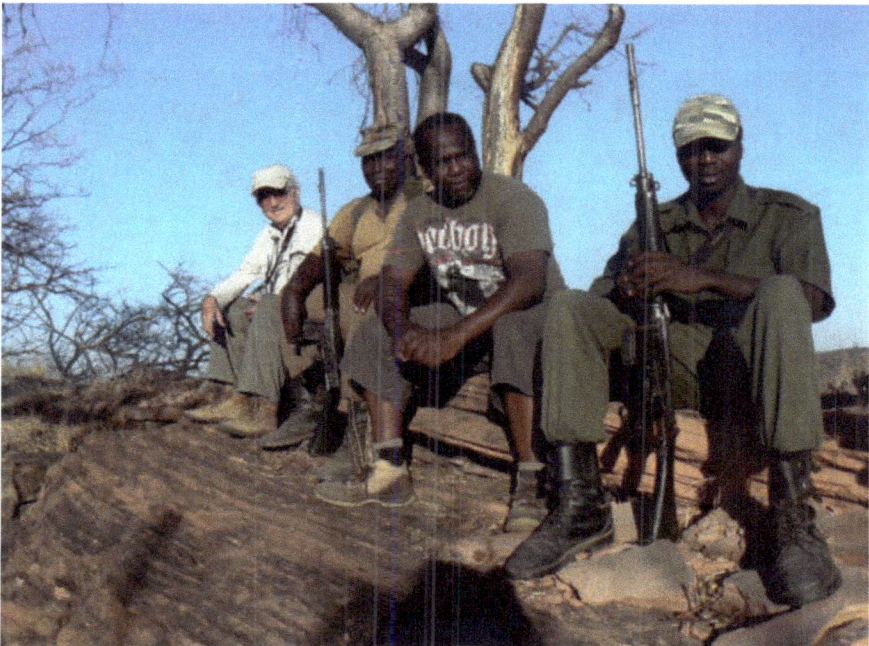

Paul with Roger Ngwenya head ranger and guide, Moses camp manager and David assistant ranger at Bumbusi high point ridge

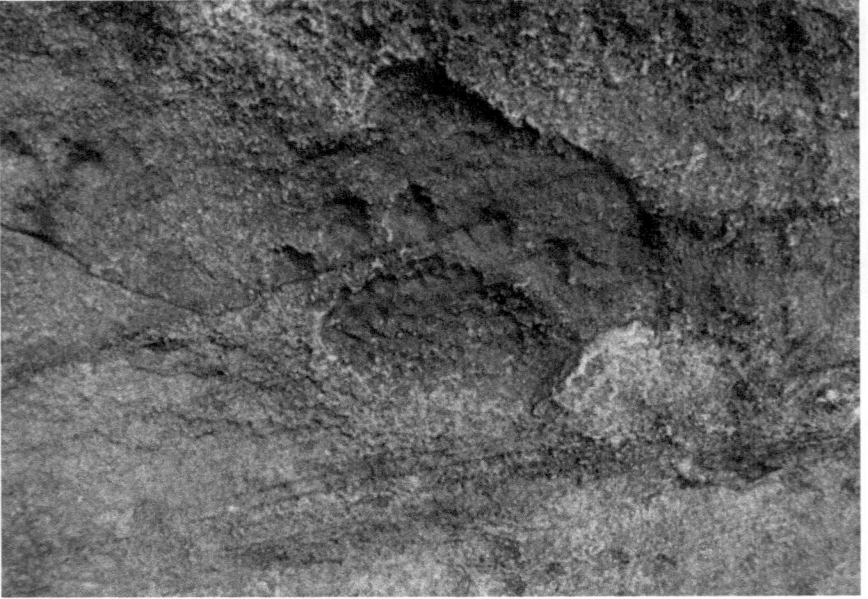

Very early Bushman engraving - lion paw perhaps?

One of the many very early bushman engravings of antelope and other game

The remainder of some walling on an outcrop

Superb Iron Age walling

We had planned to go to Jambili Pan which was not too far from the Hwange Main Camp after leaving Bumbusi. Because of the arduous drive back to Sinamatella and the shocking condition of the tar road (built in the 1960's) via Shumba to Main Camp, we decided to choose a route north to exit near the Hwange Colliery. Then to head down the main tarred road to the main turn off to Main camp. It required some careful route-finding and road negotiation, but though further, saved us travelling time. It was both disturbing and a deep concern to see the inroads and coal mining preparation development made into the National Park itself. This serious issue is being addressed by others, and it is hoped there will be a satisfactory outcome where further widespread disturbance will be stopped, and the landscape rehabilitated – time will tell. The developed road was wide and was for kilometres covered with hundreds and hundreds of elephant droppings, so clearly an area of the park well-populated with animals, particularly elephant. We did see other spoor as well.

At Jambili, we met with my daughter Heather and our son in law Robbie, and while their time was limited because they had left their school and varsity kids behind in Johannesburg, it was a great reunion and the special time camping with just the four of us was truly relaxing and special. We saw roan, sable, elephant, and numerous other animals, and camped essentially without protective fences. Under a full moon, the stillness with the occasional nightjar, owl and the nightly elephant trumpeting and splashing, and then slapping their trunks into the small pan – was an experience not to be missed. Hearing one night the distant call – a type of singular yelp of wild dog approaching from a distance, coming closer to us, then passing the pan into the night – presumably on a hunt was also a memorable experience (the sound was confirmed by the camp attendant when questioned about it the next day). We saw so many elephant, with many young ones that it was difficult to believe that so many of them were still in the reserve. The private initiative to fix, fuel and maintain the many pumps at the thirty-odd pans has contributed tremendously to the stabilisation of the herds within a reasonable distance of one another during the dry season. Visitors are not always aware of the heroic effort and private financing that goes into this worthwhile rehabilitation work to the benefit of visitors and government alike.

On our trip back via Bulawayo, we paid a special visit to the old Hope Fountain Mission (uMthombothemba), which is steeped in history, and not too far from the site of the 'Old Buluwayo' of just over six kilometres distant. It is rarely visited these days for its historical importance, but in its day, being close to 'Old Buluwayo', it was certainly on the 'bus' route into the interior, such as was Inyati Mission further north. Much has been written about the mission and how important it was for travellers' explorers, prospectors, and those seeking refuge and recovery from sickness. It was also a target during the Matabele rebellion, and was burnt down. But the faith of those that ran it, quietly, rebuilt it and provided a place for schooling and safety from harm. The testimony to those that were touched by the mission and everything it stood for is evident in the humble graveyard where graves and headstones reflect men that achieved much for the peoples of Rhodesia, that were well respected and known for their works and contributions. Great or small, they remain to remind us of our humble touch on this earth and love for our fellow man.

We met the local minister in charge the Rev. Methius Moyo by chance, as he had been away and only just returned. We had not made any prior arrangements to visit the mission, or phoned, but it was as if he had been quietly waiting for us in an open area as we had walked up to the local residence. What a delightful man, most humble and unassuming. He kindly showed us around the church which had framed portraits of past ministers and their brief histories on the walls of the church interior.

Lobengula the king of the Matabele and the successor to Mzilikazi on his death was approached by a Scottish Presbyterian, James Boden Thomson a few years after Lobengula was appointed king and requested permission to establish a mission in Bulawayo. He was finally granted permission to find a suitable site and was assisted by two of Lobengula's indunas and, hunter-explorers Thomas Baines and Henry Hartley. Together they selected a pretty valley about six kilometres from 'Old Buluwayo' and were then eventually granted permission to build. Lobengula stated:

"I give your society (the London mission), leave to occupy that valley as a mission station as long as they like under me as chief, and no trader is to build on it"

That was in 1870. The outlook for Thomson was not an easy one given the resistance to people being taught the Gospel where different ideology held sway – social interaction with a missionary was generally to ask for trouble. Notwithstanding this, he had the courage to call the place 'Hope Fountain'. Much is written about notable persons connected with the Mission such as Helm, Reed and Carnegie, but two figures stand out to which I make a brief but special note of because they were most remarkable in what they achieved often under most trying conditions.

Rev. Mtompe Kumalo was born around 1875 to 1880 in the royal kraal of eNyathini in the area of present-day Burnside a very pretty suburb in the south of Bulawayo. He was a distant relative of Lobengula (his isibongo or clan name was the same as that of Lobengula), and he was a cattle herdsman at the time of the battle of the Shangani patrol. During that troubled time, he went north with the retreating Lobengula, and was close to the scene of the decisive battle and only returned to the mission when all was lost.

When the rebellion of 1896 broke out, he and his family who at the time had a kraal close to Hope Fountain moved into the Matopos and lived amongst the rocks at the foot of Inungu (which is in clear view of Malindidzimu (View of the World – where Cecil Rhodes lies buried). They suffered harshly with little water and subsisted on wild fruits, and occasional dassie (rock rabbit) or klipspringer, and at times when they slaughtered a beast (Nkomo/Mombi) they had good meat. It was a terrible time when crops had not been planted or reaped, and with the Rinderpest, cattle were few. When Rhodes declared that the fighting was over and implored all to return, there was still doubt, but Rev. Carnegie (without arms) with the threat of distrust and being killed encouraged them to return home. It was Carnegie who fed them until they were able to again plough and plant.

Kumalo schooled at Hope Fountain and after some journeying when he worked with Tom Meikle a transport contractor, learnt to read and write. Subsequently, he was sent to Tiger Kloof in South Africa for further training and after a short interval completed his training. He then returned to Tiger Kloof on a course for native ministers which took three years, he was ordained into the Christian ministry in 1917 which he served faithfully thereon until his death on the 2nd October 1949 whilst preparing a sermon. He was a good linguist and could speak Sechuana, Sekalanga, Shona, English, and his native tongue IsiNdebele. He was respected within his own clan and always spoke with a well-ordered mind. He became a close friend with Rev. Neville Jones, and they worked together for over twenty years, and it is from this relationship, that Jones was able to capture the detailed history and ancient lore of the Matabele of which Kumalo had extensive and personal knowledge. They were similar in age, and therefore contemporaries in the sense of this, and the events and history of the day. Jones in collaboration with Kumalo urged him to recount the wealth of information on the Matabele that otherwise may have been lost in the passing of time. Such close association between two different races and cultures and in the writing of his book 'My Friend Kumalo', was a remarkable achievement.

Neville Jones was born in London in 1880. Much later, it was only whilst conducting geological work in Madagascar and after meeting missionaries from the London Missionary Society (LMS) that he then studied for the ministry. He came to Hope Fountain in 1912 when he took

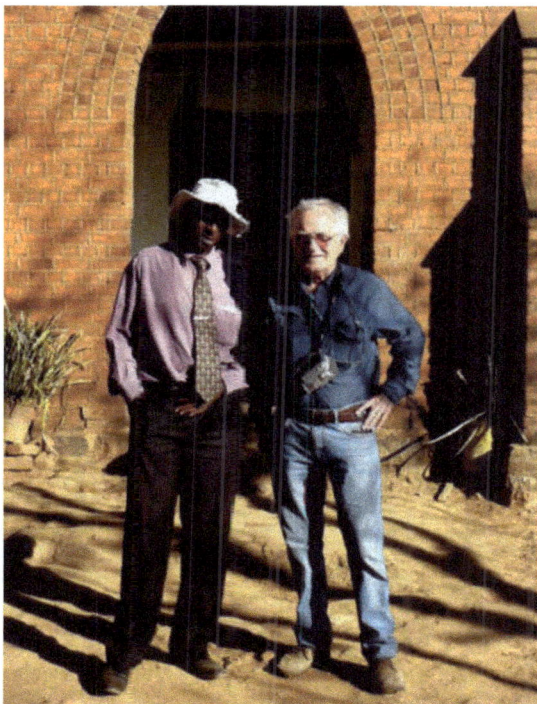

Paul and Rev. Methius Moyo in front of the church

Old sketch of Hope Fountain Mission by Father Croonenbergh in 1880
It was burnt down during the Matabele rebellion in 1896

*Hope Fountain Mission near Old Bulawayo (Gubulawayo)
as it stands today*

Interior of the Hope Fountain Mission

Some happy children at Hope Fountain

Framed view of the valley granted to James Boden Thomson of the London Mission by Lobengula. Finding this location was assisted by two Indunas, and hunter- explorers Baines and Hartley

over from Rev. Helm from 1913 to 1936. He had a remarkable knowledge and interest in ethnography, prehistory, entomology, anthropology, botany, geology and archaeology. His interest in archaeology was sparked off when he found stone implements at Hope Fountain. This led him, over the next forty years, on numerous expeditions and assignments and resulted in numerous scientific articles, reports and books on the subject and more. His previous studies were not lost and only enhanced his understanding and contribution to history, anthropology and archaeology. For his works, to which he was internationally recognised, he was awarded an Honorary Life Fellowship of the Royal Anthropological Institute of Great Britain. Quoted from his book – *My Friend Kumalo* – "at that time only one other man in the world, Dr L S B Leakey of Kenya, had traced on his own, a complete prehistoric succession for a territory". One of his earliest scientific papers related to Taungs area of the Northern Cape, where later, the first man-ape fossils were discovered. It is notable that in 1935, the University of Pretoria placed him in charge of work at Mapungubwe, the great iron-age burial ground in the Limpopo valley – now the iconic World Heritage Site within the Mapungubwe National Park in South Africa. The site is most famous for the many gold artefacts, beads and of course, the Gold Rhino.

His other discoveries of note include the Bambata cave, Nswatugi cave (with its beautiful rock paintings), and inter alia, he was also the president of the South African Archaeological Society in 1953 – 54. He retired in 1948, when he continued his interest in wildflowers and succulents. His life's work was crowned in 1953 when the University of the Witwatersrand conferred on him an honorary degree of Doctor of Science. He was the author of major publications such as the *Stone-Age in Rhodesia, Early Days and Native Ways in Southern Rhodesia, The prehistory of Southern Rhodesia, The guide to Zimbabwe Ruins,* and the *Rhodesian Genesis.* He was known as "Mhlagazanhlansi" ("he who blows on the embers and stirs the fire"). A fitting name indeed.

Why all this detail, one may ask? Well, it reminds us of the roots or foundation of a stable and civilized country, and to some of the dedicated people that helped in that quest.

We walked through the somewhat aged but lovingly maintained walled graveyard in the late afternoon, and we noted that the first burial was of a tiny child named Willie Thomson – that had died in 1875 in infancy at the age of 1 year and 5 months, a child of the first missionary couple – James Boden Thomson. Missionaries lost many young children to disease and illness in those early days, and it must have been a great hardship and sacrifice fcr them. *You will find the graves of remarkable people that had contributed so much to the history and foundation of Rhodesia, now Zimbabwe,* and though I did not at the time see the grave of Rev. Kumalo, I am sure he was laid to rest there with Dr Neville Jones – humbly and quietly as referred to earlier, amongst the many other ordinary folk that were also connected to and had contributed so much to the Mission and the country.

The present renowned and successful education and training centre for girls has grown and is built on top of a hill close to the Mission. Hope Fountain did not escape the wrath of land grabs in recent times. The Mission has always tried to be self-sustaining because of the shortage of resources and income, and they used some land in the valley below the old residence and church to breed and sell turkeys (and no doubt for consumption at times)   As described during the early days of Rev. Thomson – circa 1870 (sometimes spelt as Thompson), there grew 'waving fields of English corn, maize and oats, and grazing up the valley, bullocks, cows and goats' including plenty of good vegetables and potatoes. It had been granted to them by Lobengula, as said, in 1870, nearly 150 years ago! This land was taken away from them by the present government then under President Robert Mugabe. We were deeply saddened to look down from the old stoep of the residence in the afternoon sun and see the land now lying fallow. Such are the times of poor judgement, leadership, and lack of compassion!

Whilst in Bulawayo we also took the opportunity to go to my old stomping ground and climbing area of Matopos which brought back many happy memories of times spent in the granite domes and granite block stacked hills as well as the treed and well-grassed valleys with fellow hikers and climbers. Times have changed, and folk have moved on in life along their various paths, but the atmosphere of that wide range of hills, remains. The crystal clear and brilliant blue sky, the trees, the light-yellow grass, the luminous yellow, orange and red lichens were stunning to behold, almost like a painted landscape. It was still as beautiful as ever and retains an incredibly special peace and immunity from the harm so often evident because of poor management, over usage, or political interventions. On climbing up the 'View of the World' or more correctly as known by the Africans from time immemorial ago as Malindidzimu (Dwelling Place of the Spirits) in recent time, reminded me of the peace that unfolds as you climb up and survey the magnificent 360-degree vista. Many years before, I had climbed up the normal path to the boulders at the top and watched the sun go down in the west until it was dark. Such an experience is truly uplifting, an experience of a lifetime. On that occasion when I had descended, I spoke to the African caretaker outside his small grassed hut and asked him if ever he went up there at night, and he replied that he had never, because of the spirits that emerge there at night. I felt not the least bit uneasy at the time, but more so uplifted, and during our last recent visit there, I asked the attendant at the small tourist shop what the meaning of Malindidzimu meant, and he said it was the place of 'peaceful spirits'. It truly is a place of peace and always will be to me. The fact that Cecil Rhodes had asked to be buried there with a simple headstone, at first consideration, appears to be an affront to the sanctity of past Africans, but when quietly and contemplatively seated at that place one realises that the peace that followed the troubled times between the Ndebele regiments and the colonial settlers, removes the warring aura that might have prevailed. Cecil Rhodes although at times criticised for some poor decisions, was not a hateful person, but was an astute businessman and thereby, generated much wealth. He had sufficient wealth that he could have afforded to stay in the most luxurious places on earth, or return to England, and desire to be buried there, but he did not, he found that special solace in the Matopos, at Malindidzimu. We are all human and have failings, and we are also quick to judge others, but upon finality, realisation or wisdom, what is important is to find peace within yourself and with others – for this to be fruitful, it is necessary to have the door to peace to remain open for those that are willing to enter. He, I like to believe must have sensed that. His wealth was we know, ploughed into infrastructure, institutions, bursaries, and much else to all peoples within his keep of the time and into the future.

Generations good or bad may come and go, but the sanctuary of such places like the Matopos will remain. Just to witness a beautiful Black Eagle (Verreaux's Eagle), reminds one of the importance and freedom they enjoy aloft within the security of those impressive granite hills and almost inaccessible wilderness.

Being jolted back into reality, we were stopped at a police roadblock (a common occurrence along main roads) just outside Bulawayo on the Matopos Road. We were told that they wanted to search our vehicle.

'What are you looking for' I asked.

'We are looking for offensive weapons,' they said.

We were eager to get going because as we still had to try and draw money from the bank and fill up with fuel for the trip back via Plumtree.

Having just come from Matopos, we were hardly on a military mission, but we did have our camping equipment and did look rather like gypsies.

They started searching, and soon found a catapult hanging from behind the driver's seat. 'Ahaa the policeman cried', 'what are you doing with this, this is an offensive weapon and carries a fine' I explained that it was for chasing off vervet monkeys and baboons when we were camping (I had had to use it in Matopos at the Maleme dam camp because the monkeys were particularly bothersome and forcefully tried to prise open closed windows in our chalet, and had also tried to enter the bakkie). 'No! this is an offensive weapon, he again stated. 'No problem' I said, I shall cut it in pieces. 'No! You cannot do that' he stated. I had a penknife in my hand which he said nothing about, as I was ready to cut it apart. The atmosphere was somewhat tense which seemed absurd given that it was such a quiet morning and apart from one lone motorbike, we were the only people returning from the Matopos at that time, but the standoff was broken when they spotted an egg (which had been boiled) on the back floor – where it had fallen, then asked me why the egg was on the floor. 'I need to snack when travelling because I get light-headed if I do not eat', I said. The three policemen and one policewoman thought it funny and laughed. The one fellow then said 'I am going to let you go because you did not try to conceal the weapon. I was relieved of a court case, and perhaps a long spell in the Chikarubi prison! The successful ZANU-PF presidential elections were going to be held in a few days, and we intended to cross the border before voting day. We were allowed to go, and apparently, the search was because the elections were going to be held and they did not want any threat or potential assassinations I suppose. For a long trip, I did have an axe for chopping firewood, a battery charger, braai tongs and forks, so I count myself lucky that these were not discovered!

A little further on and just at the municipal boundary near Hillside, an African waved us down and humbly requested a donation of money because he was filling in potholes in the road – privately, he demonstrated great initiative (could be applied in South Africa) and was probably earning a few bucks a day in so doing.

We were not out of the woods though, with all charges being in US Dollars, (which is quite tough when South Africans only get paid in Rands) we had run out of cash. Credit cards were not accepted, so we went to a bank where we had arranged sufficient credit to draw from the ATM – no such luck, the bank had no money available – we were advised not to try and draw money at month end because that was when all the civil servants were paid, and it was a Saturday morning at that.. After trying another bank, with the same result, we just had to drive off with no spare cash but had been lucky to obtain some fuel near the showgrounds that accepted South African Rands (also legal currency in the country). It was interesting to note that where tourists are charged more than locals, there was no consideration for South Africa being one of the SADC countries!

We had seen hundreds of election posters with a noticeably young person displayed, and only after seeing quite a number, realised that 'Photoshop' software was alive and well in Zimbabwe and had been well utilised! We could hardly be blamed for not recognising the aged Mugabe, who then in 2013, only looked about fifty years of age, though dead and securely buried in 2019! Oh, for computers and modern technology. We will not talk about the police roadblock a few kilometres before the border beyond Plumtree, where we were asked where we were going... and much more...

We had thoroughly enjoyed our time in the bush, which was much more important than any haranguing, and would continue to do so whenever possible. The seasonal yearning for the bush remains...

23

Quo Vadis – Where to from here?

So where to now, does the journey of new experiences and discoveries ever end?

It most certainly does not end, and even trying to keep pace with the ever fast-moving and changing world and climate within which we must get up and survive every day, there still remain desires and new and even old horizons to be explored. Do not get me wrong, I am exceedingly happy to have been able to do the things that I and my family and friends have done thus far.

In parallel with my interests in nature and the bush, there are also the exciting frequent discoveries in technology and science – developments are moving so quickly, that one needs to keep an eye open and ear to the ground. Alternative and sustainable energy such as solar water heating, photovoltaic collectors, hydrogen fuel cells, wind farms, fibre-optic cables (already laid throughout South Africa, and across oceans), telecommunications and High Definition Television, advanced computers, and their storage capabilities including 'flash' drives, digital cameras, GPS, Electromagnetic Fog including EMF and EMR (and the dangers thereto including 5G), nanotube and carbon fibre technology, and of course the never-ending story of multifunctional phones, robotics and Artificial Intelligence, high energy storage Lithium ion batteries, medical technology, Thorium – for nuclear energy etc. The list goes on and on. Externally to our planet, is the study of the heavens, UFOs, UWOs, our planets and their detailed mapping and geological and other explorations and discoveries, the Square Kilometre Array (SKA), the radio telescope identification of the now many distant star planets, gravitational waves? These are all a wonderment to follow and enjoy in this incredible phase of the 'Technological Revolution'

Running or should I say sprinting in parallel with all of this is the concerns of the fact of global warming, and hinged directly to this is the population explosion, and the risks associated with that. Over-exploitation of resources, and the threat to wilderness areas – the flora and the creatures that live in them, from the smallest to the largest. No sooner is one hole in the fence closed, when another is opened. But I am confident that sanity has to prevail, and man makes a plan when it is at his doorstep, but the current rate of change does not allow enough time to listen to those of wisdom that can see the big picture and the consequences and be sensible enough to take sufficient and timeous preventative action.

Wilderness areas are becoming more and more threatened, even the existing tourist wilderness areas are being subjected to over-usage, poaching of animals (and plant life), but they are there, sometimes in inaccessible or sterile places where there are no covetous and commercial development eyes, even the smallest of these areas are worth exploring and soaking up. I recall a tour guide having said at least twenty years ago now, that some Japanese tourists travelling along one of our national roads had requested the bus to stop, so they could get out and take some pictures. When asked why, they said that they never see empty roads in Japan, and it was a delight to see so much open space! We still have lots of them, and I know some of the folk including the biking fraternity enjoy just riding off into the distance and enjoying the openness of the country. We all need that from time to time. Yachtsmen must feel the same in the open and vast sea, and those that go scuba-diving or snorkelling enjoy the silence and wonderment of what the oceans beneath the waves have to offer.

'Bucket List' has the connotation of things to do before you kick the bucket – so to speak, perhaps that interpretation is correct, but I still have lots of exploration I would desire to do, all things being equal:

To go back to Chizarira and explore some caves, see a large extinct volcano/crater in Malawi north of the Zambezi river, see the huge 'Inselbergs' in northern Mozambique (politics permitting), see the 'squashed' (my Google interpretation) of extinct volcanoes in Western Mozambique on the border with eastern Zimbabwe (this area may very well be the extension or tail end of the rift valley that passes through Malawi and southwards); look for some ruins as described in an old explorers book; explore around the Sengwe valley, another trip to the Bumbusi archaeological site, and of course to visit Scotland, the ancestral origin of both Jean and I. I must get a move on because we have been so busy here, I have not even been back to England, the country of my birth!

We never stop learning, and there is still so much to do, to discover, and so little time!

So, do things while you can folks, obviously between spells of work and necessary income to get you there...

'*Those with an enquiring mind and a sharp eye,
shall find treasure*'

*Walking boots – 1996 and still going strong
Photo: Olivia Kensley*

Bibliography and References

The Argus – photograph of Rescue of Jill Graafland –
20th December 1998

Baines, T. – The Gold Regions of South Eastern Africa – Map – 1877

Catholic Commission for Justice and Peace – Gukurahundi
in Zimbabwe – 2007

Clinton, I. – "These Vessels... " The Story of Inyati 1859 – 1959

Davison, T. – WANKIE, The story of a Great Game Reserve – 1967

Deacon, H.N. & J. – Human Beginnings in South Africa – 1999

Els, P. J. – Saturday's Soldiers – The Hunter Group – 2010
Els, P. J. – We Fear Naught but God – 2014 Fourth Edition

Fuller, B. – Bid Time Return – 1954

Gibbs, P. – A flag for the Matabele – 1955

Gray, J. – Master of Philosophy (Archaeology) Thesis –
Understanding the farming community sequence from the Mateke
Hills, South-East, Lowveld, Zimbabwe – 2008

Haynes, G., Makuvaza, S., & Writson, T. – The Bumbusi Engravings and
Paintings in Hwange National Park Zimbabwe: Preliminary results
of recording and rock shelter excavations – No. 2 June 2011 –
Zimbabwe Prehistory

Hemans, H. M. – The Log of a Native Commissioner – 1971

http://nambya.org – Internet reference

Jones, N. Dr – My Friend Kumalo – Mhlagazanhlansi – 1972

Jones, P. – Donkeys for Development – 1997

Kenneth Bradley – The Diary of a District Officer – 1966

Nobbs, E. A. Dr – The Matopos – 1956

Ransford, O. – BULAWAYO Historic Battleground of
  Rhodesia – 1968

Silvana Olivo – ZAMBEZI VALLEY The Lost Stronghold – 2018

Tabler, E. C. – The Narrative of Frederick Hugh Barber 1875 and
  1877 – 1878, and The Journal of Richard Frewen 1877 – 1878 –
Chatto and Windus London – 1960

Tabler, E. C. – To the Victoria Falls via Matabeleland – The Diary of
  Major Henry Stabb – 1875 – 1967

Van Waard, S. – The Hell – 2000

Ward, W. – Personal account – Honoris Crux (Silver) Bravery
  Medal – Recce 2 – 1976

Wright, A. – Grey Ghosts at Buffalo Bend – 1976

Wright, A. – Valley of the Ironwoods – 1972

*Note: the majority of references have been drawn from my collection of
books which have sparked many of my interests and accompanying
journeys.*

Acronyms and Glossary of terms

Acronyms

CSIR	Council for Scientific and Industrial Research
CT	Communist Terrorist
DC	District Commissioner
EMF	Electromagnetic Frequency
EMR	Electromagnetic Radiation
OP	Observation Post
OP	Operation (as in OP Tangent)
PLT	Platoon
SA	South Africa
SAAF	South African Air Force
SADC	Southern African Development Communities
SB	Special Branch
R & R	Rest and Recuperation / Rest and Retraining
RDU	Rhodesian Defence Unit
RLI	Rhodesian Light Infantry
TS	Training Ship
UFO	Unidentified Flying Object
UDI	Unilateral Declaration of Independence
UWO	Unidentified Underwater Object
ZANU – PF	Zimbabwe African National Union – Patriotic Front
ZIPRA	Zimbabwe People's Revolutionary Army

Glossary

Buluwayo	The earlier spelling of now Bulawayo
Guyo	A grindstone base
Huyo	The upper grindstone Pestle/stone
Madala	An old man
Middel-mannetjie	The ridge in the middle of a dirt track
Multum In Parvus	Much in Little – Lat.
Nkomo or Mombi	A cow
Quo Vadis	Wither goest thou – Lat.
Skinner	Gossip or scandal - Afrikaans
Tagati	Supernatural/witchcraft - Shona
Tsoro	A game played with pebbles on a 4 x 8 number of holes, ground in to stone, also called Marabaraba or Isifuba

A grand Baobab - The bastion of the lowveld that symbolizes life.

Sketch: Olivia Kensley

www.ingramcontent.com/pod-product-compliance
Lightning Source LLC
Chambersburg PA
CBHW071417090426
42737CB00011B/1492